East Side Dreams

by

Art Rodriquez

To Diane, Flora says you Are a very nice person. Enjoy!

10-14-08

Dream House

Acknowledgments

I would like to apologize to anyone who was affected in a negative way or pained as a result of my actions during my youth.
For those of my dear family and friends who are no longer alive, they will always live in my heart and mind.

Copyright 1999
Art Rodriquez

Published by Dream House Press
2714 Ophelia Ct., San Jose, CA 95122
E-mail: dreamhousepress@yahoo.com

ISBN: 0-9671555-0-9

Library of Congress
Catalog Card Number: 99-93257

Sixth Printing
Printed in the United States of America

Edited by
Margie Maestas-Flores
Greg Runion

Cover Illustration and Production by
Hiram Duran Alvarez
Alvarez Design & Illustration
alvarezdesign75@yahoo.com

Dedication

This book is dedicated to my dear wife Flora who helped me and encouraged me to write. She aided and motivated me in educating myself.

Thank you, Flora.

Contents

THE WORST DAY OF MY LIFE 1

THE BEER POURING 4

THE SWINGING KNIFE 7

THE BIG FIGHT 11

THE GETAWAY 15

THE JOY RIDE 20

EARLY YEARS 26

THE INTERROGATION 29

THE FIRST FIGHT 33

THE BEER RUN 39

THE FIGHTER 43

THE REPORT CARD 50

THE CRUISE 58

BEHIND BARS 63

THE MAT 65

MANOS NEGRAS [BLACK HANDS] 70

THE ROCK FIGHT 80

OLDIES BUT GOODIES 89

THE MONSTERS 97

PERKINS 101

THE B-B GUN 106

PRESTON 110

REBELLION 117

THE FIRE 126

THE SHOWER ROOM 131

BLOW YOUR HORN 140

RUNAWAY 146

THE ANTS 153

FREEDOM! 166

CURLY HAIR BRAT 177

LOVER'S LANE 183

A KID'S NIGHT LIFE 186

LOS ANGELES 190

MY UNCLES 194

BACK TO SAN JOSE 202

REDONDO BEACH 210

CHANGES 216

THE DEAL 218

A NEW LIFE 228

FIRST JOB 232

A GOLD MINE 238

A NEW VENTURE 244

THE CRASH 254

THE HEART ATTACK 260

THE FORBIDDEN PLACE .261

THE WORST DAY OF MY LIFE

April 8, 1966. I was sixteen years old. My mother was already divorced. My sister Tita was home and so was my little brother Victor. I used to hang around with my friends in the neighborhood. Sometimes I would go out with my brother Eddie who was two years older than I was.

My friends in the neighborhood didn't have cars to get around in yet. On the weekends we would go out, but to get to the parties and dances we would do a lot of walking. Driving during 1966, sometimes the guys borrowed a car from someone or would take a car without permission. That's what I would do occasionally.

I used to drive my mother's 1956 Chevy every so often. Even now, when I see someone that I knew then, they'll say, "I remember your 1956 Chevy." I would tell my mother I was going to the store for her and not come back for three hours. When I returned, she would ask me what took me so long. I would answer, "Mom, you know how long the lines are at the Pink Elephant." She would look at me as if she didn't know if I were lying or not. The Pink Elephant was a family-owned shopping center on King Road, at Virginia Place, in San Jose's east side.

On one spring day, Redhead came by to see if my brother Eddie was home. Redhead was a long-time friend who we gave a nickname of Redhead because of his red hair. I told Redhead that my brother Eddie went with Robert, and I didn't know if he was coming back. Redhead said he would come back later to see if he was home.

Redhead asked if I wanted to go with him.

"Sure! What time?"

"In a couple of hours. I have to take care of some things. I'll come back for you, and we'll find out where some parties are."

"All right, party time!" I thought.

I was excited. I didn't get to go with these older guys very often. Once in a while, I would go with Eddie because he invited me out with him and his friends; but I would never go with these older guys by myself. When you're sixteen and your brother is eighteen, there is a big difference.

I kept looking out the window to see if Redhead was there yet. I asked my sister to let me know if she saw him drive up.

Tita and I were getting close at that time. She was two years younger than I was, but we had the same friends. We hung out down the street at the Lopez girls' house. Next door to them lived my friend Dennis, and on the other side of the Lopez girls' house lived my other good friend Art.

I was a junior in high school and had just started a part-time job after school helping the janitor clean classrooms at Mayfair School. This was my first week working. My school work wasn't going very well at the time; I had a very difficult time in school.

"Arthur, your friend Redhead is here," Tita called out.

I went to the kitchen where my mother was, gave her a kiss, and said, "Bye, Mom, I'll see you later."

"OK, mijo, we'll see you later. Be good."

Little did my mother know that we weren't good boys. We were troublemakers in the streets. My father wasn't around anymore. He went back to Mexico after their divorce. We didn't hear from him very often.

It was still early in the evening, about five or six o'clock. I ran out to the car and got in, saying, "Hey, man, how's it going?"

"All right," Redhead said as he was backing out of the driveway. "Did Eddie come back yet?"

"No, I haven't heard from him. I don't know where he went," I said.

Redhead went on to tell me he didn't know where anyone was. But not to worry, we'd find something to do.

As we were driving down Virginia Place, it felt as if something wasn't right. What it was, I didn't know. Something just didn't feel right. As we came to the next block, we drove by my friend Art's house. I saw him and Dennis talking out on the front grass.

Redhead's car was lowered, so it attracted attention. Art and Dennis turned around, saw me in the car, and waved. I felt as if I should tell Redhead to pull over because of the weird feeling I had.

When I was with my younger friends, we would like to look for fights. When I was with these older guys, we would get in big fights. The fights were with older guys their age.

As we were driving down King Road, I remember we were talking about Redhead's car. He wanted to sell it. I asked him how much he wanted for it.

"A hundred dollars."

"Sold!" I said excitedly. I didn't have any money, but I asked if he could hold it for me for two weeks. With my new job, I'd have enough to pay for it.

We went to a friend's house and bought some beer. Then we drove around for three hours drinking. We stopped at another guy's house and bought grass and rolled three joints that looked like cigars. Redhead lit one, and I lit another. I remember getting so loaded that I couldn't think straight or see straight. We still had another one to smoke.

We left there and drove around drinking and loaded. Back in those days, if you were pulled over by the cops with beer, no big thing. They would usually just make you dump it out and let you go. However, if we had marijuana and got caught, we could go to prison.

THE BEER POURING

Thinking back during this time, I remember some friends and I once went cruising. We decided to buy two cases of beer, then we went up the mountains. We parked in a nice, quiet place looking down at the lights of San Jose. We put the eight-track player on and opened our beer. The four of us were having a good time.

We were there for about an hour, telling stories about old girl-friends and our big fights. All of a sudden, out of nowhere there were lights all over us. It went from night to daylight. At first I thought it was a UFO on top of us. Then we saw these three big things coming toward us from the direction of the lights.

"What in the heck is this?" I thought.

The door opened on the other side, and I heard a voice say, "Boys, get out of the car!"

Three police cars appeared with all their lights on us. We all followed the order and got out of the car.

The street we were on was a city street. It was on the way up to Mt. Hamilton, just after you make the turn that's almost a U-turn. Some city streets had been put in for houses; however, there were no houses as of yet.

One cop was hard. Pointing his baton, he said, "You guys all line up here and take out your IDs."

No one said anything. We came up here to drink our beer, not bothering anyone and we're busted!

The third cop was standing there watching us, with a troubled look in his eye. I think he was a rookie trying to learn the job. As we were standing there, the mean cop and the rookie were searching the car. There was beer all over the place.

After they searched, they came back to us. The hard cop asked us in a sarcastic way, "Where did you get the money for the beer?"

I looked at the cop and said, "Officer, we work."

I think that's what helped me with the cops when I was growing up in the streets. I always knew what they wanted to hear. I had some friends who were smart alecks with the cops, and the cops always found something to arrest them for.

The hard cop walked by each of us with our IDs and fired questions at us giving us a bad time. I noticed the other cop stood there shaking his head. It looked as if he was thinking, "OH BROTHER! What is this guy doing?"

Then the hard cop said to the other one, "Come on, let's check these guys out." As they were walking toward their car, he turned half way around and yelled at the cop who was with us, "Make sure they pour out all that beer!"

The cop yelled back, "Done!" Then he looked over at us and said, "OK, boys, you heard the man. Get those two boxes of beer and follow me."

In front of our car where we parked was a steep cliff. The cop stopped in front of us and looked over at us, saying, "OK, boys, push that beer over."

I had the first box. I looked at him and asked, "Push it over?"

He looked at me and said, "That's what I said!" I then pushed the whole box over, and my friend pushed his. They slid over the side of the hill about two feet. It was dark, and we couldn't see over the cliff.

We got up and went to the car and stood there, waiting for the other two cops to check us out on their radio. One of the cops told us when we left there that we should go home, so we wouldn't get into any trouble.

The cop that checked us out started to give us our IDs back; he said we checked out OK. He told us to keep out of trouble because he didn't want to see us anymore that night.

"Let's go," he told the other cops. As they were walking away, he turned to the cop who had us push the boxes over and asked, "Did they dump all the beer out?"

"They sure did," he replied. He then turned and looked at us, winked, and said, "You boys be careful."

There are not too many cops like him anymore.

That night we stayed there and drank all our beer before going home.

* * *

As Redhead and I drove around town, we lit up the last joint. We passed by Robert's house. No one was there. We cruised around for another hour and drove by Richard's house again. We saw Tino in his brand new 1966 GTO. He was backed in the driveway. In the GTO was my brother Eddie, Robert, Roy, Art J., and Tino. Redhead and I pulled up and backed into the driveway next to them. We had the windows open as we talked and listened to music.

I remember that I was really stoned. It seemed as if it was going to be a very quiet night. We were drinking, not bothering anyone at that time. Out of nowhere a car raced around the corner. We all turned to see who it was. The car stopped right in front of the driveway; four guys were in the car. One of them had blood on his forehead; it was Ceasar. He had just been in a fight at a party, and they threw him out. Ceasar didn't like it one bit. He had tried to keep out of trouble lately, since he was just released from prison. They said that he was imprisoned for chopping some guy's head open with a machete. One of the other guys was Isaac, Ceasar's younger brother. The third guy was Steve.

THE SWINGING KNIFE

Ceasar had some friends I didn't like, Noah and Indio. Noah was my sister's boyfriend who hung around with Indio. Every time I saw Indio, he was with all his friends, about six to ten of them together at one time. Indio would give me hard looks when he saw me. He would put his chin up and nod his head. Two times I stopped and told him I noticed he always had his friends with him. I didn't like him, and I knew he didn't like me. I told him one day I would catch him by himself. Both times when I told him this, I thought he was going to take a swing at me. I was always ready, even though I knew his friends would jump in. I had heard he stabbed a couple of guys. So it wasn't the time to fight him, not when he was with all of his partners.

One day Eddie and I were cruising with Rudy and Joe, the cuates (twins). We passed the house that the guys hung out at on Virginia Place, a few houses down from King Road. When we passed the house about ten o'clock at night, I noticed Indio was outside standing by the front porch.

"Joe! Pull over! There's a guy here I want to get!" I said.

We pulled over about two houses down and got out of the car. The cuates stayed behind us as we walked to the front of the house.

"Which one?" Eddie asked.

I pointed him out. Eddie was right behind me. I started to walk to the house. As I walked closer, Indio saw me approaching.

"Orale ese," Indio said as I pulled the right side of my body back. With all my might, I swung my fist to knock him out. As my fist approached his face, he couldn't move fast enough to do anything. I hit him with such force that it felt as if his feet left the ground. He went flying back like a puppet. As soon as he hit the ground, I was over him, hitting him repeatedly so he wouldn't get up. Then instantly the door to the house opened.

Noah jumped from the front porch toward me. Before he could get to me, Eddie was on him. Next, some other guy was out of the front door. I knew Indio wasn't going to get up anymore, so I turned and started hitting the other guy. A right. Left. Right. Left. He went down. I went over to Eddie and Noah.

There was a knife swinging. I started hitting Noah in the face as hard as I could. One of the times I hit him, I felt a sharp pain on my right wrist; I didn't know what it was. Noah was there covered in his own blood, and Indio was lying on the ground. The sharp pain I felt was the knife entering my wrist.

Ceasar ran out of the house where we were, not knowing what to do. "Hey, man! What's going on! Break it up, man! Break it up! Hey, man! STOP! STOP!" he yelled as he came out and saw his friends on the ground. Ceasar wanted us to leave.

I had done what we wanted to do anyway, so we said "OK, man. Let's get out of here!"

Indio was tall and thin, and Noah was medium size and stocky. Eddie was tall and on the thin side himself. I was 5'11" and medium built. Ceasar was on the short side, but he was a dangerous guy. He had a bad reputation. Nobody messed around with him.

Two of the guys took Noah to the hospital right away.

The next day Tita was upset at Eddie and me because of what we did to her boyfriend. Noah was in the hospital for a while. They said he almost died.

* * *

At first we didn't know who Ceasar was when we were at Richard's house. He wasn't a close friend of ours. Through the years we knew him as one of the guys from east side San Jose.

With Ceasar in the car when he drove up was Steve, Ceasar's younger brother Isaac, and Phillip. Ceasar knew we were fighting guys, and he needed help.

They parked their car in front of the driveway on the street, the motor running, and the lights on. The doors flew open, and all four walked toward us. The blood on Ceasar's head was starting to dry. He hadn't wiped it off.

He came up to the cars. Breathing heavily, he said, "Hey, man, I need your help! I need help from the east side!" He went on to tell us he was jumped at a party because he was from the east side. In those days there was a lot of fighting between the east and west sides of San Jose.

Everyone in the cars looked at each other and asked, "Should we go and help him?" None of them really wanted to go. For one thing, they really didn't know Ceasar and his friends; and it didn't look as if they were in a fighting mood that night. However, there I was, a young kid in the back seat, loaded, and wanting to go and do something that night.

"Let's go, man! Let's go and help him!" I said.

Someone replied, "I don't know, man."

"Let's go!" I said anxiously.

"Come on, man! You guys got to help us," Ceasar said.

Then someone else said, "Let's do it, man, for the east side."

"All right, let's go," one of the other guys answered.

Before leaving, we had a plan. My brother Eddie, Robert, Tino, and Fred were going to go in the GTO. They were going to arrive first, go into the party, and be there when we arrived. When we arrived with Ceasar, they would see he was back; they would then start fighting with us. This plan would allow our guys to be inside and start fighting from inside the house.

Most plans don't work out the way you want them. Ceasar, his brother Isaac, Steve, and Phil were in the first car; Redhead and I were in the car following them. The GTO was behind us. On the way to the party, we lost the GTO; but Ceasar had given them directions. They knew where to go. Ceasar kept looking back at us to make sure we were following him. He looked hyper, moving around in the car ahead.

We didn't know who we were going to fight. It seemed it was like that all the time. Every weekend we were fighting someone. I thought, "One of these days we are going to kill someone. Then what are we going to do? What would become of our lives?"

We passed the KLIV radio station with its tall antennas and red lights. Story Road turned into Keyes Street somewhere around there. By then I didn't feel as drunk as I did before. We were getting close to the place; we were close to Happy Hollow Park.

I was in deep thought anticipating a fight and wondering who we were going to meet at the party. Did we know them? If we knew them, maybe we wouldn't fight them. This bothered me because I was looking forward to a fight. Those guys weren't good guys either. They were street fighters like us. They kicked Ceasar and his brother out because they were from the east side.

When you are young and dumb as I was, you don't think of the consequences of your actions. When I think back to this night, I think, "I didn't even know Ceasar well enough to give my life for him, and what if we did kill someone? For what? For someone I didn't even know? For a cause that wasn't even noble?"

THE BIG FIGHT

Back in 1966, Story Road was like a small country road and so were Senter Road and Keyes Street. At Keyes and Senter there were little houses that looked like small cabins or cottages, about six of them on the north side of Keyes Street. On the west side of the little cottages next to them, there was an old bar. Next to that bar there were some railroad tracks.

When we arrived, we drove in between the tracks and the bar. We parked and got out of the cars.

The guys climbed out of the car Ceasar was in and opened the trunk. We walked up to their trunk. I grabbed a big bar; someone grabbed the jack; someone else pulled out the tire iron. As soon as everyone had a weapon, the trunk was closed.

"Let's do the job!" Ceasar said.

He started walking to the sidewalk and around the bar. The door to the bar opened, and I saw a lot of men sitting on stools and drinking.

Walking down the sidewalk, we found it was dark and quiet. I couldn't see if Ceasar had a bar in his hand.

No one said anything. It looked kind of scary. I wondered if they were waiting to ambush us. I looked around for the other guys in the GTO, but there was no sign of them yet.

Ceasar was mad and wanted blood because these guys dishonored his reputation. He wasn't going to wait for anyone. Maybe the other guys were already inside the party. But they couldn't have arrived that fast.

The small houses were white, and some of them had a little grass in front of them. In front of the houses by the sidewalk were big trees; behind the cottages was a big field with large trees; behind the field was the creek. In those days that was considered the end of town.

We heard loud noises coming from the house. Everything looked dark around the area. The door was closed, and the curtains were drawn. It seemed they knew we were coming because it was too quiet for a party. Everyone knew Ceasar and the way he was. I was sure they were expecting him back.

We were now in front of the house. It had about a ten-foot walkway approaching the porch and door. Ceasar started up the walkway to the door, and I was right behind him. In my hand I carried a heavy bar. I wondered what was going to happen.

The door was locked. Ceasar pounded on it. Everything was quiet inside. Then Ceasar kicked the door; the first kick didn't do anything. I stood there and waited for the door to open. As soon as it opened, I was ready to start fighting. Ceasar took a step back and gave the door a hard kick, then another. The door swung open. Some guy came charging at Ceasar as soon as the door opened.

I saw Ceasar charge back at him with his body low. Both of them went into the house struggling. I was in the door as soon as there was room to enter. The other guys were behind me.

Someone was coming up to hit me. My bar was already on the way. Boom! It hit him right on the head, and he went back and down. I took another step into the house, and there was another guy coming at me. I swung my bar hard. Just as it was going to hit, I saw someone charging at me. My bar hit him instead of the guy at whom I was aiming. This guy went down too. Pure, slow motion.

From the corner of my eye, I saw a shadow springing toward me, swinging a big pipe, three feet long. There was nothing I could do; it was on its way. This bar headed straight at me. It seemed as if I were suspended in time.

As I started to turn my body toward the bar, I saw the guy swinging it, taking another step toward me in slow motion. BOOM! Direct hit. I felt my body spinning, and there was a loud ringing in my head. I took a step back, hanging onto the door frame with one hand. I felt my back and my neck wet with blood. I took another step back, and I was on the porch. Then I was half way down the steps, hanging onto the railing. The next thing I knew I was on the ground in the front yard covered with blood. Everyone was fighting around me. I felt someone grab me from the back and pick me up. I turned to see who it was; it was my brother Eddie. I saw Robert, Tino, and Roy running to the house.

"What happened? I thought you guys were going to wait for us?" he asked as he picked me up. He told me to go back to the car.

After those first few minutes, my head started to clear up from the blow. I was sober by then. I picked up my bar and started swinging it again, hitting whoever was in the way. There were a lot of people fighting in front of the house as I headed for the car.

I saw the guy who hit me lying on the porch, covered in blood. Another guy was being hit with a jack. There were a lot of people, a lot more than we had thought.

Things weren't very quiet anymore. People were yelling, and bottles were breaking. I also heard music coming from somewhere, either from the party or the bar.

I later heard one of the guys with us went into the bar and threw a beer bottle at someone; therefore, they came out to fight against us too. The whole place was full of people yelling and fighting. I was fighting close to the car when Steve came running by me. His eyes were wide open.

"Let's get out of here!" he yelled.

Isaac came running by, and he said, "Get in the car! Let's go!"

It was time to leave. They were scared because they saw people dying. I saw Redhead running to the car, and we both jumped in at the same time.

"Lock the doors!" Redhead yelled out.

I reached over and locked the door on my side. As soon as I did, there were about five guys trying to open it. Redhead was trying to start the car; he was having a little trouble.

Some big guy came to the front of the car and had a big log in his hands. By now my head was hurting and bleeding even more. I could hardly move. The car still hadn't started. The big guy in front of the car raised the log over his head and threw it right at the windshield. Both of us thought the windshield was going to break. As the log came toward me, I thought, "This is it. It's going to hit me right in the face!" Redhead's arms went up to cover his face, and he bent over my way. I couldn't bend over; I was in bad shape, with my head bleeding heavily. The log hit the windshield. Boom! It didn't break it but bounced off. What a relief! Redhead turned the key again, and the car started.

Another guy ran to the back of the car. He must have been drinking too much because he put both hands down on the bumper, trying to hold the car back. We weren't going to wait for him to get out of the way, so Redhead put the car in reverse and let the clutch out. We started to back up very quickly. The guy on the back bumper wasn't as strong as he thought he was. He couldn't hold the car. I was looking back, saw him one second, and didn't see him the next. The next thing I felt was the car thump over something, and the guy under the car yelled. Perplexed, Redhead and I just looked at each other.

"What should we do?" I asked.

Redhead put the car in first gear and moved forward. Again we felt a thump. By this time there were about 10 to 15 guys surrounding the car. We looked at each other again and gave each other a look of, "Oh well!" Redhead put the car in reverse and let the clutch out, burning rubber. As the car was burning rubber, backing out, we felt a thump from the back wheels and a thump from the front wheels.

Years later we heard this guy was still having surgery on his stomach to remove the rubber.

THE GETAWAY

We were backing into the street. Our car came to a stop, and Redhead changed gears. I could see the other car with Isaac, Phil, and Steve. They were backing out in front of us. It looked as if there were about 25 guys around and behind them. It didn't bother them at all, even if it meant backing out and running over them. They were leaving, and that was it!

As we looked east on Story Road, I saw red lights flashing and racing toward us. Also from the other direction and Senter Road we saw red lights coming.

"So how are we going to get out of here?" Redhead screamed.

I looked around to see where we could go, then I said "Go through the railroad tracks!"

Redhead stepped on the gas and started down the tracks. It felt like a giant vibrator, especially since I had a four-inch open wound on my head. I was trying to hold my head as we were bumping down the railroad tracks. It seemed like a long time before we got off the tracks. I'm not sure where it was that we got off.

The next thing I knew, we were headed down San Antonio Street. From far away we saw police cars flying through the streets. We knew someone back there had to have died. One police car was coming toward us. We turned our lights off, turned the corner, and parked.

Redhead said "Lie down!" I went down toward him, and he leaned toward me.

The cop car came around the corner slowly. We saw his head-lights, and we didn't move. He kept moving down the street. We stayed there for a few more minutes, just in case he came back. He didn't return, so Redhead started up the car again. We started back down the road, headed down San Antonio Street not too far from King Road. We were behind another car when out of nowhere a police car came up to the car in front of us. The police officer was flagging the car to stop in the middle of the street. Right away I leaned over and down, so he couldn't see me.

We stopped behind the car in front of us but couldn't hear what the police was telling the guy. Redhead then said, "Don't move; here he comes."

The police car moved up to ours. The street was dark and quiet. The cop car came very close. As we waited there, it sounded as if the cop had his head in our car. He asked, "Where are you coming from?"

"From work, officer," Redhead answered, trying to act normally.

"Have you seen any trouble?" the cop asked.

"No, officer, no trouble around here," Redhead said, trying to sound convincing.

"OK, go straight home," he said as he sped away.

We again started driving down the street behind the other car. When we arrived at Jackson Avenue on the east side, another police car raced by us. Finally we were back at Robert's house.

All the other guys were there waiting for us, except Steve, Isaac, and Phil. They were in the car in front of us in the driveway when we left the fight. Everyone else made it back. Ceasar had jumped in the GTO and returned with my brother and the other guys.

The guys wanted to see how bad I was hurt. Ceasar and I were the only ones injured. We were telling each other how many cops we saw out there. Someone said they knew someone had died. Everyone was talking a mile a minute.

What were we going to do? We decided they would take me to the emergency room, and someone else would take Ceasar to another hospital. We agreed to say we had been at Robert's house, and Ceasar and I became angry at each other and started fighting. We would say I fell and hit my head on a rock. A good story. But would it work? Everyone said we'd try it so that at the hospital it wouldn't be connected with the big fight.

Redhead agreed to take me to the emergency room. We rushed into the car and told everybody we'd see them later—we hoped.

As we drove down Capitol Avenue, my head was still bleeding. I knew it was a big wound. Back at Robert's house, everyone looked at my head. They told me it looked bad; they felt it would be necessary to sew me up with a lot of stitches. By this time Redhead's car seat was full of blood.

We turned down a side street to Jackson Avenue because we wanted to avoid all the cop cars on the main streets. Things just didn't look good again. I had a feeling things weren't going to end up too well that night. We had been in a fight and hurt some guys pretty badly, and I was on the way to the hospital.

What was my mother going to say? It seemed she had always trusted us, and we were always doing bad things behind her back. My poor mom. I dreaded her finding out what happened that night.

As we were riding to the hospital, I wondered how I was going to tell them what happened to me. Would they believe me? I had become a pretty-skilled liar by that time.

We were now on Bambi Lane; everything seemed to be cool. I wasn't talking, just thinking. Redhead wasn't saying anything either. He was more than likely thinking the same thing I was.

We were coming up to Jackson Avenue, and out of nowhere lights appeared all over the place. I turned to look behind us; there was a cop car following. He was right on our bumper. I mean on our bumper! If he came any closer, he would be pushing us.

"Redhead! There's a cop behind us!" I yelled as he looked in his rear-view mirror.

"I know! I know!" Redhead answered, sounding alarmed.

I looked across the street on Jackson Avenue. There was Art's car, the one Ceasar was in earlier. The doors were open, lights were on, and four cop cars were around it. Nobody was there, not the guys or the cops. They had run out of gas in their stolen car and were pushing it. When the guys saw the cops, they took off running through the field behind Lee Matson School. The cops went after them on foot.

By this time our car came to a stop, and we were surrounded by cop cars. We had just made the turn to Jackson Avenue. In those days the freeway wasn't there. It was a big field. Everything was lit up with the cops' lights. An officer marched to my side of the car first.

"OK, where's Ceasar?" the cop asked.

Before I could say anything, he opened my door. As he opened it, I said, "Who's Ceasar?"

He pulled me out of the car by my arm. "Where's Ceasar?" he asked again.

Just then he noticed the blood all over my head and down my back. "Hey! This one is all full of blood!" he said to the other cop.

At that time Redhead was being pulled from his side of the car. "What happened to you?" the cop asked me, as he dragged me toward the front of the car.

My eyes met Redhead's; and since they already knew about Ceasar, I didn't want to say anything about getting into a fight with him. I replied loudly enough so Redhead could hear me, "We were cruising down Capitol Avenue, and these guys threw a bottle at us and told us to pull over. We did, and this guy hit me over the head with a bar."

Redhead was being pulled to the back of the car; therefore, he couldn't hear me anymore. I hoped he heard what I said because I wasn't going to change my story.

"What were you doing on Keyes Street?" the cop asked harshly.

I looked at him in the eyes and said, "I wasn't on Keyes Street."

"We know where you were tonight, kid!"

By this time more cop cars were arriving and parking all over the street. They told me to put my hands on the hood of the car, and they frisked me. I looked toward the back of the car. I saw Redhead already handcuffed and being led away to a police car. As he got in the police car, the cop pushed his head down to force him in. Four cops surrounded me, all asking questions at the same time. I told them I didn't know what they were talking about.

"What fight on Keyes Street? I don't know anything about any fight on Keyes Street!"

"Turn around, boy!" He put handcuffs on me—so tight that they hurt. All my circulation was cut off.

"What are these for? I didn't do anything wrong."

One of the cops asked the other, "What are you going to do with him?"

"First we'll take him to the hospital; then we'll take him downtown."

Going to Juvenile again.

THE JOY RIDE

I had been in Juvenile Hall twice before. Paul and I had gone to Tropicana, on King and Story Roads, to see if we could steal a car. Tropicana was a newly built shopping center at the time; it had many different stores. It's still there today.

Paul took half of the parking lot, and I took the other half. We walked by all the cars to see if anyone left their keys. After a little while Paul yelled at me, "Come over here!"

When I walked to where he was standing, Paul was smiling. "The guy just went in and left his car keys in the ignition."

I looked at Paul and said, "Let's go!"

"You drive," Paul replied.

So we jumped into the 1957 Plymouth, a nice car with a push-button transmission on the dashboard.

We drove the car all over town; then the gas marker showed we needed gas, fast!

"Let's go to Bobby's house. He'll like this car. And you know him; he'll have money for gas," Paul said. We all liked Bobby. He was all right, always ready to do what everyone wanted to do. We then drove to his house.

We called him Bobby X because he went around with our friend Sandy. When he broke up with her, he became her X. The name stayed with him.

Bobby X lived around the corner from Robert, off Capitol Avenue by the old Payless Drug store. We drove up to his house. Paul got out of the car to call Bobby. I watched them at the door talking to each other. Bobby came outside for a minute, and Paul pointed at the car. Bobby went back in the house, and Paul started for the car. He looked like a little boy with a new toy as he walked toward me with a smile.

"What happened, Paul?" I wanted to know.

"He'll be right out. He has to tell his father that you just got your license to drive, and your uncle loaned you his car." Bobby's father wouldn't let him go with someone who just stole a car.

We went back to my house because I wanted to take a shower and change clothes. Before arriving at my house, I pulled over and told Bobby to drive the car. If my father saw me driving, he would have a fit.

During this time my father wasn't home very much. He and my mother weren't getting along very well, and my father was planning to go back to Mexico as soon as the American Can Company closed down.

When we pulled up to my house, I told Paul and Bobby to return in about an hour. My father was standing at the front door with a frown on his face. I remember thinking "OH NO! My father doesn't like this."

I started around the back because my father was very strict about some things with us at this time. He had his rules. One of them was that we kids had to use the back door. If my father looked as if he was in a bad mood, we had to watch our step.

"Arturo! Come here!" my father said in a rough tone. I walked over to the front door where he stood. Looking toward the car, he said, "Whose car is that?"

"What car, Dad?" After all, he could have meant another car in the street. My father didn't like my response very much.

He said with a stronger voice, "The car you came in!"

Bobby and Paul were now driving away from our house. Looking at the car, I said, "That's Bobby's uncle's car. He always lets Bobby use it."

My father stayed there and stared as they drove away. He wondered why he had never seen it if Bobby's uncle always let him use it.

My father looked at me and said, "OK."

I continued around the side of the house to the back door.

About an hour later, I was in my room ready to go. I heard my father's Cadillac start up. I thought to myself "Good! He's leaving and won't come back all night."

During this time my father and I didn't get along very well. He was never home with us; he was always with his friends. When we were young, he spent a lot of time with us but not when we were teenagers.

I made sure my father had left. If he was to tell me I couldn't go, then I would have to wait a little while and sneak out. I waited by the window to make sure he didn't forget anything and didn't come back.

"All clear," I thought. I started walking down the street towards the Lopez girls' house. Paul and Bobby were there. Just as I walked down the sidewalk, they drove up the street.

Moving slowly, Bobby yelled out of the window at me, "Hey! Kid, you want a ride in my new car?"

I ran to the car. "What took you so long? It's been longer than an hour."

We kept that car for three days and were caught three times with the car. What do I mean that we were caught three times? The first time was 3 p. m. the next day. We went to The Jose Theater on Second Street where we used to hang out. We parked the car on Third Street at a parking lot behind the theater and walked around the corner to the show.

When my two brothers and sister were children the Jose was the theater we would always go to every Sunday. During that time our parents would drive us to the theater. The admission was a dime. We would watch three movies, and in the evening we would walk out and look for my parents' Pontiac parked along the curb. At times when our father was late, we would walk across the street to see what was playing at the Lyric. We gave the Lyric a nickname, the Flea House, because it only cost five cents to get in. The Jose was a much nicer theater. The Lyric was owned by an older couple. One worked the booth where tickets were sold, and the other worked the snack bar. I entered the Lyric a few times and would have more appreciation for the Jose.

During the time I was growing up, the Jose theater was well maintained. It had ushers who walked around in their uniforms, red vests, white shirts, and black pants with a gold stripe running down the side. They would walk around with their flashlights. If one was talking when the movie was playing, the usher would approach and ask us to keep quite. The Jose was one of the hangouts for the youth during that time.

In a while Bobby and Paul wanted to leave the theater because they missed their new car. We left and walked back around the corner.

Three cop cars had surrounded the car. They had the doors and trunk open, as if they were looking for a body or something. We walked within a few feet to see if we could hear them talking and stood by the wall and watched. They thought we were kids just looking to see what was going on. After a while they were done. They closed the trunk and locked the doors. We heard one of the cops call a tow truck on his radio. Here we were watching them with the keys to our new car in my pocket.

"Let's go. The car will be all right. The tow truck will be here in a few minutes," one of the cops said. They took off and left us with the car. We waited a few minutes. Once it was all clear, we jumped in the car and took off.

Later on that night we were cruising around looking for parties with our new car. We ended up at the IES Hall on Alum Rock and 101. There was always something going on there, either a dance or a wedding. First we cruised into the parking lot, circling around a few times to see if there was anyone we knew. I told Bobby to go around a few more times while Paul and I went inside to check things out. If it was all right, we would return and tell him to park the car and come inside. Bobby didn't mind driving around the parking lot; he loved driving that car. We went in the building and checked out the party. It wasn't very good, even though we knew a lot of people; therefore, we decided not to stay.

We went outside to find Bobby. As we were walking through the parking lot, we saw the car right in the middle of the parking lot. All the lights were on, the driver's door was open, and the engine was running. A cop car was behind it, but there was no Bobby and no cop. I asked a guy who was standing there with his girlfriend, "Hey, what happened to the guy who was in this car?" He told us a cop pulled up behind Bobby and made him get out of his car. The cop had Bobby put his hands on the hood while he went back to his car to radio for help. The guy who had his hands on the hood took off running and jumped the fence. The cop then ran after him around the corner.

I looked at Paul and said, "Let's go! Get in the car! I'll drive! Hang on!" We jumped in the car and took off, turning the corner really slowly. A police car went by us fast, but the cop didn't notice we were in a stolen car. He thought it was in the parking lot. Then out of nowhere, as we were moving down the road very slowly looking for him, Bobby came running into the street waving his hands. As we were still moving, Paul opened the door. Bobby jumped into the back seat, got down, and screamed, "CLOSE CALL. LET'S GET OUT OF HERE!"

That night I dropped Bobby off at his house and took the car home. I parked it a block away so my father wouldn't see it.

The next day, Sunday, we went to the show. The Jose Theater was packed with young people we knew. We liked spending our Sundays at this theater.

Later that evening we had big plans. Our friends, the Lopez girls, wanted to go cruising with us. "No problem, man! We'll take you girls cruising anytime with us!" I said.

Taking the Lopez girls home to Virginia Place, we found we were overcrowded in the car. I was in the back seat with someone on my lap. It looked as if lights were on us. Bobby couldn't see out the back window because of all the heads, so I turned to see who was approaching from behind.

A cop car was behind us! He was so close it seemed as if he was on our bumper. I didn't know what I expected Bobby to do. He pulled over right there in the middle of the street, right on the corner of Virginia Place and King Road—the street I lived on, where everybody knew me. The cop jumped out of his vehicle and immediately ran to the side of our car. As soon as I opened the door to run, he was there, squatted down with his gun pointed right at my head.

"HOLD IT! HANDS ON THE CAR OR I'LL SHOOT!" He wasn't messing around.

We all got out very slowly and placed our hands where he directed us. We stayed there until he received backup. In the meantime everybody from the neighborhood wanted to see the show. We told the cop the girls had nothing to do with stealing the car and asked if he would let them go. He agreed.

All the surrounding neighborhood saw a cop holding his gun on these guys on the corner in the middle of the street. It was really embarrassing.

This was the first time I went to Juvenile Hall. Now I was going in for a lot longer and for a much more serious crime.

* * *

As we were driving away from Jackson Street where we had stopped, the cop asked me again, "Where's Ceasar? We know you were with him tonight."

"Ceasar who? I don't know what you're talking about. I told you that we were jumped on Capitol Avenue."

He told the other cop who was with us that we were going to the hospital first. He turned and asked me my age.

"Sixteen." I answered.

When we arrived at the hospital, I was asked the usual questions. We sat there for a while. I really didn't know what we were waiting for until I saw my mother enter the emergency room.

"What happened, Arthur?" she asked with a look on her face which said, "My poor mijo." My mother didn't know what was in store for her, all the worrying she was going to experience for the next few years.

The cops took me into the room, so the doctor could treat me. It took a while because they had to take some x-rays to make sure my skull wasn't fractured. My mother had to sign some papers in order for them to provide treatment. Twenty-four stitches were needed on the back of my head.

I heard the cop tell my mother I couldn't go home with her. She wanted to know why. "There has been some trouble tonight, and we want to make sure your boy wasn't involved in it," he said. I was still handcuffed.

My mother came over to give me a kiss and said, "Don't worry, mijo, everything is going to be all right."

As we were leaving the hospital and driving out of the parking lot, I saw my mother standing there looking sad and hurt. On the way to City Hall, my mind kept flashing back to when I was a small kid.

EARLY YEARS

My two brothers and sister and I were born at San Jose Hospital. I was born in 1949. My mother had a difficult time delivering me. In fact, she had a difficult time with all four of us. My oldest brother Eddie is two years older than I am. Following me in age is my sister Tita whose real name is Mildred. I think it was my little brother Victor that couldn't pronounce Mildred and would say Tita, so the name stayed with her. Victor is about four years younger than I am and two years younger than Tita.

Every time my mother had a baby, she would go blind for about three months. Why? She never found out. Eddie was her hardest birth. Both Eddie and my mother almost died at the time of his birth.

I was now thinking back to everything my parents had done for me. Here I was going to cause them so much pain, especially my mother.

My father was from the state of Chiapas in southern Mexico. He would tell us stories of his childhood and how he grew up in the jungles. When we watched Tarzan movies, he would say, "That's what it looked like when I was growing up." We really didn't believe him because we watched cowboy movies, and they showed Mexico as a desert. We went on vacations to Mexicali, and the country didn't look the way my father described Mexico.

My father came to the United States when he was a young man

in his twenties. He left his home town as a young man and went to Mexico City to work. His father was a lawyer and a doctor in the town of Venustiano Carranza. Venustiano Carranza was where my father was born; his five brothers and three sisters were also born there.

My father often talked about all the fun he had in the jungles. He would tell us about the giant snakes and the giant ants. That's right! The ants were so big a person could ride them like a horse.

Later on in life when I was a man, I took my family to Chiapas to visit. I told my relatives I came to see the giant ants for myself. They wanted to know which giant ants. I said, "The ones you can ride like a horse." They all laughed.

My mother was born in New Mexico. She had four brothers and four sisters in her family. When she married my father, my father only spoke Spanish. My mother only spoke English. Regardless, they fell in love and were married. They must have spoken in sign language.

As we were growing up, my father worked at the American Can Company. My mother worked at the cannery during the summer months.

My earliest memories reflect back to living on San Fernando Street. I have pleasant memories of our home, an apartment building built in the twenties. I remember we had a big yard on the side of the apartment where we played a lot. To run across the yard took a while. The yard seemed really big. In my memories the yard was like a football field, although it really wasn't.

My father built a swing set for us in that small area. He also added a small room to the side of the building for Eddie and me. It was only a one-bedroom apartment with a small kitchen and one small bathroom. I was four years old then.

I also remember the day my little brother Victor was born. My mother came home from the hospital, and we all wanted to see the little baby. That's all I remember of that day; I don't remember my mother going to the hospital or being away. I only remember little flashes of scenes.

One day we were in the bedroom with my father, and one of us let out some gas.

"WHO STUNK UP THE ROOM?" my father wanted to know.

"Not me!" Eddie said.

I looked at my father and said, "It wasn't me either!"

My father looked at both of us and said, "I'll find out who the guilty one is." He went over to his dresser and brought over this thing. I didn't know what it was. (When I became older, I found out it was a roulette game for gambling.) My father wanted to know if we wanted to change our minds.

"Not me!" I said.

Eddie, my brother, repeated the same thing.

"OK," my father said. "We'll find out." He spun a little b-b in the middle of a round thing. It spun and made a whirling noise. I couldn't believe my ears!

It made a noise and said, "AAAA-RRRR-TTTT-HHHH-UUUU-RRRR!" My father looked at me, and I stood up.

"Arturo, you lied to me!" my father said, staring at me.

How that thing could say my name, I don't know. Later when I was grown up, I asked my father how that thing knew my name. He couldn't remember. I think I imagined the noise saying my name, and my father saw the guilty look on my face.

These were funny memories I had of my earliest years. Now look at me, on the way to the police station, probably for murder.

THE INTERROGATION

The police didn't say too much to me on the way to the station. The other two times I was arrested, I went straight to Juvenile. This time it was different. I was on my way to the police station.

We drove to the front of the building and came to a stop. There were two other police officers waiting for us at the front door. I looked around to see if I could see Redhead or anyone else. It looked as if I was the only one there. The police who were waiting at the police station door came over and opened the car door. They asked the cops who brought me in if I had given them any trouble.

"How could I give them any trouble with these handcuffs on so tight," I thought as he was taking me out of the car. I asked the cop if he could remove the handcuffs.

"In a minute, kid, when we're inside."

He probably thought that if he removed them outside, I would run. If that's what he thought, he was right. I would have tried to get away.

When we entered the station, they told me to walk down the hall. As we approached the end of the hallway, they told me to turn right, down another hallway. There were many rooms through that hallway. Some of the doors were open; they looked like small interrogation rooms. All the doors had small one-way windows. One could look in through the outside of the door; but when you're on the inside, it looks like a mirror.

We stopped at one of these rooms, and they told me to step inside. When I was inside, the cop told me to turn around. He took off the handcuffs.

"My hands feel better now," I said in a low voice. My hands felt as if they were dead.

The cop told me, "Sit down on that chair, and don't get up!" He left the room and closed the door. It was very quiet; I could hear them talking outside the door.

In a little while one of them entered the room and sat down on one of the chairs.

"Do you want to tell me everything you know?" he asked.

I nodded.

"Go ahead," he said, feeling good and thinking I was going to give him information he didn't have.

I looked at him, and at the same time I could hear someone outside of my door. I said, "We were coming down Capitol Avenue when these guys were...."

He stopped me. "Hey! Don't tell us that story! We know that you were at the party on Keyes Street!"

Just then the other cop entered the room. I looked at the first cop right in the eye and said, "What party? I told you that I don't know anything about Keyes Street."

The questioning went on like this for about an hour. It was as if they were playing ball with me. One had me and then threw me to the other one to work me over.

"We know you were there."

"I was not there."

"Yes you were!"

By this time there were three cops in the room. In about an hour the phone rang, and the detective stood to answer it.

"Yeah, — yeah, — Oh no! Really? — OK, — OK." He hung up the phone really hard and looked at me for a long time, not saying anything.

He then walked over to the table. In front of me he stretched over the table with both arms spread out. He leaned over to me, about five inches from my face, and said, "One of the boys who was at the party is dead!"

I looked at him, frustrated, and replied, "What party?" His face turned red.

"Look, kid, this is not just a fight anymore. It's murder now, and this is big time! Do you want to go to prison for the rest of your life?"

"No I don't! But I don't know what you want me to say. I wasn't at that party! Is that what you want me to say, that I was there?" As I was talking, I knew someone was watching outside the door. I could hear them leaning against it.

Another officer barged into the room, rolling up his sleeves, as if he was saying, "Now we're going to take care of business." He grabbed another chair and sat down on it backwards. I waited to see what he was about to tell me.

"OK, Arthur, let's talk. Your friend told us everything. He's scared. He doesn't want to spend the rest of his life in jail. He told us you boys were on Keyes Street, and he gave us the names of the other guys who were with you. He also told us about Ceasar." He continued, "He already saved himself, and we want you to have a chance to save yourself."

I didn't say anything for a while. I thought to myself, "This cop is lying to me. I know he's lying to me. I know Redhead wouldn't rat on us... they're probably telling Redhead the same thing."

I looked at the cop and said, "I don't know what you guys want from me. You probably scared him into telling a lie. I don't know what he told you; but like I told you earlier, we got jumped on Capitol."

This interrogation went on for about another two hours, in and out of the room. I was told what Redhead told the police and that I should tell them everything I knew. They had some things right about what happened, but not everything. I felt if Redhead had really talked to them, they should know everything the way it happened.

I made up my mind. Even if they knew everything, I wasn't going to tell them anything because they could have heard it from someone else.

The detective said, "We know you were there, Arthur."

I repeated, "I wasn't there!" over and over again.

The phone rang again. The cop stood up to answer it. "Yeah — yeah — OK" and slammed the phone down hard on the table again.

He turned to look at me, "The other kid just died! This is a double murder now! Do you know that there has never been a double murder in San Jose? We're going to give you some time to think this over. When we come back, if you don't want to tell us what happened, we're done talking to you. We're then going after you for murder one!"

They all left the room, and again it was very quiet. I couldn't hear anybody by the door. I wondered what time it was. It was probably three or four in the morning. I was really tired and felt like getting on the floor and going to sleep.

How did I get into this mess? Why did I like to fight so much? When did this start?

THE FIRST FIGHT

When I was in the sixth grade, I attended Lee Matson School. At Lee Matson Junior High, I knew a lot of the kids in my same grade level.

One day at lunch, I was on the baseball field, sitting on the grass and talking to a friend, when some eighth graders came over and said they needed two more players for a game of football. I really didn't want to play with them because they were older than I and because I really didn't know them very well. However, they insisted I play.

"OK, I'll play!" I said. These guys were a lot bigger than I was. The other kid I was with was smarter; he said he didn't want to play. It seemed to me that when I played with these older guys, they would pick on me.

On one play I had a kid who was about two years older than I who got in front of me. My job was to try to pass him and tackle the guy with the ball.

"READY, SET, HIKE!" This big guy was laughing. He said he was going to cream me on that play. The play started; the guy came at me and kicked his leg in between my legs!

I went down and didn't get up. The kid who kicked me was laughing at me. I was hurt badly.

Some kid told me, "Come on, you can get up! You're going to get us in trouble. Come on, get up."

I tried, but I couldn't. A teacher had to carry me to the nurse's office. I wouldn't let her see where I was hurt, so she had to call my mother.

My mother came to take me home. She wanted to know what happened. She was angry because a big kid did this to me. "When your father gets home, you tell him what you told me."

I thought, "My dad is going to go to the school and beat up this kid for me." I really didn't want this to happen.

I was in my bed when my father arrived, still unable to walk. My father and mother were talking in the living room. I couldn't hear what they were saying, but my mother was probably telling him the story. In a little while my father came into my room with a frown on his face. He wanted to know what happened. He took a chair and sat down next to my bed.

"Let me see, mijo." I stood and showed him my injury I had down there. He frowned more. He looked at me, feeling sorry for me, and asked, "Do you know who this kid is?"

I told him he was a big kid in the eighth grade. He said "big" had nothing to do with it.

I thought, "Oh yes it does!" He asked if I knew who the kid was, and I replied that I did.

My father said, "You stay home a few days until you get better, and then you can get him back."

I thought to myself, "I can get him back? My father is going to have ME get him back?" I should have known.

In a few days I was well enough to return to school. My father said I would have to confront this kid after school. All day I was nervous. How was I going to do this? My father said he didn't care how I was going to do it, but I had to fight this kid.

Before my father left to work, he decided to talk to me. He came into my room, quietly saying, "Arturo, Arturo."

I opened my eyes, "What?" I thought to myself, "Maybe he's changed his mind now."

"Listen, remember I told you to get that kid?"

"Yeah." I answered hopefully.

Standing by the door, he said, "Don't forget what I told you. You have to get him. I don't care how you do it, even if you have to pick up a board and hit him with it! OK?"

I thought to myself, "This guy's a lot bigger than I am. If I start anything with him, he's going to get me."

My father wanted a reply, so with a stronger voice he said, "OK?"

"All right, Dad, I will." I answered.

I was worried about what was going to happen after school. The day went by fast. I wished I could have stopped time; but I couldn't, even if I had wanted to. I saw this kid a few times during the day. He didn't even know who I was.

I was watching the clock when the bell rang. Two-thirty. School was out. I left right away, ahead of all the kids, walking fast. One block from Lee Matson School was Mayfair, an elementary school. As I was walking to Mayfair from Lee Matson, I came to a big walnut tree. I stopped and waited for the kid. Down the street other kids were walking toward me. My stomach had butterflies; I was very excited, thinking I was going to be beaten up really badly. As I turned my head the other way, I looked up the street and said to myself, "Oh no!" I saw my father's Pontiac parked about a half block away; he was sitting in it. He left work early to see how I was going to take care of this.

"Here comes the kid," I thought. I was standing behind the tree hiding. There were some boards and sticks lying on the ground. I picked one up and stood there waiting. Seeing the kid walking toward me with a couple of his friends, I came out from behind the tree.

"Hey!" I yelled. He turned and saw me running toward him with the stick in my hands. I swung it at him, and he raised his books to block the blow.

"Hey, kid! What's wrong with you!"

I took another swing at him. He was running backwards. I don't think he remembered who I was.

He crossed the street, shaking his head, saying, "Dumb kid!"

I turned and saw my father driving away. I thought, "Dad should be satisfied."

When I came home, my father wasn't there. In fact, he didn't come home until late that night. The next day he didn't say anything to me; this meant he was happy with the outcome.

At school the next day, I talked to all my friends about the fight. They told me how bad I was to go after that big kid. They didn't know how scared I really was; but, nevertheless, I loved the praise. Everyone told me what a good fighter I was.

I think this is what started my love for street fighting. After this confrontation every time someone gave me a bad time, I would try to knock him out with the first punch. Then the fight would almost be over before it really started.

Now, here I was, such a good fighter and loving it. Look where it got me—at the police station being questioned for murder!

* * *

My eyes were getting heavy after a while. I wondered what time it was. I knew it was getting late, or I should say, early in the morning.

All this time I was in the interrogation room, I heard people in the hallway. Every so often someone would stop and look at me. They probably didn't think I could hear them. However, the room was so quiet that I could hear a lot of what was being said outside. I couldn't hear what they were saying all the time; but if they talked clearly and close to the door, I could make out some of the conversation.

About 7 a.m. two detectives came into the room. "Arthur, do you want to tell us anything?" This time they asked me in a different way.

"Not really," I said, anticipating their playing ball with me again, throwing me back and forth and trying to wear me down.

One of the detectives opened the door to the room and said, "OK, come on."

"Good!" I thought, "I'm getting out of this room. He's probably going to take me to Juvenile." As we were walking out in the hallway, I saw another door open. I realized he didn't put handcuffs on me. Out of the other door came another detective. Behind him was Redhead. Redhead looked as surprised as I was when he saw me. He walked to where I was standing, looked at me, and said, "Hey, how's it going, man?" We're looking at each other's eyes as if we were saying, "Hey, man, we did it."

"All right, man, how about you?" I asked. He shook his head.

The detective started to walk down the hallway. We followed

closely behind him.

"We don't want you boys to leave town, in case we have any more questions to ask you."

We made a left turn towards the big front doors of the building. I could see daylight outside.

"Can you get a ride home?" the detective asked.

This is where our big mistake happened. As we approached the front doors, Redhead asked the detective, "How can I get my car back?"

Stopping by the doors, the detective responded, "What happened to your car?"

Redhead replied, raising his hands, and motioning to the detective sarcastically, "You guys towed it away." Redhead looked as if he were saying, "Don't you remember, dummy?"

"I don't know what happened to your car, but I'll find out. You boys can sit right over there. I'll be right back." We sat where he told us to sit.

A window was in front of us. It looked as if a nice spring day was beginning.

"It's a nice morning out there," I told Redhead.

We were both wondering what was going to happen, even though we were now going to leave. Redhead looked at me. He sure looked tired; I knew I looked the same.

"What are you going to do now, Art?" Redhead asked.

"I'm going to Mexico, man! My father always wanted us to go there with him. Now I'm calling him when I get home and telling him that I'm coming. What about you?" I asked him.

"I don't know. Maybe they won't find out."

Just then the detective whom we asked about the car returned, joined by two other officers walking next to him. I noticed they were walking quickly toward us. As we started to stand, the detective asked Redhead, "If you weren't at the scene of the murder, why was your license number taken?"

Redhead looked at me, not knowing what to say. Moving his hand hesitantly, he said, "I guess we were at the wrong place at the wrong time."

Nodding his head, the detective said, "You're both under arrest for murder."

On the way to Juvenile Hall, I thought, "What a mess I got myself into. I'm going to Juvenile Hall again."

I had been to Juvenile two other times, once for stealing the car and another time when I was about fourteen years old.

THE BEER RUN

My friend Art, the one who lived next door to the Lopez girls on Virginia Place, Bobby, and another friend Henry, wanted to get drunk. Art had an idea.

"Let's go to the market on Alum Rock, get in through the back door, and get some beer."

"Yeah right!" I answered. "They're going to leave the back door open? They're not that stupid."

Art looked at me excitedly and said, "Yeah, man! A friend of mine worked there for a while, and he said they always leave the door open."

Looking at him, I thought for a few seconds and said, "If that's true, let's go! I'm ready!"

"I don't care. I'm ready too," Bobby said, moving his shoulders excitedly as he always did. Henry said he'd go too.

We left Virginia Place and walked down King Road. In those days King Road was a country road. It had no sidewalks, just a barbed-wire fence next to the road. It was late and dark. If we saw a car coming up the road, all of us would hide in the tall grass. We were always on the lookout for a cop car. Walking up the road, we reached Alum Rock Avenue and continued about a block where we came to the Alum Rock Store.

The store had a long driveway next to it that went all the way to the back where somebody lived. Two of us decided to go around the back while the other two waited in front. Once inside we would open the door for them. In the meantime they watched for cops.

Art and I walked around to the back. It was dark along the side of the small store. In the little house in the back, someone was home. I saw lights on, and I could hear voices in the house. We walked slowly and looked cautiously in front of us, so we wouldn't trip over anything and draw attention. We were approaching a ripped and dirty screen door. I reached to open the door, then I tried to open the main door. It was locked. I looked over at Art, but he was looking the other way because he thought he heard a noise in the back yard. I whispered, "Hey, Art." He didn't turn around. "Hey, Art! The door is locked! I thought you said it was going to be open."

He turned, pointed to the back of the building, and said, "Look, a window over there."

I went over to the window and checked to see if it was unlocked. It was. I pushed it up and crawled in. Art followed me. As soon as I was in, I opened the front door.

We were all in and looking around, checking out the store. I walked to the front window to make sure all was fine in the street. I looked back at Art who was breaking open the cash register with a bar. I said, "Art! What are you doing? I didn't want to take these people's money. I wanted beer!" Just then I heard the cash register break open.

"Hey! This thing doesn't have any money in it!" he said. By this time the other two guys started taking out the beer and putting the six packs in bags.

"We are going to party tonight with all this beer!" I said.

We didn't want to go out with all this beer through the front door because someone would see us with our arms full of bags and think they might be full of money. We decided to go out through the back door. We didn't want to cross the street because some people lived nearby, and the door of their place was open. So we started around the block, deciding to cross at Alum Rock where it was quieter.

As we turned the corner on the back side of the block, we were laughing at how easy it had been to steal all that beer. Just then an undercover-cop car drove by us really fast.

"Hey, man! Did you guys see that? That was a narc!" Bobby exclaimed.

"Are you sure?" Art asked. Each one of us had 4 six packs of beer in two bags.

"I'm sure!" Bobby said.

Just then a police car drove very slowly alongside us. There were two cops in the car. The driver of the car had his window open. Moving close to the curb, he asked, "What do you boys have in the bags?"

I thought to myself, "What are we going to do, answer him? He probably knows where we got this beer." Just then all of us dropped the bags at the same time and ran.

I ran toward a house. The people who lived there had a six-foot fence between their homes. I thought to myself, "I only have one chance to make it over." Not looking back at my friends and running as fast as I could, I went for it.

Already the cops were out of their cars and after us. I heard other cars racing down the street. I was barely making it over the fence. Over. Down the other side. I could hear yelling and a lot of police cars all over the street. I thought to myself that it was probably better not to run anymore. The yard had a lot of bushes. I stayed at the point where I had jumped the fence, falling down right there and not moving.

Around the side of the house, two cops came running. They stood there in the middle of the yard. One of the cops walked over to the back of the fence and started talking to another on the other side.

"He didn't come over to your side?"

"No, he didn't come over here. I was here waiting when they started running."

I thought to myself, "They had this well planned out and did it quickly. They must have started when we were in the store."

I could see them, but they couldn't see me. One grabbed his flashlight and started from one side, moving the light very slowly along the fence. He was getting closer to where I was. I didn't know if I should get up and run or take my chances where I was lying. If I stayed, maybe he'd miss me. I should take my chances, I decided. The beam of light passed over me. He didn't see me. Good!

I waited for a long time, thinking after a while they would give up and leave. Then I could go home and never do this again.

Lying there for about an hour, I could hear police talking out front. They were laughing and telling jokes to each other. Then I heard a car pull up; and someone said, "I got him!"

"All right!" one of the others exclaimed.

I thought to myself, "Got what? What are they talking about?"

I heard the side gate open. Their lights were shining on the fence. Then I heard it—a dog was barking at me. The cop hadn't let go of the leash. I knew I couldn't hide now.

I jumped up and climbed the fence to the front yard. The street was all lit up with approximately ten cops, all standing by their cars. I still continued to run past all of them. Three cops grabbed me, threw me on the ground, and handcuffed me. "Where are you going, kid?" one of them asked as he laughed.

This was my second visit to Juvenile Hall.

* * *

Now look at where I was. Murder!

"You're under arrest for murder!" the cop said.

"Maybe they'll find out I was just fighting with those guys, and I didn't actually kill anyone. Maybe they'll let me go," I thought to myself.

The last two times I went to Juvenile, I was released. The first time I was in for two days; the next time I was released in three days.

One thing you learn growing up in the streets is that you never rat on anyone, even if everything is riding on it. A rat is someone who tells on you. If you do rat on anyone, you might get off with a light sentence, but you might not get out of prison. Everybody knows you're a snitch and not to be trusted, so they put what's called a "jacket" on you. It's like wearing a school jacket with a big name on it; everybody knows who you are. When you leave the county jail to prison and arrive at a prison, everyone is waiting for you. They know who you are, what you're in for, and how long you'll be there. Sometimes they'll put a contract on you right away—they'll send someone to kill you. Therefore, you don't tell the cops anything.

THE FIGHTER

Here I was, waking up in my cell in Juvenile Hall. "Again!" I thought. "How long am I going to be here? I'll probably be out in a few days; I'm just here for fighting at a party. I didn't kill anybody. Even if I had, there were so many people there, the cops wouldn't know who did what. In a little while people who work here are going to come to get me and take me to my unit."

I lay on the bottom bunk bed thinking about a lot of things. I remembered the last time I was in Juvenile I was in Unit B-2. In those days there were three units they put kids into. There was B-1 for very young boys, B-2 for boys from 13 -16 years old, and B-3 for boys from 16-18 years old.

The last time I was there, I was in B-2. I had to share a cell with a guy who was getting into trouble because he wanted to go to the California Youth Authority. (CYA which I'll refer to YA) He said he was a champ of a fighter; and in YA if you beat up the guy in charge, then you take his place and are in charge of everybody. When I went to YA later on, I found out this wasn't true.

The first day I was with him in the locked cell, he told me he was going to let me get settled in for a day before he started to practice on me. He said he wanted to be in good shape by the time he was sent up to YA.

I was worried about him, hoping he wasn't a good fighter. He didn't look like one. He was a short, white guy, kind of stocky, and had one of those faces that looked as if he didn't have a chin.

They came to all the rooms and unlocked the doors. I didn't know what was going on; so he told me, "We're going to go out to the day room for a while; then we'll go to eat in about an hour. I try to get in a fight at least once in the morning and once in the afternoon." I didn't believe him. It seemed like talk. If it were true, then I could see what kind of fighter I was up against.

It didn't take long. I was sitting on a big chair watching TV, not talking to anyone because I was new and didn't know anyone. My cell mate walked up to another Chicano sitting on one of the chairs by me and said, "Hey, man! Get out of that chair! I want to sit down!" The Chicano looked like one of those tough guys; he just sat there looking at him. The white guy slapped the Chicano. The slap was just to get him angry and to get him out of his chair.

The Chicano sprang to his feet! As he got up, he showed his anger and took a swing at the same time. The white guy took a step back, and the swing missed. Then this short, stocky, white guy let into him hard, like a tank, both arms moving in and out fast, with jabs in and out, in and out! The Chicano guy went down! The white guy was on top of him in a second with more jabs, in and out! All the counselors were running over to break it up. Three of them had to pull the white guy off the Chicano, and still he wouldn't let go of him. He looked like a pit bull on speed.

Right there I felt a bucket of acid drop in my stomach. I was in the same cell with the white guy!

We were waiting in line to eat our dinner. My cell mate told this big guy that when he got his food, he wanted his dessert. The big guy said, "No way, man!" So my cell mate slapped the big guy in the head. My cell mate wanted the big guy to start fighting first. It was the same encounter which took place in the day room earlier. My cell mate was sent to lockup for the night and the next day. Lockup was a padded and dark cell at the end of the hallway.

The next day when my cell mate was released from lockup, I started thinking about my next move. The guard brought him back to our cell. Once the door was locked and the guard walked away, I asked him something. As he turned around to answer me, I hit him as hard as I could. He went down, but he didn't stay there for long. He got up, and we fought for a long time. Every time we tired from fighting and stopped to rest, I thought we were finished and that was it, however; in a little while we started again. I was fighting in anger, but he was just having a good time. In the next two days, we spent most of the time fighting. Sometimes he won. Sometimes I did.

The day I left Juvenile, we were like good friends. He said I was one of the best fighters that he had had the pleasure of locking horns with. He said no one ever hit him as I did when they first locked us in the cell. He shook my hand and said, "I'll see you one day in YA."

* * *

My door opened and I jumped up, startled. A guard with a breakfast tray entered. I thought I would have been assigned to my unit by then. I looked at the guard and reached for the tray, asking, "When am I going to my unit?"

Closing the door, he said coldly, "Not today, buddy!"

After breakfast I was doing the only thing there was to do, lying on my bed. About an hour later my door opened, and I was told to come out. I thought the other guard was wrong because it looked as if I were going to my unit. He told me to walk down the hall.

"In here," he said, pointing to a small room with a little window on the door.

When I walked into the room, I saw two detectives sitting there. They told me to sit on the chair. I sat down.

"Here we go again!" I thought.

One of the detectives started talking, "We would like to ask you some questions, Arthur. We want to know what happened at the party. We want you to know we want to help you. If you cooperate with us, we'll put that in our report."

"Sure, officer, I'll tell you anything you want to know. I don't want to get into any more trouble than I'm in already," I said, trying to put on a sad face.

The detective asked, "Who all were with you at the party?"

"What party?"

Agitated, he looked at me and said, "The party on Keyes Street where the two boys were killed?"

"Oh, that party. It was Art (Redhead) and me," I said in a matter-of-fact way.

The other detective added, "Who else was with you besides

Art?"

"That's all that was with us. There were a lot of other people there that I didn't know. But as far as Art and me, we're the only ones that were together."

Both detectives were now staring at me with blood in their eyes. One of them said, "Tell us the real story. What really happened?"

Answering him with a sober look on my face, I said, "I don't know."

"What do you mean, you don't know?"

"Well, it went like this. We went to this party. As we were walking up to the house, somebody came from behind me and hit me over the head with something!" I said, as I pointed to the stitches on the back of my head. Actually, when the guy hit me with the pipe, it had an elbow on the end of it. It looked as if I was hit on the back of the head from behind.

Looking at the other detective, he looked back at me and asked, "Who started the fight?"

"I don't know!"

The detective looked at the other one and said, "We're not getting anywhere with this smart aleck." Getting up from his chair, he said, "Let's get out of here. This is the first party I've heard of where there was a fight, and everybody who was there didn't see anything or hear anything!"

They left the room and walked away. I stayed until someone came after me and took me back to my cell.

The next morning after eating my breakfast, my door opened. I was told to come out, and I did what I was told. The guard said I had a visitor. He walked me to the same rooms where I previously met with the detectives.

The guard told me which room to enter. There were about four rooms in a row. Walking into the room, I saw a man sitting there with a lot of papers in front of him. I thought it was another detective. More questions. I already gave them all my answers. Now what did they want?

This man was middle-aged with thin, brown hair. He was wearing a gray suit, slouching in the chair, and taking a puff of his cigarette as I entered.

"Hi, Arthur!" he said as he let smoke out. He continued, "My name is Mr. Anderson. Your father and mother hired me as your lawyer."

A lawyer for me? I wondered why. My father wasn't here; he was in Mexico.

"You said my father and mother hired you?" I asked.

"Yep, that's what I said. They called me this morning."

"But my father's not here; he's in Mexico." I said.

"I don't think so; I think he's here." he answered.

"Well, Arthur, let's get started. What can you tell me about what happened the other night when you were arrested?"

I thought for a minute. Then I repeated the same thing I had told the detectives. I didn't know this lawyer, and I didn't trust him either.

"So what you're saying is you didn't see anything?" he asked.

"No, I didn't. If I did, I would tell you so." I said.

I was thinking to myself, "Why did they get me a lawyer? I should be out of here in a few days. The police didn't know what happened at that party. If they didn't know, then they have to let us go."

I was going to ask him how long I was going to be locked up, thinking I should be out in a day or so, no more than a week. He said, "What's making this thing worse is the newspapers. You kids have been front-page headlines for two days already."

"Front page? What do you mean front page?" I asked.

He went on to tell me more bad news. "Your brother's case doesn't look very good because of his age, but ..." He stopped talking for only a second. I couldn't believe my ears, my brother. They got my brother? They must know more than I thought they knew.

"They got my brother?" I asked.

"But your age," he continued, not even listening to my question. "I have to do more research; but I think because of your age, they can't give you the electric chair!"

"The electric chair," I uttered in a low voice, not believing my ears! Here I was thinking I was going to be getting out of this place soon, and now this guy was talking about the electric chair!

"Oh, yeah! I think I can save you from it because you're sixteen. I think, but don't quote me on this, if you are sixteen, they can't give you capital punishment."

The lawyer ended up doing a very bad job on our case. My

father and mother didn't know anything about lawyers. He was the same one they used when they got their divorce and the only one they knew to call.

Still not believing him, I asked, "You mean you're telling me I'm not getting out in a few days?"

"I think if I get you off with life, then you'll be doing well. We'll see how it's going to go later."

After I heard this, I forgot the rest of the conversation. I do remember him telling me not to talk to the detectives anymore. He said if they came by to talk to me, I was to tell them to call my lawyer. That sounded good to me.

The week that followed I stayed in the cell, only coming out once briefly when the detectives returned to talk to me. After they took me to the small room, I told them what my lawyer had told me to say.

"Are you sure? If you talk to us and tell us what we want to know, we can help you get out really fast."

"Hey, you should let me out because I already told you everything I know." They didn't say anything, just stood up and left the room.

In about three days I was called out of my cell and led to the main lobby of Juvenile Hall. When I entered the room, I saw Steve, Isaac, and Phil all sitting and waiting. Steve was the driver of Ceasar's car when they first drove up at Robert's house.

When I saw them, I said, "Hey, man, how's it going?" I was glad to see them. I thought I was the only one locked up in Juvenile.

Some detectives were there, about five or six. One of them looked at me and said, "Hey, no talking!"

I took a seat on one of the chairs. Just as I sat down, another detective opened the door from the outside of the building and said, "OK, we're ready."

The other detective said to us, "OK, come on, let's go."

I didn't know where we were going. Looking at Isaac I asked, "Isaac, where are we going?"

"I don't know. They just told me let's go. They didn't even give me time to wash up or comb my hair. I was sleeping." His hair was standing up in some parts.

Walking outside, we saw there were ten policemen waiting to

escort us. We walked down the street and then turned the corner, entering a building through a side door. We went in through some double doors that swung open.

As soon as the detectives swung the doors open, I was blinded by the flashes. Not just one flash, but it seemed the cameras wouldn't stop. At first I didn't know what was causing the flashing. After a little while they all stopped to change their bulbs. In those days the reporters had the old cameras that required bulbs to be changed after every picture. The next day's newspaper printed photos which appeared as if we were trying to cover our faces from embarrassment. This wasn't so. The flashes had blinded us.

Where were we going? To court? When I was in Juvenile in the past, I had to go to court in the Juvenile facility. Because this case was so serious, we went to the main court.

Walking into the courtroom, I saw my brother and all the other guys sitting together. I saw my mother and some of our friends. The family and friends of the boys who died were there also.

The pretrial hearing didn't last too long. We stood up and said, "Not guilty!" Right after we pleaded not guilty, the hearing was over. We walked out, walked through all the cameras again, and went back to our cells. I didn't talk to my lawyer.

The following Sunday my mother came to see me. She didn't look well. She looked tired and worried from all that had happened. I tried to look positive, even though I didn't like it there at all. She asked me, "How's everything going over here, mijo? Are they feeding you OK?"

"Sure, Mom, I'm fine. I have my own room, and it's clean. I eat three times a day." I didn't tell her I wasn't eating well. Not that it wasn't good food, I just wasn't hungry. I told her I had my own room; however, it was really a cell.

After my mother left, I was sad, not for me but for her. I went back to my cell and sat on my bed doing nothing, just as I did all the other days. After one week in that cell, I knew it very well, every crack on the walls. I even knew how many concrete bricks were on the walls. All I could do was count them, over and over again.

THE REPORT CARD

When I was in the fourth grade, I had a difficult time in school. I couldn't learn my math and spelling words, was always clowning around in class, and was getting into trouble.

Every time my mother went to teacher conferences, I would get hit with a belt by my father. My father didn't give love taps. In fact, once he went to Mexico to visit and brought back a real leather whip. He hung it where he usually hung his belt, on the hot water heater.

My mother was scheduled to talk with my teacher on this day. All day I was worried because I knew what was going to happen when I arrived home or my father got home.

All through my school years, I had a difficult time learning. Things just wouldn't stick in my mind. Through my years in school, all the same guys were in the same group; we were called the slow group. In class we played around and were sent to the principal. At times I would really put forth an effort to try to learn, but I just couldn't.

That's what I used to tell my father, but he wouldn't believe me. The day before my mother went to talk with my teacher to see how I was doing in school, my father called me into the living room where he was lying on the couch watching television. "Arturo, Arturo!" I was in my room with my brother Eddie.

"Arthur! Dad wants you!" Eddie told me.

I listened and said, "No, he doesn't want me." If my father

wanted me, then I was going to be hit for something. He hit us almost everyday.

If we made my father wait too long after he called us, then we'd also get hit for making him wait.

"Arturo!" my father yelled, sounding irritated. I ran to the living room.

"What, Dad?" Hearing his tone, I stood there feeling afraid of what he wanted from me.

"Where were you?" he asked.

"I was in the room," I answered, pulling the side of my pants and feeling scared.

Trying to decide what he was going to do because he had to call me twice, he stayed there thinking. After a while he said, "Your mother is going to school to talk to your teacher tomorrow. How are you doing?" I didn't know why my father would ask me such a question. He knew how I was doing. I think there was never a time in all the days I went to school that I did well; however, I sure wasn't going to tell my father that. I would have been hit even more.

"I don't know, Dad," I said.

"Arturo," he said, "if I were you, I would go to school tomorrow and tell your teacher 'Please tell my mother I'm doing good in school! Please! Please! Because if you don't, my father is going to hit me with a whip! A real whip!' If I were you, I would get down on my knees and tell my teacher that."

I didn't want to get hit; however, I knew I could not go and tell my teacher this. Or could I? Maybe she'd lie for me. No, she didn't like me. Some teachers were cool, but this one was extra mean with me.

As I walked to my room, I stopped to look at the whip hanging by the hot water heater. "What an ugly thing!" I thought. I even thought of getting the whip and hiding it, so my father would have to hit me with a regular belt. No, if I did that, my father would have a fit and tear the house up looking for it. Then all of us would get big spankings. If he hit all of us, then he'd know he spanked the right one. One of us would be the right one.

The next day at school, I was waiting for the right opportunity to talk with my teacher. The more I thought of the whip hanging there, the more I knew I had to try to prevent it. The lunch bell rang. All the kids ran out of the classroom. Usually I was one of the first ones out the door. Not today. I stayed in my seat.

Three girls also stayed in class and went to the teacher's desk to talk with her. They were having a good time laughing and didn't notice me sitting there waiting. About five minutes later the girls left the room. Now it was my turn to talk with the teacher. I stood up from my chair and headed slowly to her desk. Her eyes looked up to meet me with a look on her face that said, "What do you want! I don't like you! So what are you doing here!"

When I reached her desk, she was looking at me over the rims of her glasses, waiting to see what I was about to say. My stomach felt as if it was going to turn upside down!

"Mrs. Heagan," I said, "I want to talk to you about my mother coming to talk to you today."

She looked at me with a sarcastic look and nodded her head, waiting to see what I was going to ask. Mrs. Heagan was an older lady with gray hair. She was a strict teacher, and she didn't like it when things didn't go her way. She didn't put up with it. If we were out of line, she would stand up, go to the phone on the wall, pick it up, and say she was sending someone to the office.

Through the years some teachers would try to help me learn, helping and showing me how to do what I was supposed to do. But not Mrs. Heagan. She gave me my work; and if I didn't do it, even if I didn't understand, it was too bad.

"Mrs. Heagan, if you tell my mother that I'm not doing good in school," I said, "my dad has this whip that he brought over from Mexico. And he's going to beat me with it. So please tell my mother that I'm doing good; and if you do that, then I'll try harder to do my work."

All she did was nod her head, not up and down, but back and forth, as if I were lying about the whip. I knew what she was thinking, so I continued. "He does have a whip! He used it on us already. My uncle in Mexico gave it to him. My uncle did give it to him but not to use it on us."

Nodding her head, still looking at me over the top of her glasses, she said, "I have to tell your mother how you're doing. If you want to get a good report, you'll have to try harder."

"But I am trying!" I answered.

I could tell that wasn't going to work. Mrs. Heagan didn't care what happened to me. My father was probably going to kill me for this, and she didn't care.

She didn't feel sorry for me at all. In fact, it seemed as if she wanted me to get hit with that whip! Through all my years in school, I remember her as my meanest teacher.

Later that day my mother went to talk with Mrs. Heagan. I was in my bedroom waiting for her to return; my father wasn't back from work yet. I was in my room, and I didn't feel well. I heard the front door open and close, and I hoped it was my mother and not my father. I sneaked in the hallway to see who it was. If it was my father, I didn't want him to see me. I might get hit early, and I didn't want that to happen. My father would always find something wrong.

My mother was sitting on the couch looking at some papers when I entered. I walked over to give her a kiss. She was always good with us. She would feel really bad when our father hit us the way he did, but there was nothing she could do about it. When he hit us and went to the point of abusing us, if my mother said anything to him, he really became upset with her. I guess it didn't matter much because he was always angry with her anyway.

My mother put her arm around me and said, "Why don't you try harder in school, Arthur."

"I do try, Mom, but ...." I didn't know what to say. When I was in school, I wanted to learn; but it was difficult for me to remember things.

My mother and I knew what was going to take place when my father arrived home. She told me to go in the backyard or to my room until he arrived.

I knew what I was going to do. It might work! My father loved to see us kids working. My plan was to go outside and start pulling weeds in the yard. When he got home, he might say, "Oh what a good boy! I think I'll let him off and won't spank him because he's pulling weeds!" I thought hopefully.

I started pulling weeds in the front yard. Next to the driveway we grew some rose bushes that always had crab grass around them. By doing this, when my father got home, the first thing he'd see would be me working. I made a good pile of weeds then stopped and watched for him to drive down the street. I felt nervous and sat waiting on the street curb.

Our house was the second to the last one on the dead-end street. The asphalt from the street ended right before it reached our house. In the winters the street was a muddy mess. Our backyard was big with nothing but dirt when we bought the house. At the back of the yard was a barbed-wire fence. On the other side of the fence were fields with a lot of cows.

Looking down the street two blocks where Virginia Place started, I could see a car turning the corner that looked like my father's car. I stood up and kept looking. The car was getting closer. The closer it got, the more it looked like him. My stomach felt as if it had butterflies. I ran to the rose bushes and started working. The car was only a few houses down now. I kneeled down and pretended I didn't see him. I waited for a few more seconds, but it wasn't him.

I ended up waiting for about two hours before my father drove up. When he did, I started to work extra fast.

"Hi, Dad!" I said, sitting on the ground with weeds in my hand. He stood there for a minute and just looked at me. At the time I thought I was impressing him, but now I know what he was really thinking. He didn't say anything and walked into the house. I sat there wondering what was going to happen. "I hope! I hope!" The front door opened.

My father was standing there. "Arturo! Come in here!" he said harshly.

"Here we go!" I thought as I stood up. I walked to the door and saw the whip in his hand. I felt like running. Where would I run to? I had been through this so many times in the past. I hated it! I walked in the door, and I was already crying. My father became angry at me and told me to be brave. I couldn't! I knew he was not going to stop hitting me. He went wild when he hit us. He then told me to turn around and give him my back. I did because I knew if I didn't, it would only make it worse.

"I told you to tell your teacher to tell your mother you were doing good!" my father yelled, as I felt the first hit on my back. "Answer me!" he shouted. I didn't know it was a question, or I would have answered him. With that first hit to my back, I went down. Another blow hit me as I was going down. I felt my back sting. It was the whip! It hurt worse than the belt. He paused for a second and said, "From now on I want good grades!" and resumed his beating. I saw the whip coming down, so I put up my hand to protect myself. My father became angrier! He yelled out that every time I put my hands up, he was going to hit me two more times! I really tried not to put my hands up, but I had a hard time.

"Help! NO! STOP, DAD! STOP! PLEASE! MOM! MOM!" No one came to my rescue. My mother had a hard time because my father was so overpowering. She tried in the past, but it only made things worse.

Like a broken record, this kind of thing went on all through my childhood. If it were not for school, it was for other things.

By the time I went to high school, I wasn't interested in school work. I went to school to be with my friends and to check out the girls.

* * *

Waking up in my cell, I felt a pain shoot through my mouth. A toothache! It hurt so much I couldn't eat my breakfast. I told the guard I had a toothache, but he didn't seem to care.

Around noon one guard came to my cell to see how I was doing. I told him I wasn't doing very well; my tooth was getting worse. He opened the door and entered. He was a young Chicano. I liked this man because I could see compassion in his eyes. He talked to me in a mild tone; it showed his feelings for me. He seemed to be the nicest guard of all.

"How you doing, kid?" he asked. He wasn't that old himself. He looked as if he was about twenty-five years old.

"I need to go to the dentist!" I said, holding the side of my jaw.

"I'll see what I can do," he said as he closed the door and locked it.

The rest of the day the toothache didn't go away. I couldn't eat anything, and I lay on my bed moaning. I heard the keys and the door open, but I was in so much pain that I didn't look up. The Chicano guard came in. Standing next to my bed, he said, "How you doing, partner?" I couldn't answer him; the pain was so bad. Thinking back to this, I don't think I was ever in so much pain before or after this time. He said, "I'm having a hard time getting them to take you to the dentist. They say they have to get a court order and a special escort. I just wanted you to know that I'm still trying."

I said, "I'm lying here rolling in pain! This is two days already. If they can't take me to the dentist, then they should bring one to me."

All night I didn't sleep. I rolled around on the floor in pain and kicked the door. Maybe they'd come and shoot me to take this pain away! Every so often the guard would stop to check on me. I couldn't talk very well because my mouth was swollen and there was so much pain. Once, one of them came and opened the door, standing and looking at me. After a long time he said, "Just checking on you. How are you doing?" I was angry. Why were they checking? To see if I was dead yet! Rolling around on the floor, holding my face with both hands, I yelled, "What the heck do you think, man! I need a doctor!"

The morning light started to come through the window. As I continued to roll on the floor in pain, I heard someone outside of my door, but I couldn't look up. I felt as if I were in a torture chamber, and they would come to look at me to see if I was suffering enough. Three days passed with that pain. I felt like dying. I wanted to die. Part of the time I was rolling around; and some of the time I was on my knees against the brick wall, banging my head on it to relieve the pain.

About midmorning I was lying on my bed, kicking the wall and kicking the top bunk. I hadn't slept for two nights and was tired. Then I saw green! What a beautiful park. I had seen this before! It had a lake and a lot of ducks on the water. I saw people playing in the distance. I went to lie under a tree. "What a nice place this park is. My tooth doesn't hurt here! No more pain. I feel really good!"

I took a deep breath. "I hear something! What is that noise?" It sounded like keys. Keys here?

"OK, Arthur. Let's go!" a voice said. Waking up from a deep sleep, I realized where I was. Something felt different in my mouth. The pain was gone! My tooth didn't hurt anymore.

"Where are we going?" I asked as I woke up.

The guard whom I liked was the one who opened my door. He said, "We finally reached a judge to sign a court order to take you to a dentist." With my hand I felt my face. It was hard to believe all that pain was gone. "Should I tell them it's gone?"

As I was washing up, the guard was waiting, holding the door open. I held my jaw as I walked out of the room, so they would think it still hurt. I thought to myself, "I'll let them take me out of here anyway. It will be like a field trip."

They had two detectives and a regular police officer escort me. Before leaving, they put shackles around my body as they would a wild animal. Shackles are chains that came up around my back then over to my hands and around my body.

At the dentist's I had to wait in the waiting room with the three officers while wearing the shackles. The other people who were waiting couldn't take their eyes off me. I didn't care. I was glad to be out of that torture chamber.

The dentist said the reason the pain stopped was because my tooth died; the nerve in the molar died. He looked at me and said, "You must have had a lot of pain. How did you put up with it?" He had to pull the molar even though it was dead because it would have caused blood poisoning.

Walking back into my cell with a big wad of cotton in my mouth, I sat on my bed. The cell didn't look so bad now that I wasn't rolling around on the floor. I rested on my bed, thinking back to when I was a kid.

THE CRUISE

When I was five years old, we moved from San Fernando Street to Spencer Street. Spencer crossed Virginia Street, one block from Delmas Street. My father had a small house he bought for a really low price. It was a small one-bedroom home with a kitchen, one bathroom, and living room. The living room was where Eddie and I slept. Tita and Victor slept in the room with my mother and father.

Outside of the house there was a big backyard with a lot of weeds. Eddie and I later grew to know the reproductive power of those weeds very well; we did a lot of weed cutting through the years. Also in the backyard there was an old boat with a broken bottom. When we first moved into that house, it wasn't in such bad shape. Through the years we kids rode the boat around the world. By the time we moved, it couldn't be sailed anymore.

My father worked at the can company. He would make us bank cans; the tops had holes like a piggy bank. We had one bank in the house that already had a lot of money in it.

I gave the bank a lot of thought. I decided I was going to rob it. I was going to ask Eddie if he wanted to do it with me. After thinking it over, if I asked Eddie, he was going to want half of the money. Knowing my brother, he was going to want most of the money. So I decided to do it by myself.

I waited until the next day. I thought it was well planned out. I would take the money and run! Who knows where I would run, but I would run!

My father was working, and my mother was sleeping because she worked nights at the cannery. I walked into the house, got the bank, and made my getaway on the boat! I stayed in the boat for a while, then I ran into the house and took a knife from the kitchen. It was hard to break the bank open. I was only able to bend the top of the can to make the opening bigger. Once I removed the money, I filled my pockets and went to the corner store on Virginia Street and Delmas.

Having all this money, I felt like a big shot. I couldn't fit all the candy in my pockets and decided to give every kid around our house some candy and gum. My brother wanted to know where I got the candy. I told him a man at the park gave it to me.

The neighborhood store was only a block away. The park was across the street from the store. In those days it was very different from today. We kids walked to the store anytime. When we went to the park, we were careful with the cars because we had to cross the main street.

With all that candy, I went to my boat and went on vacation. It was sure nice with no worries, just cruise on my boat around the world, lying in the sun. I imagined the tall weeds around the boat were the waves; they never came into the boat. What a life: my mouth full of gum and my pockets full of candy!

"What is that I hear in the distance?" I thought. "Is it someone calling me?"

"Arthur! Arthur! Dad wants you!" Standing up very quickly, I spit the gum out of my mouth. I didn't know what to do! "Oh no!" I thought. "Why didn't I think about what I was going to do when my father got home?"

Again, Tita yelled at the top of her voice, "Arthur, Dad wants you!"

As I entered the house, my father was sitting on my bed holding the can. How did he get that can? I thought I threw it away on the sidewalk in front of our house. How did he get it? My father was looking at me as I entered the room. Eddie and Tita were next to him.

"Arturo, did you take the can and the money?" he asked with a very serious look.

"What can, Dad?" I said, trying to look surprised.

"Come here," he said, motioning his hand to draw me closer. His eyes were fixed on my pockets that were bulging with candy and money. He emptied my pockets on the bed. At the bottom of my pockets was some money I hadn't spent yet. He sat there for the longest time staring at me, waiting for me to say something. Finally he said, "Where did you get the money, Arturo?" He continued, "Don't lie to me because if you lie, you're going to get it worse." Standing there, I planned my answer in my mind. I knew what I was going to say to get out of this mess.

"Dad, I found the money in the boat. It was all on the floor in the boat."

He looked at me for a second, his looks expressing doubt. "Who put the money in the boat?"

I didn't have any time to answer my father. He stood up and started walking to the back door and said, "Come with me!"

I followed him to the boat. Standing next to the boat, my father asked me, "Where did you find the money?" My father handed me two pennies. I took the pennies, stepped into the boat, and put one on a spot very carefully. I looked up at my father. He was standing there with one foot on the side of the boat, wondering where I was going to put the other penny. I stood there for a second, thinking it looked as if he believed me.

"Why would he bring me out here, if he didn't believe me? He could have spanked me right away. I better make this look really good," I thought.

I bent over and put the other penny down on a spot and said, "I found this one right here!"

"Are you sure you found that one on that spot?"

I picked up the penny and moved it over about two inches.

"It was right here!" I said. When I looked at my father, he was already walking away.

"Arturo, come in the house!" he said without turning around.

This was the endless spanking that wouldn't end. I must have been hit about ten times with the belt.

As a young boy this was something that also happened a lot with my brothers and sister. My father had his way of raising us. Even though he was abusive when we were growing up, we loved him very much, especially when we got older. Once we asked him, as adults,

"Dad, why were you so hard on us when we were young kids?"

"Mijo, you guys were little devils," he answered. "I couldn't treat you normally. You guys were wild!"

Thinking back to my childhood, I know we were kids who were hard to handle. I also know we were dealt with more harshly than other kids. However, we grew up loving my father very much; and he loved us dearly.

* * *

I heard a voice on a speaker outside my door, "Mr. Jones, call receiving." I was back in my cell from my trip through time.

There was nothing to do in that cell. It had been two weeks since I arrived and had been waiting to see what was to happen. The day before they let me out for a little while to stand in the hallway. While I was in hallway, I saw Isaac and Steve in the cells next to me. All this time they had been there, and I didn't know it. I thought they were being held somewhere else. Isaac was trying to tell me something through his small window on his door.

I didn't know Isaac very well. I went to Mayfair and Lee Matson school with him. Although we were in the same class, we didn't hang around with each other. I had heard of his brother Ceasar who was two years older than I. He was supposed to be a tough guy.

When the guard returned me to my cell, he told me I might be moved to the county jail soon. This was the first time I had heard this. I asked, "What is the reason?"

He told me we were going to court the next day. They were going to decide if we were to be tried as adults in Superior Court instead of juveniles. He didn't know when I would be moved.

It had been two weeks since we got into trouble. My mother had come to visit again last Sunday; she didn't say anything about going to Superior Court. Maybe she didn't know.

The next morning they came and took us out of our cells just as they had when we previously went to court. Isaac, Philip, and I went into the main lobby. The friendly guard was working on that day; he came over to talk to us for a while. He said, "How are you boys doing?"

"I'm OK." I answered. Isaac and Philip told him the same thing.

"I'm sorry to see you boys go. I think it would have been better for you if you could stay here," the Chicano guard said.

"This is all news to me," I said. "Someone told me yesterday I might be moved, but he didn't know when." That's what happens when one has a bad lawyer; he doesn't come around to tell you anything. All it seemed he did was collect money from my parents.

"You mean we're not coming back?" I asked.

"Didn't you know?" the guard asked.

"No, I didn't know. Did you guys know?" I asked, looking at Isaac and Phillip.

"I didn't know," Isaac said. Phillip nodded his head, indicating he didn't know either.

"Yeah, you boys are going to court today; and you're going to be moved. You're going to Superior Court to be tried as adults. In fact, I hear they have a place for you over there." He paused for a second, knowing he had our attention. He continued, "I understand they're getting it ready right now. Right after court you're going straight over to the jail and not coming back."

Steve wasn't going because he was too young. The newspapers were wrong about everything they wrote, even Art's age. He was the youngest of all of us. Because he was fifteen years old, the law stated he couldn't be tried in Superior Court.

I thanked the Chicano guard for being cool. I thought he was the only one who was straight-up with me.

We left through the main doors of the lobby just as we had before. It was almost a repeat of the first time, with all the cameras and the flashing lights blinding us. The court room was crowded with people we knew. The older guys weren't there this time, just us younger ones. Again, court didn't last too long. I remember it was as if they were speaking a different language; I didn't understand anything that was said. After court it was just as the guard had said; we went to jail.

BEHIND BARS

After court we didn't have to exit through the door with all the reporters. There was a door in back of the court that went down a tunnel to the main jail.

As we were walking through the tunnel, we passed a lot of holding cells with prisoners in them. The prisoners were sitting down on benches in the cells waiting to go to court. When the three of us walked by them with the sheriff who was escorting us, the prisoners stood as they saw us coming. They walked over to the bars to talk to us. We were special to them because we were youngsters.

A lot of the prisoners were in their fifties and sixties. Some of them said, "Hey, kids, how you doing?" Others said, "You kids take care of yourselves, you hear!" They heard we were coming from Juvenile Hall. These old timers treated us very well through our stay. They were the ones who brought food to our cells, and they gave us as much food as we wanted.

Coming into the main jail, we heard someone call out, "Hey, here they come!" It looked like a dormitory; everybody came over to the bars to look at us. I kept looking for my brother, but I didn't see him. I thought, "He's in here somewhere." Little did I know they had all our friends upstairs in small cells in Max Row, short for Maximum Security.

The sheriff led us up three flights of stairs; then we came to a holding cell. Everybody was dressed in the same kind of clothes. We waited in the holding cell for about an hour. Phillip, Isaac, and I were talking about things that happened at Juvenile Hall. I told them about my tooth, but they already knew about it.

"How did you guys know about it?" I asked.

Isaac said he could hear me down the hall. I made a lot a noise. He also heard me yell at the guard and get away with it.

"I was hurting, man!" I said. I then asked Isaac, "What did your lawyer say?"

Isaac nodded his head and said, "I don't know, man. He hasn't come around." He continued, "I think he's talking to my family."

Our holding cell had four walls of bars, like a cage with a bar door in front. It also had a bench all around the inside. Across the hall from us, there was a desk with a sheriff sitting behind it. Prisoners were all around him talking. Some prisoners were waiting in line to use a pay phone on the wall next to the desk. Other prisoners were mopping the floors. We stopped talking for a while to check things out.

Looking at the guy mopping, I was reminded of a time when my dad became really angry with me.

THE MAT

My father had a rule with Eddie and me. On Saturdays we had to be working in the yard before the sun came up in the morning. If my father woke us up, that meant we would be hit with the belt. We would have to work until the sun went down. If we finished all the work there was, then we had to turn over dirt. We would never tell my father we ran out of work.

My father was working on his car. I was in the front yard pulling weeds, minding my own business.

"Arturo! Arturo, come here, hurry!" my father yelled out.

Running over to where he was by his car, I said, "What, Dad?"

"Go in the house and get me a mat. Hurry!" my father said, wanting me to run, not walk.

Not wasting any time, I ran in the house, eyes wide open, and scared because my father said "Hurry!" When he said hurry, he meant HURRY! "Mom, Mom, Dad wants a mat!" I declared.

I was sure he wanted a mat, even though he couldn't speak English very well. My mother looked at me and said quite calmly, "If your father wants a mat, Arthur, take him a mat."

Not knowing what to do, I said, "What mat, Mom?"

My mother looked at me and said, "Why are you so excited, Arthur?" She continued, "Get the mat from the front door." She didn't finish saying the words when I took off for the front door. I didn't want my father to wait any longer then he had to. Grabbing the mat, I ran to the car where my father was working.

"Here, Dad, here's the mat," I said, holding up the mat and hoping I did the right thing.

My father stopped working for a minute, sat there, and looked at me without saying anything. The longer he looked at me, it seemed the angrier he became.

I stood there holding the mat, thinking, "I'm going to get it!"

My father stood up from the side of the car, moved over about three inches from my face, and with fire in his eyes said, "Estupido!" [stupid] I told you the mat!

Not knowing what he meant, I asked, "Dad, what mat?" Now he was really angry.

"THE MAT! THE MAT! ESTUPIDO, GO GET ME THE MAT!" If his brown face could turn red, it would have.

Not wasting any time, I ran toward the house. When I entered the house, I let the mat I had in my hand drop where it may. "Mom! Mom!" I yelled with terror. "Mom, Dad wants a mat!"

My mother turned to look at me and said calmly, "Did you take him the mat from the front door?"

Then I said hurriedly, "Yes, but that's not what he wanted!"

My mother stood there, nodding her head back and forth at me. She said, "Well, you have to ask him what he means when he says the mat."

"I did. He only got madder!" I stated.

"Then he probably meant the back mat," my mother answered.

Taking off again, I headed to the back door, knowing by now I was taking too long for my father. This meant I was going to get the belt. I grabbed the mat from the back door and thought he must want to sit on it or something. Out of breath, I reached him and said, "Here's the mat from the back door, Dad!"

My father looked at me and said in a furious undertone the word he loved to use, "Estupido!" He stood up and took off his belt.

"Dad, you said the mat! This is the mat! Just tell me what mat you want, and I'll go get it! Please, Dad, I'll go get it! Please, Dad!" I pleaded with him.

My father took the first swing with the belt and struck me around the shoulder. I took a step back.

"Dad! I'll go get the mat. I'll get whatever you want!" Another swing hit me around my legs. I started to fall on the grass. Just then my mother ran out the front door.

"Joe! Joe! Why are you hitting him?"

My father looked at my mother and said, "I told the ESTU-PIDO to bring me the mat, and he brings me the MAT!"

My mother asked, understanding the way my father pronounced certain words in English, "What is it you want?"

"THE MAT! THE MAT!" he yelled.

"Oh, you mean the MOP," my mother said.

I was hit again for nothing. My father would tell us he knew we did a lot of bad things and got away with them. However, when he hit us for something we didn't do, it really wasn't for nothing. It was for something we had done and for which we didn't get caught.

* * *

Sitting in the cell checking things out, I realized my life had really changed. Some of these men looked like old timers. I hoped I wouldn't turn out to be like them.

Just then a sheriff came to the bar door with his keys. Unlocking the cell he said, "OK, boys, let's go!" Not knowing where we were going, we were led down a hallway.

On both sides of the hallway were big cells with about 20-30 men in each one. It looked as if everyone there smoked. Some were sitting in chairs around a TV. A lot of the prisoners were gathered around tables playing cards, and some were on their bunks sleeping. Turning left down another hall, the sheriff said, "This way, boys." The hallway we just turned down wasn't too long. At the end of the hall there was a door with two sections. The top half was opened, and the bottom half looked as if it had a shelf. To the left of the door was a big room with a tile floor, tile walls, and benches around the sides. When we reached the door, I knew where we were—the showers.

A man came to the door that was half open, and the sheriff told him, "Hey, Williams, fix these boys up." The man behind the door was not a sheriff but a prisoner too.

"Yes, sir," he said. Then the sheriff went back to get our things. He came back with pants, shirts, underwear, shoes, and towels. He must have been doing this for a long time. All the clothes he gave us fit just right.

"OK, boys, go in there," the sheriff said, pointing his finger to the showers behind the wall of the other room. He continued, "I'll be back in a little while. Don't take too long."

The sheriff walked away. The prisoner who gave us the clothes went back into the room to whatever he was doing when we arrived. I thought to myself that this was all right. This was the first time they had left us alone since I had been locked up.

While we were getting undressed, we started talking about things that happened at the party. We also talked about our future. Phillip thought we'd be getting out. Isaac thought we'd go to San Quentin or some other hard-core prison.

"I don't think so," I told them. "I think we're too young." I continued, "I think we'll go to YA."

"I was there before," Isaac said boastfully.

Walking into the shower, Phillip, asked, "Oh yeah, how is it? Is it as bad as I heard?"

Isaac, now wanting to do all the talking, said, "Hey, man, you can't even take a shower like this."

"Why not?" I asked.

"Because of all the homos that are there," he answered.

"How disgusting! Hey, man, if a homo comes by me, man, I'll knock him out!" I said.

"Oh no, they won't come at you. They'll just stare at you," Isaac answered.

Not saying too much now, just thinking about what he said, we continued taking our showers.

After a little while we turned off the showers and got out.

"I don't think I want to go to YA," I said.

Isaac responded, "It's not that bad. You just have to go by all the movidas [moves]."

"What do you mean movidas?" I asked, getting dressed.

"Well, movidas are rules the guys tell you you have to follow," Isaac explained.

I still didn't know what he meant when he said movidas. "What are some THINGS you have to do?" I asked.

"Well, like when a white guy or a black guy gets up from a

chair, you have to clean the chair before you sit down," he said.

I thought that was silly. "Why would someone want to do that?"

"Because we don't like blacks, and blacks don't like us. And whites, well nobody likes them," he said, meaning in the prison system.

MANOS NEGRAS [BLACK HANDS]

When I was growing up, my father and mother almost never brought up things about other races. We weren't raised with any prejudiced feelings. On the east side of town, there were a lot of blacks; some whites, but not too many; and a lot of Chicanos.

Once, not too long before we got into trouble this time, my friends and I had a problem with the guys from Meadow Fair. Meadow Fair was a tract of homes where a lot of rough kids lived, not too far from King and Tully Roads. A lot of these kids went to our high school, W. C. Overfelt.

During lunch time my friends Art, Ray, Bobby, Dennis, and I walked around the campus talking to girls and to our other friends.

Dennis was medium built with curly hair and a baby face. Art was on the small side, but don't let size fool you. He was tough; and one thing about Art, he was never scared of anything. Ray was Art's cousin. Ray was on the thin side and was always ready to back up his friends. He was always there when we needed him. Bobby X was medium built; and no matter what he was doing, he never messed up his hair. If he did, he would pull his comb out and fix it.

Every time we walked by the guys from Meadow Fair, we received dirty looks from them. They didn't like me very much because I had been in a fight with one of them not too long before this.

I saw Dennis later in the day. Dennis told me that Roy from

Meadow Fair wanted to fight him at the park that night.

"What happened?" I asked. He didn't know why. Joe from Meadow Fair told him to be at Meadow Fair that night, ready to fight. Dennis told him all right; he'd be there. I told Dennis not to worry; I'd get all the guys together.

That evening I called our friends who lived not too far from us on Story and White Roads, Frank, Bert, Richard, and a couple of other guys who lived in their area. From where we lived, there was Dennis Art, Ray, Danny, Bobby, Tommy, and his brother John. I thought this would be plenty of guys since we were all good fighters.

We all met on Waverly Avenue where Art lived, since the park was behind Art's house. While we were waiting, one of our guys who came to meet us asked who else was coming. I told him all the guys who were supposed to come and help. He stood there shaking his head and said, "Oh no!" I wondered what was wrong.

He looked at me and said with a worried voice, "Hey, man, those guys have around 20 or 30 guys on their side."

"How do you know?" I asked, not believing him.

"Because I know one of the guys from Meadow Fair," he said, trying to convince us. He continued, "He told me a little while ago on the phone that all the guys from Meadow Fair are going to the park to fight!"

All our guys were standing around thinking the same thing I was. "We need more help!" They were all waiting to see what we were going to do.

"Hey, this fight is between Roy and me," Dennis said.

"Dennis," I said, "we'll back you up, man!" I continued, "If you want to fight him alone, that's OK. If anybody jumps in, I'll jump in; and so will everybody else, man! Right, guys?"

Everybody nodded their heads and said, "Yeah, hey we'll back you up. That's why we're here, man."

"Look," Dennis said, "I want to fight him alone, just the two of us." That was where it stayed, but we had to do something because the guys from Meadow Fair outnumbered us.

"Hey, my neighbor, the black guy, has all his friends over right now." Art continued, "I know they'll help us or at least be with us to make it look like there's a lot of us."

"Sounds good to me. Go ask them, Art," I said. Everybody said the same thing.

Art went to talk to them. In a little while he came back with about eight black guys. When I recognized them, I said, "Hey, man, how you doing?" I shook one of the guy's hands. "I know these guys. They're in my classes."

One of them said, "What's going on, Art? I hear you need some help?"

We now looked like a big mob. We started walking to the park to meet the guys from Meadow Fair at 8:30 p.m.

The park was really dark and quiet. All of us walked to the middle, near some picnic tables. We sat and waited with our bats and bars. Art had this wicked thing that looked like a sword. At the time I didn't know what it was, but now I do. It was a long knife sharpener he had filed down and made to look like a sword. I asked Art if I could use it that night. At first he didn't want to trade me for my bar, but I talked him into it.

We were waiting for the longest time and thought maybe they weren't going to show up. While we waited, we made a plan. We asked Dennis if he was sure he wanted to fight Roy by himself. He said he did. Well, it was OK with us. If he didn't want to fight him or if he was losing the fight, he just had to look at me and say, "OK!" That would be the sign to jump in.

It was getting late. We thought we'd better leave, since it looked as if they chickened out on us. Just then a Chevy low rider raced down the street really fast. I didn't think they could see us because we were in the middle of the park, and it was dark.

"It's them!" Bert said. We were all quiet, just looking.

"Was it them?" someone asked. Then the car came back a little slower.

"Hey!" someone said, "If they want to fight and they only came with one carload, they're going to have a hard time!" We all started laughing.

The third time the car came down the street, it was moving about ten miles per hour. On the passenger side someone was standing outside of the car on the running board. He yelled out, "MEADOW FAIR!" He was moving down the street a little farther and again yelled out, "MEADOW FAIR!"

"Hey, man, they're telling us who they are; and they want to know who we are," Richard said.

Then someone else said, "Yeah, man, who are we?"

"Good question, who are we?" I asked.

Looking around at everybody who was there with us, I looked at all the black guys who were there as our right hand. I thought, "Las Manos Negras! [The black hands!] That's who we'll say we are."

The car came down the street again. Standing up on the running board, a guy yelled out again, "Meadow Fair!"

I yelled out, "Las Manos Negras!"

We could hear the guys in the car saying, "It's them, man!" They spun away around the corner where the guys from Meadow Fair were waiting.

We waited about five minutes; then a whole group of guys came walking around the corner. They seemed to have only about seven or eight guys more than we had.

It's funny the way I remember it. It was just the way it was in the cowboy movies. They were on one side, and we were all on the other. One of their guys walked out to talk to one of us. I walked to the middle.

The guy from Meadow Fair said, "Hey, man, how do you want to do this?"

I looked back at Dennis for a second, looked back at the guy, and said, "Hey, man, we don't care either. We all fight, or the two of them fight."

"Well," he went on, "Roy wants to fight Dennis in a fair fight."

These guys didn't want to fight us. They had heard of us, and they were a little scared. I told him to tell his guys that if anybody jumped in or even threw a kick, I was going to throw blows—not with the guy who threw the kick, but with him, the guy who was talking. I said this because I loved to fight, and I was itching for some action.

Dennis was ready and so was Roy. Dennis was a pretty good fighter. So was Roy, they said. Roy was one of those guys who all the girls liked. From the way he acted, I knew he thought he was tough. This was the kind of person I liked to fight.

The fight started with just the two of them. At first they danced around each other for about fifteen minutes. Everybody started to egg them on, to try to get them to start swinging. One of the guys from Meadow Fair started to overdo it, telling Dennis things. My blood was already boiling, wanting to fight! I looked at the guy and told him if he said anything else, it was going to be he and I fighting. We were not going to dance around. Just then Dennis and Roy started swinging. They both were swinging hard and connecting their blows.

It turned out only the two of them fought that night, a fight that ended in a draw. They were both tired. Neither could pick up his arms to swing anymore. They both had bloody faces. "What are the girls going to say about those faces?" I thought.

This was a Friday night. On the following Monday we went to Overfelt High School. Right away in the morning, I heard people talking about the fight. Roy was telling everybody he won. His friends were also talking and said the same thing. I was angry.

On our first break I met with Dennis, Art, Bobby, and Ray. All of these guys were the same as I—they loved to fight. I thought to myself, "We're going to have a good fight today!"

We had to pick up a paper for Dennis at the office for being late to one of his classes. As we were walking away from the office, around the corner came Roy with his friends, about ten of them. They liked to walk in groups. It made them look tougher.

They saw us walking toward them. We stopped when we reached them. Looking at Roy and pointing my finger in his face, I said, "Hey, man, it's my turn! I'm going to get you!" One of his friends who was with him was a guy named Jim. The way Art and Jim were looking at each other, it looked as if they were going to get into it right there.

All morning while I was in class, I looked forward to fighting Roy. At lunch we all joined up, Dennis, Art, Ray, Bobby and me. We were walking around the campus the way we always did. The guys from Meadow Fair hung out in one spot by some lockers. We stopped at the snack bar and bought some food. Art was eating a sandwich and had a small carton of milk. We then walked by the guys from Meadow Fair. Jim was standing there with Roy and some other guys. He was giving Art a hard look.

"I'm going to get that guy, man!" Art said.

"Get him right now. Why wait? We're with you right now," I said.

Art started to walk toward him. I was checking Roy out. Art walked toward Jim and said, "Hey! What are you looking at man?" With a half smile and a sarcastic look, Jim answered, "You! You don't like it?"

Stepping in front of Jim, Art pulled his arm back with the milk in his hand. Swinging it as hard as he could, Art smashed the milk right in his face! Just when he did, I hit Roy in the jaw with all I had. Then I hit him with another left. With those two punches he fell backwards. From then on in the next few seconds, everything went wild! Fists were flying!

All the girls and others who were there crowded in and broke up the fight before the teachers arrived.

All of us were together again, Art, Dennis, Ray, Bobby, and me. The bell rang, and everybody started going to their next class.

We were walking to our class; Art, Ray, and I were together. It just so happened the guys from Meadow Fair were in front of us. Roy turned, saw us behind them, and said, "Hey, man, after school we'll meet you. After school, man!"

There was someone behind me. His name was Chris. Wanting to see a fight get started, he egged me on, "Now! Now! Now, Art, why wait!"

There were a lot of people around also wanting to see a fight. They also were saying, "Yeah, now, now!"

I thought to myself, "If I wait after school, he's going to have way too many guys there. I might as well get him right now."

I looked at Art and Ray. They both said, "Go ahead, we're right here to back you up!" I knew we were outnumbered, but at this point I didn't care. I wanted to knock Roy out.

Everybody was now walking at a slower pace, anticipating a fight. Roy turned around to say something else. I don't know what he said. I was just thinking where I was going to hit him, knowing I wanted the first hit to count.

With all my might I reached back and let go! I connected right on his nose; he fell back. From this point things happened really fast. All I saw was Art and Ray fly by me toward them. The next thing I knew, I was fighting three guys at the same time. I danced around in a big area. Boom! Boom! I hit one guy. Boom! Boom! I hit the other guy. I danced to another guy. Boom! I loved it! I had this problem, as you may have noticed already. I loved fighting.

The fight didn't last too long. Everybody broke it up, so we wouldn't get into trouble. I went to my next class. My knuckles were bleeding a little, but they felt all right. Ten minutes into the class, a teacher came in and asked if there was an Arthur Rodriguez in the room. I stood up, and he took me to the front office.

Everybody was in the office. Roy was sitting there quietly with a bloody nose. All of us were suspended for a week, except Art. From then on they called him the "Milkman" because he started the whole thing by throwing the milk at Jim. He received a two-week suspension, which he liked; he didn't like school either. All of us considered a suspension a vacation.

As the years went by, the guys from Meadow Fair became good friends of ours. We backed each other up in several big fights.

* * *

We were sitting there dressed in jail clothes, ready to go, when the sheriff walked up. Shaking his keys, he said, "OK, boys, are you ready to go? Let's go." He turned around and walked back down the hallway we had come through. We stood up from the bench where we were sitting and followed him, walking back down the hall near the big cells.

"I hope they don't put us in with these guys," I thought. They were loud and getting carried away, yelling and playing cards. Some were sleeping on their beds. "How could they sleep with all that noise," I wondered. "If they put me in with them, I'm going to get in a lot of fights."

Walking up to one big door made of bars, the sheriff said, "OK, here we are." The place they took us, where we were going to spend the next six months while we went to court, was called Mini Row. Upstairs they had Max Row. That was where my brother and all the other guys were jailed.

Walking into Mini Row, I could see there were five small cells and one big one. The small cell was where we'd be for a few months. They have a bar front, with a bar door. The walls were concrete. Inside there was a bunk bed, and against the wall were a sink and toilet. The toilet didn't look so good. It was really big and all ceramic with no seat and no cover. At least we had one.

Something I noticed right away but didn't know if it worked was the radio on the wall. It would be cool if I had a radio. In Juvenile they didn't have anything. The radio worked. It was set up with a volume control and a knob for four stations.

We all went into our cells. They had other prisoners in there, but they moved them out to make room for us. They wanted to keep us juveniles separated from the rest of the inmates.

Once we were in our cells, the sheriff walked out and went past the main door at the end of the hall. He hit a button; and all the doors made a loud, locking noise. From inside the cells, we couldn't see each other or couldn't see down the hall. In front of us was a wall. On that wall about five feet up, there were windows. I could sit on the top bunk bed and look out at the city. I couldn't see much, just the top of buildings. I could also see the garage where the police cars were kept. Throughout the months that followed, we saw the cops start their shift and come in at the end of the day. During those times we kept track of which cops were working, who was coming, and who was going. There was nothing else to do.

The first few days of being in Mini Row weren't too bad compared to where we were before with nothing in the cell. Phillip, Isaac, and I got to know each other really well through the next few months. We couldn't see one another because of the concrete walls in between us; but we would stay up some nights and talk, telling stories of our lives.

Right down the hall from where we were, there was a door that went outside to a sun deck. This was where they took the prisoners out to get sun. They gave us special treatment because they took us out two times in the six months we were there. I say special treatment because we never saw anyone else out there.

Twice a week someone with a little cart came by to see if we wanted to buy anything. On the cart there were things like pencils, pens, writing tablets, and other small personal items we might want. It wasn't that we could have them free of charge. We needed someone on the outside to send in money which would be placed in our account. The jail personnel would then subtract the purchase we made from whatever we had.

I was in my cell all the time. The only time I got out was on

Sundays and whenever we went to court. I think my lawyer came to see me two or three times in the six months I was there.

I looked forward to visiting with my mother and family on Sundays. We were only allowed one, one-hour visit a week. The visiting room had a small stool to sit on, with a plate of glass in front, and a phone to talk through. This was no fun. My mother always looked tired and sad.

Time went by slowly during this period. There wasn't too much to do in my cell for those few months. I wrote a lot of letters. Those who received my letters had a hard time reading them, since I didn't know how to spell. All I did was write letters; lie on my bed; and listen to the radio, listening to hits such as "When A Man Loves A Woman." I always had daydreams I was home with my family and friends.

In my cell, on the walls and ceiling, there were prisoners' names carved. I wanted to let people know I'd been there too. I took my time and carved my name on the ceiling. This cell became my home for four months.

We went to court maybe once every two weeks, sometimes once a month. Court was one big blur. I just remember going and looking for my family and other friends. The only time we saw and talked to the older guys was while we were in the holding cell waiting to go to court.

I wrote a lot of letters to my girlfriend Patricia. Our letters got to the point where we were writing a lot of romantic and sexy things to each other.

One Sunday morning they called me to get ready for a visitor just as they always did on Sundays. I walked down, looking forward to seeing my mother. I was really anticipating her visit. There were things I wanted to ask her, and I also wanted to know about the rest of the family and my friends.

When I walked into the visiting room, at first glance I didn't recognize anyone sitting there. Looking back at the sheriff, he pointed to one of the spots against the visiting wall. It wasn't my mother. It was Carla, the mother of my girlfriend.

As I was walking over to sit on the stool, I noticed in her hand one of my letters. "Oh man!" I said in a whisper. I felt like turning around and walking out rather than dealing with this.

Picking up the phone on the wall, I said, "Hi, Carla! How are you?" She had the phone up to her ear, not saying anything, just staring at me and looking very angry. I didn't know what to say. I knew she knew what I wrote in the letter. I hoped she wasn't going to read it to me.

Finally she broke the silence and said, "Are you going to marry her?" I guess she thought we did something sexual because of what I wrote in the letter.

I said, "I can't because I'm in here." She didn't like that answer very much and started to tell me I should be ashamed of myself for writing these letters. I didn't want to tell her it wasn't only me, but her daughter was also a participant. It was a two-way street. She was angry enough, and I didn't want to make her angrier. She told me she didn't want me to write anymore letters like the one she had in her hand.

"OK, Carla, I won't," I said timidly.

She hung up the phone without saying anything else and stormed out of the visiting room. I stayed sitting there, thinking to myself, "That's it? That's my visit I've been waiting for all week?" I was only allowed one visit a week. Now my mother or anyone else wouldn't be able to visit me.

I tried to argue with the sheriff who was working at the time, telling him this wasn't the visit I was expecting. I almost got into trouble for not shutting my mouth. Finally he told me to shut up or I was going to the hole. The hole was a padded cell with a hole in the corner to be used for a toilet. I didn't want to go there, so I had to shut up.

I returned back to my cell and reflected on how much I missed my family. I lay on my bed, thinking back to when I was growing up in my neighborhood.

THE ROCK FIGHT

Shortly after I started my own business in 1985, I made a delivery on Thirty-Fourth Street, off of San Antonio. The delivery was to one of the last houses on the street. An old man came out to accept the order. While I was standing there waiting for someone else to bring the money, the old man sat on the porch. Waiting and looking around, I recalled a lot of memories of when I was a kid. I asked the old man how long he had lived there.

"I've been here many years. I raised my kids here."

"Did you enjoy raising you kids here?"

"Oh yes," he said.

I asked him if he remembered the rock fights with the kids from the other side of the field. When I asked him, he got up from his chair and wouldn't stop talking about it.

On Virginia Place there were kids living in almost every house. The street always had kids doing something. It was a lot of fun growing up on that block.

Virginia Place was surrounded by fields. We were always doing something in the fields, either building forts, playing in the swamp, or just hanging out. At times we played in the field that was between Virginia Place and San Antonio. We could see the kids from the other side of the field once in awhile, although we never really got to know most of these kids very well. They had their own friends to play with. The big division between us was "THE FIELD"!

During that time the city was laying big pipes underground, from Thirty-Fourth on the San Antonio side, through the field, and over to the Virginia Place side. The construction company had a big crane that dug big holes about 20 to 30 feet deep. Close to the San Antonio side they had a big hole exposing a large pipe. On the Virginia Place side, they were working daily to put in a few pieces of ten-foot sections of pipe. It took them a while to complete the job. The pipes were about five feet wide. We played in them all day, going in through one side and coming out of the tunnel on the other side.

There was a lady who lived on the corner of Virginia and Thirty-Fourth. Thirty-Fourth was a small section of street that was between the two blocks of Virginia Place. We called her "Crazy Mary." I don't think she was really crazy, just loud.

One day we were playing in the pipes, and she saw me come out on one side. When I walked by her house, she stopped me.

"Hey, boy," she said, "did you know there are small snakes in that pipe? They crawl up your behind. You can't feel them. They eat you up from the inside, so you better not go in there anymore!" I looked at her as if she were crazy for saying this. I went home thinking she was really crazy, but later that evening I started to feel sick to my stomach. It started hurting. I didn't want to go near the pipes again.

One summer evening we were playing in the street. Someone came running down the street to tell us about the rock fight that was going on. Every so often we had rock fights with the kids from the other side, from San Antonio Street. We stopped what we were doing and ran to the end of Thirty-Fourth Street. Everybody was throwing rocks at the kids from the other side of the field. We all joined in on the fight. Even my little brother Victor, only four years old, was there throwing rocks at those big kids.

Victor was the baby of the family. Whenever he came out in the street to play with us, we had to watch him. That was our job.

I remember about 20 or 30 kids on our side. On the other side they had about the same number throwing rocks back at us. In the construction of the underground pipes, the construction workers were using some sort of steel washer about the size of a quarter and a quarter-of-an-inch thick. All the kids were also throwing those steel bombs.

A lot of rocks were flying at us. We had to be careful as we were picking up the steel washers and rocks to also watch for incoming missiles. It was a small war!

Since he was so small, Victor ran all the way up to a guy with one rock, got about eight to ten feet from him, threw his rock, turned around, and ran back. He kept doing this, back and forth.

"Victor! Get back over here!" Victor didn't care. He wanted to win.

Kids were yelling and continued throwing rocks. Sometimes the rocks would hit us, and they hurt.

Victor wouldn't listen to us. "Victor! Get back over here, or they're going to hurt you!"

The kids from San Antonio Street were being pushed back a little. We were winning. I tried to pick up four or five rocks at a time. With all of these, I ran a few feet forward, throwing my rocks. I forced a guy from the San Antonio side back a little ways.

Victor flew up into the combat zone! "Victor, get back over here!" Sometimes he tried to obey, but he had a hard time. Every time he tried to listen and not to get too close to them, he just couldn't reach them with his rocks. He was just too small. This was definitely a bigger kid's fight.

I think we made Victor tough at home. He could handle a fight like this. When he was a young kid, he often showed a hot temper.

There was a little girl, Donna, who lived down the street from us. She was about Victor's age. I never saw her when she grew up, but I heard she turned out to be a very beautiful woman. At the time Victor was little, she had long, stringy hair; had no teeth in front; and wore big glasses. Eddie, Tita, and I teased him about Donna all the time.

"Victor! Go get me some water!" I would demand.

Victor would say, "No! Get it yourself!"

Then I chanted, "Victor likes Donna! Victor likes Donna!"

Victor began breathing heavily, looked at me, and yelled, "You better stop Arthur! You better STOP!"

Next I opened the door and yelled at the top of my voice, since Donna lived about six houses down, "VICTOR LIKES DONNA!" Victor charged at me, swinging with both arms in a big circle and with his head down. I held him back by stretching my arm out and holding his head back, so he couldn't reach me.

We were a little mean to him sometimes, but at the same time we were good to him. He was the baby of the family.

Again he charged to the front lines. "Victor, don't get too close to that guy; he's going to get you!"

We were doing really well out there. So far we'd backed those kids up about two thirds down the field and were getting close to the houses where they lived.

We'd been out there throwing rocks for a long time. It was hard work fighting like this, but it was fun because we were winning.

Kids were yelling. Some were getting hit with rocks and crying. I really hadn't seen anybody on our side hit badly enough to draw blood and to stop them from throwing rocks.

Then I saw Victor from the corner of my eye, with his one rock in his hand, running up to a kid.

"Victor!" someone yelled. He was running toward a big guy.

Earlier the kids on the other side weren't really paying any attention to him. They were probably thinking the little kid couldn't do anything. Victor ran up to a big kid, sliding on the dirt as he approached him. Dust came up behind him, as if he were sliding home on a home-run hit. He threw his rock, turned around, and started to run back. As Victor was running back, the big kid turned his way, took aim, and threw his rock hard. A direct hit! Victor fell down crying; blood was running down his head. "Dad and Mom are going to be mad," I thought. We ran and threw rocks at the guy who hit him.

It was hard to get Victor under control. He was full of blood, but he didn't care. He was crying, not because he was hurt but because he was mad. Because he was having a temper tantrum, we had to carry him back. He was crying bloody murder and wanted to pay the guy back. Victor was a tough kid.

The rock fight kept going. We were pushing those kids all the way back across the field. They didn't give up and start running but kept right on fighting.

Now they were hiding behind the fences next to the field on the other side. We were throwing rocks, missing them, and hitting the houses. I heard glass break. We really were having fun winning the fight. We had been in other rock fights in the past but not like this one—pushing the other guys back all the way to their side.

More glass was breaking! Now the men and the women started coming out of their houses, and they were furious. That wouldn't stop us now. We were winning. I remember the older ladies with their aprons, running down the stairs yelling at us. With rolling pins in one hand, they threw rocks with the other.

In a little while more older people came outside and started to throw rocks also. They were almost hit by our flying rocks.

What ended the fun was the same thing that always did, Law and Order! I saw a police car coming from San Antonio Street and yelled, "The cops!" We all started running back to our side of the field.

The old man I talked to years later told the story as if he were describing a war story and how he almost got shot—or should I say, rocked?

* * *

Waking up in my cell one morning while dreaming I was home in my own bed, I opened my eyes and realized I was still in jail. All the time I was locked up, I would think, "One of these days I'm going to wake up, and it will all be just a big dream." Most mornings were like this.

On this particular morning I turned on the radio to KLIV. On the news was a story about a killing that took place at St. James Park. They found another guy dead in an orchard in San Jose, a total of two killed. It turned out one of the dead men was a priest who was dressed in street clothes.

Some of the guys who killed the two were juveniles. They robbed them at St. James Park then beat them up. It was not brought out in the news media that both of the dead men were homosexuals. The priest and the other guy went at night to St. James Park and met other homosexuals. The boys they met didn't know one of them was a priest.

The juveniles were all charged with murder. We were told by some of the inmates that the boys who killed the priest were being moved to the jail with us at Mini Row.

A couple of days later, the sheriff announced over the speaker, calling our names, "Roll'em up!" This meant we had to gather our things together because we were to be moved somewhere and were not coming back.

I had been in this cell for four months. Now I was leaving it in five minutes; this was no time to say good-bye. I put my belongings in a little pile by the door because I didn't have a bag or a box.

Before the sheriff unlocked the doors down the hall, he said over the speaker, "OK let's go!" The loud noise of unlocking all the cells was heard at the same time.

When I stepped into the hallway, I saw the sheriff walking toward us from down the hall by the main doors. Not too far from him, at the end of our cells, there was a big cell. The sheriff stopped there, looked in it, and pulled open the door. It was already unlocked; he was inspecting it.

I watched the sheriff as he looked my way and pointed into my cell. "I have all my stuff, and I don't have a box or anything to put it into," I told him.

"Don't worry about it. Load your arms, and bring your stuff here to your new cell," he answered, pointing to the big cell.

This new cell was going to be our new home. Isaac, Phil, and I were going to be together now. We'd share the same room, the same space, and the same toilet. I didn't know if I would like that. I had grown used to being by myself.

As the days went by, we settled in our new home. We liked being together after all. Now we could look at each other when we talked and play cards; now we could keep busy.

The day we moved into our new cell and as we were getting settled in, we heard the big doors unlock. People were talking and walking toward us. All three of us moved toward the front bars. It was the guys who killed the priest who were being brought into our area. The first one to walk by was Jerry, then Tommy, and Gene. There were a few older ones, but they were upstairs in Max Row.

Once the juveniles were locked in their cells, the sheriff left; and we started talking to them. We learned the story of what actually happened, and what led up to it. As I now look back at these young guys, I can see they were not bad guys. I think they were all just bad company for one another.

When the district attorney's office wanted to send someone up for something, they wouldn't let go. They wanted Jerry more than the others. The newspapers made Jerry out to be the ring leader. Being there in jail with him and hearing the story, I came to realize he was just one of the group.

These guys weren't your everyday killers. They were going out and doing bad things, got caught up in it, and went overboard.

I felt sorry for Jerry because many nights I woke up and could hear him crying. Once around 3 a.m., Jerry was crying in his cell. I thought it was because he wanted to go home. The crying went on for a long time. Finally I asked him, "Hey, Jerry, what's wrong?"

Jerry said, "Oh nothing, it's just these letters I got." I noticed he had been receiving a lot of letters the past few days and thought he had a big fan club. It turned out he did, but they were bad fans. He was getting letters from all over the world, from priests, bishops, and cardinals. They were all telling him what a bad youngster he was. They said he was condemned and was going to burn in hell.

This wasn't one, but letter after letter. He read one of them to us from a priest in France. The priest said Jerry wasn't worthy to be alive; he should be put to death; and once it happened, he would burn in hell. This was why he was crying. Jerry wasn't a rough-looking kid. He was a nice kid who could have lived next door but was used as the scapegoat for the whole group.

I wondered how these priests from all over the world could tell Jerry he was going to burn in hell. They didn't know him. How did they know he was the one who killed the priest? We all felt the same; the priests didn't know what they were talking about. We didn't know anything about hell, and who's there. We also didn't know what God would have to say about it, but we knew God couldn't be that mean.

We told Jerry how we felt; the priests who were writing him were all full of it. We all talked to him about it and advised him not to open the letters from out of town or those with a return address from a church. I really don't know if he listened to us because he was in the cell by himself, but I think he felt better. We continued to hear him cry whenever he received this type of letter.

As time went by we got to know Jerry, Tommy, and the other guy very well. When we went to court with my brother and the other guys in our group, some of them said their lawyers felt the guys who killed the priest were bad for us. It looked as if something had to be done with the youth to teach them they couldn't be doing this kind of thing, "killing people." Others said that it was good for our case because killing a priest made us look less bad. "Who knows?" I thought.

Through the years we heard stories about Jerry and his friends. We heard some didn't make it through the prison system; they died.

As time went on, Isaac, Phil, and I got used to being together in the same cell. We became best friends and worst enemies.

We spent the majority of our time playing cards. Most of the time I won. I was a bad loser. Isaac and I were in a lot of fights with each other, sometimes over small things and sometimes over big things. We fought non-stop because there was nobody there to stop us. We stopped only because we were too tired to throw any more punches, or we were just tired of fighting and stopped ourselves.

Using our pens, pencils, and writing paper instead of money, we often played cards. They didn't allow us to have cash. One day we started playing poker in the early evening, right after dinner. We kept playing until late at night. At first I was winning; then things took a turn for the worse. Isaac was happy because he was beating me. I was getting angrier as the night went along. Eventually, I only had five pens and one writing tablet left. We put in one pen each to start the hand.

Isaac dealt the cards. Picking up my cards, I found I had three eights. Three eights were a good hand because nothing was wild. I threw two cards down. Isaac also threw two cards down. The cards he dealt me were two sevens. "All right," I thought, "a full house!"

Isaac picked up his cards and smiled. He was a bad bluffer.

"What do you want to do?" he asked.

"I'll raise you two," I said.

Then Isaac with a smirk said, "Here's your two, and I'll raise you three more."

I thought to myself, "I wonder what he has. He knows I started with three-of-a-kind because I asked for two cards. He has something good because of the way he smiled. Since I only have one writing tablet left, I'd better call him and save my tablet for the next game. In case I lose, I'll still have one more chance."

Throwing my three pens in the pot, I gave Isaac my hard-gambler's stare and said, "Here's your three, and I call you. What do you have?" The only thing that could beat me was four-of-a-kind. Isaac threw down four queens. "MAN!" I yelled, throwing down my cards hard on the table.

Isaac reached from behind where he was sitting and grabbed the box where he kept all his things. He put the box on the table and started packing all his winnings into it.

"Hey, Isaac, I have one more thing to play with!" I said angrily.

Isaac looked at me, shaking his head and saying, "No way man! I quit!"

I could feel myself getting red and hot in the face. I yelled, "You can't quit! You have to give me a chance to win my stuff back!"

Isaac kept putting the things in his box and continued to shake his head. He said, "I don't have to give you a chance. What if you win everything back? I quit man!"

I was burning up now. "You have to give me a chance, man!"

Isaac, not listening to me, just concentrated on putting the stuff in his box nicely and neatly.

Looking at the smirk on his face and getting angrier, I told myself he was not going to get away with this. I'd get him; and if I couldn't have my things back, then I'd break all the pens and tear up the writing tablets.

Isaac now looked at me and said, "Don't be such a bad loser, ese."

Something snapped inside of me. That was it! Diving over the table, I threw a punch right at his face. Both of us went rolling over the table and chairs, struggling, hitting each other.

We kept fighting for hours, and I mean hours. The three of us had an agreement. If two of us got in a fight, the third one would stay out of it and not break it up. Once in a while the sheriffs would take a walk through Mini Row, but they never caught us fighting.

We kept fighting although we were so tired neither one of us could pick up our arms to hit the other. We still tried. I woke up in the morning, not remembering who hit whom last. I was on top of Isaac with my hands around his neck. I must have gone to sleep trying to choke him. He didn't remember either. He didn't care. He was so tired, he didn't care if I was choking him.

In the morning we were friends again, even though we went to sleep wanting to kill each other. He even gave me a couple of tablets and a couple of pens, so I could write my letters. Isaac was all right!

Every night I would lie on my bed listening to oldies on the radio, thinking of home and all my friends.

Oldies but Goodies

When I was a young teenager, I hung out at the Lopez girls' house. They lived down the street on the next block on Virginia Place. Tita, my sister, was the same age as Sandy, the youngest of the four Lopez girls. The oldest was Stella; she was about my brother Eddie's age. Stella was a quiet girl. Then there was Margie, who later became Art's girlfriend for a while. Following her was Sylvia, then Sandy. There was little Fred too; he was the youngest of the family. He was my little brother Victor's age.

I used to go there all the time and listen to oldies. My mother was good friends with their mother Sarah.

The girls' father Fred was never home. He spent all his time at the Happy Hour bar. Whenever he arrived home in the evenings from the bar, we had to leave fast. Fred didn't like boys to be at his house when he wasn't home. Actually, Fred never knew we were always at his house because we were never caught. A few boys were at his house almost everyday whenever Fred was at the bar or at work.

They had a patio outside behind their garage. The sliding door was in the dining room that went outside to the patio. On the patio there was a big, long bar that stretched all the way across. On the bar they had their forty-five record player set up with stacks of forty-fives. It seemed we were having a party every night; there were always a lot of kids around. Someone always kept watch for big Fred. From the patio we could usually see the headlights from his car as he drove up.

Every night was the same. We listened to records, and someone would yell out, "Fred's home!" We would all start running and ducking down, so he couldn't see us. The lights to the patio would go off. Sometimes we were in the house, and one of the girls would sit and watch by the front window. The kids were dancing or sitting around talking, including their mother Sarah. I always remember Sylvia sitting by the big window in the living room, smoking. Blowing smoke, she yelled out with her big eyes wide open, "He's here!" Everybody started running in different directions, getting down as if Fred could see us from outside, then jumping out of the rear windows and hiding in the back yard. We would leave through the back. In those days there was a field; now there are apartments.

One day when I was over the girls' house, Sylvia told me a new kid moved in next door. Sylvia was a tall, thin girl. What made her look tall was her hair. Her hair was ratted and made to stand tall, about a foot high. She always liked to wear it the same. It was the style in those days.

I wanted to know who the kid was who moved in next door to the girls. She said his name was Art. Art's mother was just married, and Art was having a hard time getting along with his new stepfather. Later whenever we got drunk together, he would cry for his real father. Art didn't realize at the time that his stepfather was a good man and was trying to be a good father.

Art's real father died not very long before this. One day his father came home drunk, couldn't get into the house, and broke the sliding door to enter. He cut himself very badly with the glass from the door. By the time the ambulance arrived, he bled to death in front of Art and his family. Art suffered over this for the rest of his life.

As time went along, Art and I became best friends, always doing things together. I didn't know Dennis yet. I knew he lived next to the Lopez girls' house on the other side.

One day I was sitting out on the porch of the Lopez girls' house, and we saw Dennis come outside for something. Art asked me if I thought I could beat up Dennis. I said, "Sure I can!" I was about thirteen years old.

Art said, "I wonder if Dennis wants to come out?"

Art said he'd be right back. I didn't see where he went. He went to Dennis' house, told him I wanted to fight, and said I could beat him up.

Dennis didn't know me and really didn't want to fight me. For what? Dennis' father Tex was sitting right there in the living room and asked who wanted to fight Dennis. Tex worked with my father at the American Can Company. The next thing I saw was Dennis walking out of his house, his eyes red, and his father behind him with a belt in his hand.

Dennis was standing with his father behind him when he said, "Do you want to fight me?" I really didn't want to; I didn't even know this guy. Fight him for what? Art was standing there with a half smile on his face, moving his shoulders up as he said, "I don't know, man!"

Dennis and I boxed on his front lawn for about fifteen minutes. We didn't throw very many blows at each other. If we had, we might not have become good friends later.

As time went on, we became the best of friends. He started to hang out at the girls' house listening to oldies with us.

* * *

Over the speaker a loud voice called my name then said, "Visitor!"

"Who could be visiting me on a weekday?" I thought. The door unlocked, and I stepped out of my cell and started walking down the hall. At the end of the hall, the sheriff pointed to some small rooms where I went when my lawyer came to talk to me, which wasn't very often. Looking over there, I saw my lawyer standing outside the room waiting for me.

"Hi, Arthur. How are you?" he asked as I walked up.

"I'm all right. How you doing?"

"Come on in. I have some news for you," he said. The news was that they reached a plea bargain.

"What does that mean for me?" I wanted to know.

"Well," he continued, "what it means is that I got all the charges lowered for you."

That sounded good to me, but I asked, "Does that mean I'll be getting out?"

"No, I don't think you'll be getting out for a while. But," he went on to say, "from murder one to assault to commit murder, that's a big drop. How does that sound to you?"

He already said I was not getting out. "Did that mean I was to be getting out soon?" I wondered. "How much time do you think I'll do?"

"Honestly, I don't know," he said.

"I should be happy it's not murder one," I thought. Actually, when I went to YA, it didn't matter. They looked at my case as if I were sent there for murder anyway.

"Well, Arthur, we go to court tomorrow. I'll see you there," he said.

"So what you're telling me is that this is the last time I'm going to court. It's over, right?" I asked.

"That's what I'm telling you. This is the last time you're going to court, unless something else comes up," he said, closing his brief-case.

I got out of my chair and stood by the table. A lot of thoughts were spinning through my mind. What a short visit for such big news. Looking at the lawyer still in disbelief, I asked, "Now, if we go to court tomorrow, what does that mean? Am I going to stay here long? Am I going to serve my time here or what?"

He was in a hurry to go. As he stepped out of the room, he answered me, "From what I have been told, I think as soon as the court is over, they're going to take you to the California Youth Authority, either the same day or the next morning."

Standing there in deep thought, I felt a strange sensation come over me. I was locked in a cell with Phil and Isaac for so long, they had become like part of my family. I wanted to leave; and at the same time, I wanted to stay. I'd gotten to know them so well that I knew I would miss them. I didn't know how I would do without them.

"OK, Arthur, I have to go take care of some other things; so I'll see you tomorrow," the lawyer said, patting my back and walking away.

I wanted to ask him more questions, but he wouldn't let me. Thinking back to this, he reminded me of someone who'd just got off work and wanted to leave because he wasn't getting paid anymore. I really didn't know. Maybe he was on his way upstairs to see my brother to tell him the good news he told me.

Walking back to my cell, I was still in shock, thinking about what he had just told me about leaving tomorrow. All the things I heard about YA, now I was going to find out for myself.

I heard a lot of stories about YA from Isaac, Phil, and the older guys who came to Mini Row to serve us our food.

They all told me that when I arrived there, the first thing I had to do was start fights, fight with everybody—fight with Mexican guys, black guys, and white guys. If I'd go in as a troublemaker, after about six months, everybody would respect me and leave me alone. Then when I'd go to board (board is like court), they would say, "Hey, this guy came in as a bad kid, fighting with everybody. Now look at him; he's a nice kid. We rehabilitated him. We'll let him out early."

Some guys who were sent to YA, really didn't like fighting. They didn't do a lot in the streets, so it was hard for them to look for fights. Not me. This was going to be easy. As long as I didn't get shanked, I'd be all right.

Arriving back at my cell after talking to my lawyer, I told Phil and Isaac what he said to me. They were angry because their lawyers hadn't told them anything. We stayed there talking about all the time we were together, laughing about the things we did while we were there, and about the fights we had with each other.

Isaac warned me about other things to watch out for in YA. "There's one particular thing they like to do with a new guy, ese," he explained. "When you first arrive, you might find either a carton of cigarettes or a few packs of cigarettes outside the door to your cell. DO NOT TAKE THEM! Leave them; they're not yours! The state doesn't give away good cigarettes. They will give you a little pouch with some ugly tobacco and some paper to roll your own, but they won't give you any brand-name packs."

"Why would anybody want to leave cigarettes by my door?" I asked.

"When the inmates see the cigarettes are gone, they'll wait a while; then one of them will come back later and want them returned. 'Hey, you! Did you see my cigarettes here?' he'll ask, looking down as if he's looking for something." Isaac continued, "If you got that guy's cigarettes and smoked them, you'll say, 'I didn't know they were yours.' Then they got you!"

Puzzled, I looked at Isaac and asked, "What do you mean they got you?"

"Yeah! They got you ese! He's going to want his cigarettes back; and if you smoked them, he's going to want something else."

"OK," I thought to myself. "I think I got it."

In the prison system homosexuality is rampant. During the time I was in YA, if someone was a homosexual, he was called a "punk." I remember in Preston, an institution in the YA prison system, there was a teacher who taught classes in the school. He couldn't stand the homosexuality there. Before all his classes started, he gave a lecture about homosexuality. He tried to get it through the inmates' heads that it didn't matter if you were the receiver or the doer—you were still a homosexual. In the prison system some inmates feel if they are the doer, they are not a "punk." So when these guys came back for their cigarettes, they'd really want to try to scare the new guys into being a punk. They had to pay back in this way.

Isaac kept talking about all the things to be careful about in YA. In a little while over the speaker, they called Isaac's name to get ready for a visitor. "My lawyer!" he said. In a little while Phil's name came over the speaker, and he went to see his lawyer.

The way it turned out, the DA gave Ceasar two second-degree-murder charges which each carried about four to life. With these two life terms, he could be out in about six years if he behaved himself. Roy received one second-degree-murder charge. He could be out in about four years. The rest of us had our charges lowered.

The next day we went to court, and the sentencing went the way our lawyers said it would. Our last night together, we stayed up all night talking. We planned to get together to party after we were released.

We had no idea where we were going. There are a lot of institutions for YA all over California. The sheriff brought us some boxes for our belongings. He told us not to take too much because we wouldn't be able to take it all with us.

At 5 a.m. over the speakers, our last names were announced then, "ROLL'EM UP!" We jumped out of bed and dressed. It was going to be a big day. This was the first time we were going outside in the street since we'd been locked up.

After doing time in the county jail and eating the food there, at six feet tall I dropped down to 155 pounds. I was a bag of bones. And from the lack of sun, I looked like a white guy.

We were taken downstairs to a holding cell where we waited for awhile. I remember we were sitting in the holding cell quietly, just as the first day we arrived. After waiting for about half an hour, a sheriff came to our holding cell, opened it, and called Phil's last name. Phil stood up, looked back at us, and shook our hands. He said, "Don't forget, man. I'll see you locos [crazy guys] when we get out!" Both of us stood up and told him we were looking forward to it. They took Phil away. That was the last time I ever saw Phil.

Now it was Isaac and I who were alone in the cell. It didn't take long for another sheriff to come back to our holding cell and call my name. I said my good-byes to Isaac, and I walked with the sheriff out the front door. Once out of the doors and before going out of the main doors, they told me to stop and stand still. Two sheriff's officers put shackles on me, the same kind they put on me when I went to the dentist.

It seemed strange walking outside for the first time in six months. I climbed into a white, plain station wagon. Two officers were in the front seat. I didn't know where I was going. Someone told me I might go to Vacaville first; then I'd be sent to the prison in Tracy. Isaac said he thought I'd go to Perkins then to Preston.

As we were driving away, I looked back at the jail. Looking up to where my cell was, in my thoughts I said good-bye to my friends, my room, and the whole routine.

Waiting for the officers to stop talking to each other, I asked, "Where am I going?"

The sheriff on the passenger side said, "You're going to Sacramento to a place called Perkins. Have you heard of it?"

I had because Isaac told me about it. "Yeah, I heard of it. I've never been there before. Do you know where I'm going from there?" I asked. Actually, that was the big question. Because Perkins is a receiving place for YA, I'd stay there for about thirty days; so they could check me out. When I say "check me out," I mean check my physical health. If anything was wrong with my teeth, and there probably would be, they'd fix them. They'd also take X-rays to make sure there was nothing else physically wrong with me. If there was, they'd take care of me right there.

Perkins was a prison-system hospital. Once I arrived at Perkins, I became the property of the state; or as they called it, a ward of the state.

The sheriff answered me, "No, I don't know where you're going after this. All we know is we're supposed to deliver you to Perkins this morning."

"How long will it take to get there?" I asked. The driver, looking at me through his rearview mirror, glared at me. I was asking too many questions.

"About two hours or so. Sit back and enjoy the ride," he said roughly.

I looked at the other sheriff, and he shook his head. I thought to myself, "That's the way some of them are. Some are good cops, and some are bad cops."

"Well, I guess I'll just sit back and enjoy the ride. I haven't been out here for six months, and who knows how long it's going to be until I go for another ride out here again," I thought.

We got on the freeway. I was looking for someone I might know to drive by. Fat chance if that would happen.

In a little while we were passing the county farm. If someone was sentenced to county time, this was where they would go. I wished I had been sentenced to do my time there. Too late now, I was on my way to YA.

I wondered what was waiting for me at Perkins? Was I going to have to fight a lot there? With whom? How much time would I have to do? Where would I go after Perkins? All these questions were racing through my mind. Thinking about all these things was kind of spooky—going somewhere I'd never been before and not knowing what I was going to encounter in the unknown.

Sitting there looking out of my window as the fields blurred by on Highway 17, I let my mind cruise back to when I was a kid. What was the unknown?

THE MONSTERS

When I was about four years old, we lived in a little house on Spencer Street, one house away from Virginia Street. To get to the corner store, we had to walk all the way to Virginia. "All the way" because when you're four years old, this was a long way. We had to cross the street. The store was at the next corner, on Delmas, a whole four or five houses away. We then had to go around the corner to the front of the store.

One evening I was with my brother and sister in the living room, which was also Eddie's and my bedroom. My father was in the kitchen watching my mother cook dinner. He walked into the living room and said, "Arturo, go to the store and get some bread!"

Looking out the window, I replied, "But, Dad, it's dark outside!" I'd never been outside in the dark by myself, let alone think about going to the store by myself in the dark.

My father was already turning around to go back into the kitchen when I caught his attention with the comment. "What!" he exclaimed. "It's dark outside? Cobarde! [coward] Go to the store, I said!" My father started to undo his belt. I knew then I had to go out into the unknown.

My father gave me a dollar and said not to take too long. I could see my mother in the kitchen, so I started to cry a little. My father's frown became worse; so I felt I had better shut up, or I was going to get spanked for being a cobarde. It's one thing to get spanked for doing something wrong but quite another for being a cobarde.

I remember opening the front door and looking over at Eddie and Tita. Their faces told me they felt sorry for me. Eddie knew what I was in for out there in the unknown. The same thing had happened to him when we lived on San Fernando Street.

I stepped outside on the porch, and the door closed behind me. Everything was so quiet. Not knowing what to expect, I walked very slowly down the front steps. I was at the bottom of the steps, walking down our small walkway.

Next to our walkway at this house, we had a very large pine tree. The branches came all the way down to the tops of our heads. In the dark I could see nothing but black; I couldn't believe it. I saw something move! My heart was pounding. I ran to the front picket fence and looked back, expecting to see a hand reach out to grab me. Nothing was there. I wanted to go back and tell my father I didn't care if I got a spanking for being a cobarde! But I'd better not do that. If I did, I would have to walk by the tree again.

I started to walk down the street to the corner of Spencer and Virginia and crossed the street. The sidewalk was very dark in front of the next few houses. I was crying a little; I was so scared. Coming to the darkest part of the street, I heard someone walking behind me. I stopped. They stopped. I looked back, but I didn't see anyone. They must have jumped in the bushes. Taking a few more steps and looking back at the same time, I still didn't see anyone following me. Just then, right where I was walking, I saw two eyes glowing at me. Screaming and starting to run backwards, I fell on the ground and scratched myself. I didn't care if I was hurt and bleeding. I didn't want to be eaten by the monster in the bushes. I took off and didn't look back. I ran away from this monster! It made some kind of noise as if it were screaming and ready to eat me. I ran the rest of the way to the store. As I ran, I thought, "My dad's going to feel sorry he sent me out in the dark because I'm going to be killed out here!"

Running around the corner by the front door of the store, I stopped. Finally a lot of light appeared. Waiting a second to see if whatever was following me would come around the corner, I stood by the door. Just in case it came around fast, I could escape into the store. "What am I going to do to get back home?" I thought. Looking at my injured elbow, I saw a little red spot of blood; but it was not too bad. Straightening my shirt, I walked back to the corner of the building to take a look for myself to see if anything was there. Looking around the corner, I could see everything was quiet. Nothing. Just the dark night.

I walked into the store, picked up some bread, and went to the counter to pay. The old lady at the counter took my money. The store was a family business. She was looking at me in a funny way, as if she were reading my mind. I felt I was a brave little boy to be out in the dark fighting with all those monsters. If she only knew what I just went through, she would really know how brave I was.

I put the change in my pocket and headed out the store. I was a little nervous now, thinking about what I had to do to get back home. As I looked around, I stepped on the sidewalk and thought maybe I could go home around the block the other way. As I looked down the street in the other direction, I could see it was darker. The trees were a lot bigger. I decided it was a lot farther to go home around the block; I would be a monster's meal if I went that way.

I returned the way I came, walking around the corner a little slower. Walking past the first house, I looked at everything to make sure there was nothing that could attack me. Walking a little farther, reaching the area where I saw the eyes, I slowed down. Scanning the area really well now, I stopped. The glowing eyes were walking toward me! A CAT! That's all it was, a cat! It walked up to my legs and brushed against me; he wanted me to pick him up. The night didn't look so dark now. I looked around; I could see a lot better than the first time I walked through this area.

By the time I reached my front fence, the darkness didn't bother me anymore. Walking up to the tree, my eyes scanned it to spot whatever I heard earlier; but nothing was there.

I took the bread into the kitchen and gave my father the change. Everybody stopped what they were doing and looked at me, wondering what happened out there in the unknown. I didn't say too much. I just went in the front room and started to play with Eddie again, trying to be cool.

With this experience I found out what the unknown is. After this time the dark wasn't as bad as it looked. My father sent me to the store other times. No big thing. I was still scared at times but not as much as that first time.

Now I was going to prison, another unknown! I'd get used to it, just as I did the monsters. I hoped!

PERKINS

We reached the gate in front of Perkins and stopped in front of some big, electric doors. A guard came to the car, exchanged some words with the driver, and showed him some papers. The big gate opened in a few seconds, and we drove in.

The first thing the prison personnel did was shave my head. They do this to everybody who will spend time here, to make sure they don't come in with lice. I then took a shower and changed clothes.

In YA we had two sets of clothes. First, we had our everyday clothes—a pair of pants that looked like Levis and a blue denim shirt. To dress up for a visitor or for a special occasion such as different kinds of entertainment like movies, shows, or special performers, we had khakis and a plaid or white button-up shirt. Our shoes were black and shiny. The guys always competed to see who could make their shoes the shiniest.

Once all this was handled, I was sent to my company. As I walked into the big day room with about 60 guys in it, they turned to look at me as I entered. The noise level dropped. Everybody stopped doing what they were doing. "Oh, man, what am I going to do here?" I thought. Looking around, I saw the whites, Mexicans, and the black guys all in their groups.

There was a counter with a couple of guards behind it with some inmates around the counter talking. In one corner of the big day room was a TV on a tall stand with about 20 chairs and some couches around it. The chairs and couches were the kind one would find in a waiting room of a doctor's office, all different colors.

There must have been about 20 guys lounging around watching TV. Around the other wall there were tables with guys playing cards and other games. The doors we walked into were opened, and some guys were outside the building playing ball. The grounds were like a school with a little pavement and all green with grass.

Perkins is a California-transit prison for young inmates. Once they leave Perkins, they are placed in institutions all over the state.

Everybody was with their racial group: Mexicans, whites, and blacks. When I say Mexican guys, I don't mean guys from Mexico. I mean guys like me—Mexican American or Chicano. We proudly referred to ourselves in YA as "Loco" [crazy guy]. The white guys who hung around in their small, tough group were called "Straight." The blacks called themselves "Blood." Finally, there were those we called the "Stone Outs," the guys nobody wanted.

The Locos and the Straights didn't like goofy-looking or goofy-acting guys. The Straights were Hells Angels or skinhead types. The Bloods were a little different because they accepted all the Bloods, goofy or not. If there was a Blood and he wanted to hang around with the Stone Outs, it was OK. The guy was accepted back by the Bloods. If you were a Loco or a Straight and you wanted to be with the Stone Outs, the other guys wouldn't want you back.

Standing there looking around at everybody checking me out, I wanted to look bad. I put my head up and shoulders back and tried to look mean. I also tried to look big. I had a hard time with looking big. Jail life reduced me to weighing only 155 pounds. Since I am six feet tall, I looked like a bag of bones.

After a few seconds all the inmates went back to what they were doing. They wanted to see who I was and what group I belonged to: Locos, Straights, or Bloods. Right away the Bloods stopped looking. Then the Locos stopped looking. The Straights kept looking at me. I didn't like that very much. I looked over and gave them a dirty look.

Once I was checked into the company, I sat on one of the chairs in the big day room in front of the TV. I knew from what I had heard from Isaac that after a while the Locos would send someone over to talk to me.

Watching TV, I kept looking over in the direction where the Locos were sitting. It didn't look as if they knew I was there. I thought maybe Isaac was wrong, but I didn't care. I'd just do my time and not worry about it. However, it was good to belong to a group. If you get in a fight with a Straight or a Blood, you'll be in trouble. Everybody backs their group. If you don't belong to one, they can send someone over to fight with you every day if they don't like you. If you do belong to one of the groups, it isn't as difficult because your group will back you up in a fight.

In about an hour a Straight came over and sat next to me. He said, "Hey, man, what are you in for?"

I thought, "What does this Straight want? I'm not one of them."

He continued, "What's your name?"

"Art Rodriguez," I answered.

Looking surprised, he said, "Oh!" Not saying anything else, he stood from his chair and walked over to the other Straights. Because I was so pale from a lack of sun, they thought I was a Straight.

He went back over to the other Straights. They began talking and laughing, looking over at me. One of them stood up and walked to where the Locos were sitting. They talked for a minute, and then they all turned and looked at me.

After a little while one of the Locos came to where I was sitting and sat next to me. "Orale ese, where you from?" he asked.

"San Jo," I answered.

After that I had a smooth ride at Perkins. I got along with almost everybody.

I had a lot of things wrong with my teeth. They filled 18 cavities in two days. They worked fast at Perkins. They also had to treat two other health problems I had. They weren't problems when I arrived; I got them at Perkins. These prolonged my stay at Perkins for about two weeks.

I had been at Perkins for about three weeks. One nice morning I went outside to get some sun. After my welcoming committee mistook my identity, I had more appreciation for maintaining my color and spent the mornings outdoors.

Some of the guys were playing baseball. I went out to the field to lie down and daydream about being home. Sometimes I daydreamed so deeply, I actually thought I was home. I dreamed I was at the Lopez girls' house when I received a phone call. It was my mother. She wanted me to use her car to go to the store for her. All right! I loved using her car to go to the store. Coming right home, Mom!

"ART! ART!" I opened my eyes and could hardly see. The sun was so bright.

"Who's calling me?" I wondered. Looking up with my hands over my eyes and trying to refocus, I saw green; it was the grass.

"ART, ART, COME AND PLAY WITH US. WE NEED ANOTHER PLAYER!" A Loco was yelling at me from a distance.

"Man," I thought, "this guy brought me back from home! I was having a good time!"

I yelled back at him, "NO, MAN, I DON'T PLAY BASEBALL!" Sports weren't my thing. Now, if he had asked me to come over to help them fight, that would have been a different story.

I sat there for a little while and thought to myself, "Maybe I should play; maybe I'll like it. No, I don't think so." Standing up and watching two guys playing catch not too far from me, I said, "Hey, man, throw the ball!" I raised my hands.

The guy who had the ball looked at me and said, "No. You don't have a glove. This is a hard ball."

"What?" I asked. "That little dumb ball can't hurt me! Throw the ball, man! It's OK. Don't worry about it. Just throw it!" The guy stood there looking at me, debating if he should.

He repeated again, "No, man, you don't have a glove!"

"Hey, what are you, an umpire or what?" I yelled.

The guy stared at me for a second, then he pulled his arm back to throw the ball. I raised my hands in a catching position, with my ten fingers almost pointing at him to catch the ball. He let go! Zoom. Coming right at me. Flying right into my hands. Coming kinda fast. BOOM! The ball crashed into my index finger.

I bent over in pain screaming. I was trying to be tough. As I said, I wasn't that good at sports. They took me across the field to the doctor and took X-rays. I had a broken finger; therefore, they had to put a cast on it. I had to be there two extra weeks until they took off the cast.

The very next day I got up in the morning. It was another

beautiful, sunny day; and I wanted to go out to get some sun again. "Wait a minute!" I thought. I did this yesterday. Maybe I'd better not do this again! Look what happened to me already. "What could happen to me with this cast on my left hand?" I asked myself.

I sat on a bench to enjoy the sun, minding my own business. These guys came by me and started to throw the ball back and forth. I was watching these inmates play catch and having a cool time. "Should I? No, I better not. Yeah, what the heck!" I thought. I stood up and said, "Hey, man, throw the ball!"

Looking at me, one of them said, "No, man, you have a broken hand!"

Picking up my hand, I said, "My hand's not broken; it's only my finger. I'll catch the ball with my right hand."

"Hey," he said, "you don't have a glove on!"

"Neither do you! Just throw the ball easy. It'll be all right!" I protested.

The guy looked at me as if he were saying, "OK, you asked for it!" The ball came fast. I put my hand up to catch it with my fingers almost pointed at him. The ball came flying right at my hand. BOOM AGAIN! Now I had two broken fingers. They both broke in almost the same place. To this day both of my fingers hurt everyday in the same spots. As a result I think of Perkins a lot nowadays.

My stay at Perkins went by slowly. I lay around thinking of home and things I did when I was young. I also thought of the good times and bad times I had with my brothers and sister.

THE B-B GUN

Eddie was a good brother when we were growing up. Our parents put a lot of responsibility on him since he was the oldest of us four children. Even though Ed and I got into a lot of squabbles with one another through the years, he stood by me. When he had the responsibility to take care of us, he did a good job of it. There are a lot of good memories of our playing together, having a good time, as well as a few memories of our big fights.

One day when I was about seven or eight years old, my parents were out shopping. Just Eddie and I were home. We started off having fun, playing with the B-B gun and target shooting.

Whenever I made Eddie angry, he wouldn't let it rest until he got revenge. I remember it as always being an overkill—I was the one being overkilled. On this day I had to get away from him after making him angry; so I ran behind the garage, not realizing I had the B-B gun in my hand. Eddie ran after me. He trapped me behind the garage. I said, "You better leave me alone, Eddie, or I'm going to tell Dad when he gets home!" That should have scared him, but Eddie knew me. He knew I wouldn't tell my father. I might get into trouble too. Eddie had me trapped. He started to walk slowly toward me, so I wouldn't get away. If he approached fast, I would run. He would have a harder time catching me. He was bigger than I.

"You better get away from me, or you're going to get it!" I yelled.

I knew Eddie was going to catch me and slug me a few times. I couldn't let that happen again. I realized I had the rifle in my hands. "I might as well use it," I thought. Raising the rifle, I said, "Ed, if you don't stop, I'm going to shoot you!" That should've stopped him. He didn't think I would shoot him.

"Eddie," I yelled, "I'm warning you. If you don't stop, you're going to get it!"

I should have known this wasn't going to stop him. Ed wanted blood! He left me no choice. Pointing the gun at him, I aimed for his stomach. Thinking to myself, I said, "Should I give him one more chance to stop? Ah, I'll just be wasting my time!"

I pulled the trigger! Eddie yelled and bent over in pain. Cocking the gun, I said, "I told you to stop, Eddie; and you didn't want to!" I hoped he would give up. He looked up at me with murder written all over his face.

"I'm going to get you, Arthur!"

"Well, you should have never said that!" I replied. I aimed the rifle again and pulled the trigger. Hey, this was fun!

"I'm really going to get you for this!" Eddie yelled again in pain.

"I don't think so," I said. He was really angry now. He was breathing heavily and looked up at me with eyes that could kill. "What the heck?" I cocked the rifle again, aimed it, and pulled the trigger the third time. I don't know where that B-B hit him, but this time I took off running to the house.

Through the back door I ran into the house, and I turned as fast as I could to lock the screen door. I knew as soon as he could, Eddie was going to be up and right behind me. Sure enough, as soon as my finger was on the lock, he ran to the door and pulled on it.

Locked! Just in time! Our eyes met. We thought the same thing. The front door! I took off through the house. Eddie took off around the side of the house. Just as my finger was on the lock on the front door, he grabbed the door to open it. "Too late, it's locked!" I taunted.

Without wasting any time, I ran to the windows to lock them. Safe! I walked to the front door and saw Ed walking away toward the back. He was probably checking to see if I left anything open. I headed to the back door. There he was standing outside, angrier than I had ever seen him before.

"You better let me in! If you don't, I'm going to really get you!" he demanded. He couldn't fool me. I knew he was going to really beat me anyway, even if I opened the door.

I might as well have fun with this. "NA, NA, NA, NA, NA, NA, you can't get me; and you have to wait until dad gets home to get in!"

He was getting angrier by the second. I knew he wouldn't dare break the screen open, not with my father coming home in a little while. My father, with his belt, would make those B-Bs seem like pebbles.

Then out of nowhere the mean-killer look on Eddie's face disappeared. A big, warm smile appeared.

"Something's up," I thought. I even looked behind me to make sure he wasn't smiling at someone else. No, no one was there. Looking back at Ed, I wondered what was going on. Eddie said something in a friendly voice. "What?" I asked, not hearing him.

"Pes, pes," he said it again.

"What? I can't hear you," I said, moving a little closer to see if I could find out what this was all about.

He answered with a happy look that went along with the big smile on his face. Curling his finger to come closer, he said, "I want to tell you something." Almost touching the outside of the screen, he moved his lips to whisper something to me.

"Sss, Se," he said. I couldn't hear him.

"What?" I asked. He started to say it again, very low. I still couldn't hear him and moved closer, almost touching the screen with my ear. Through the corner of my eye, I thought I saw something moving.

"What?" I turned my head around almost facing the screen, still close to it, to see what was moving. BOOM! His fist smashed into my mouth without tearing the screen.

I rolled in pain on the floor for about fifteen minutes. That was the end of life for my front tooth. It turned black in a few days and died. I don't remember if my father found out what happened. I do remember that my tooth and my gums hurt for many days.

* * *

One day, after about six weeks of being at Perkins, they called me to the counter.

"Rodriguez!" they yelled out. I stood from my chair and walked over to the counter to see what they wanted.

"You're leaving in the morning," the guard said. I still didn't know my final destination.

"Where am I going?" I wanted to know.

"Preston School of Industries," the guard answered.

"Preston," I said in a low voice to myself.

At Perkins I got to know some of the Locos fairly well. They, like Isaac, told me what it was going to be like at Preston. They said I'd do fine there. They told me I needed to fight more than I had in Perkins. I didn't fight at all in Perkins. I couldn't with two broken fingers. I thought to myself, "I wonder where my brother Eddie's going? It will be cool if he goes to Preston too."

The guys told me stories about the castle. There's an abandoned castle which was Preston back in the 1800s and early 1900s. One of the guys at Perkins was sent to Preston in the past, and he had been in it. There's a saying about the castle: when you're released and driving away from Preston, never look back at it. If you do, you'll be going back. The day I was released from Preston and the car rolled out of the gate and down the street, I didn't look back.

PRESTON

The next day I was on the bus heading for Preston, a rough place. If someone was in another institution, messed up, or got into trouble a lot, they'd send him here. If he messed up in Preston, he'd be sent to the prison in Tracy.

As we drove into the main gate at Preston, I could see it was different than when I arrived at Perkins. As we stepped off the bus, each one of us was frisked to see if we were bringing in any weapons or drugs from Perkins.

Once inside we were all taken to receiving. I was there for about two weeks, waiting to find out how I would be classified. Classification was decided through tests taken everyday from morning until evening, tests to find out what kind of "persons" we were. Some of us were classified as manipulators, as leaders, or as followers—following the crowd. It was something new the state was trying to do to rehabilitate us.

Some of the guys at Perkins told me the same thing Isaac had said: start fights with everybody when I arrive at Preston to earn respect. Now I was here, but I thought I'd better wait until I arrived at my assigned company.

There were probably about 60 of us in receiving. Preston was a big place. It had its own school, football field, and gym. It also was big enough to have its own roads with its fleet of cars and trucks. If we became ill at Preston, it had a hospital with a lot of beds. If we needed minor surgery, we had it right there. If it was life threatening, then we were taken to Perkins, about an hour's drive from Preston.

Most of the companies were named after a letter of the alphabet. Along one side of Preston, it was hilly; and we called that side the Loma [hill]. Everything was kept up with green grass and looked nice. Yes, some referred to it as a country club. In fact I was surprised to find that when it was time to eat, a loud whistle would blow. We would file out of the building to go to the cafeteria—no lines, no one walking with us. They watched us from the tower overlooking us. If there was anything going on, such as a fight or someone getting shanked with a knife, they called down. The guards would be there in seconds. Once in a while if it was suspected there was going to be a riot, we had to line up and walk in lines to the cafeteria.

There were some inmates who had their stay at Preston planned out. They got out, partied with drugs, and stayed out every night, almost to the point of burnout. They had nowhere to live. About six months later, they were caught for something small. Therefore, they came back with a program to rest. The courts sentenced them to a program in Preston; it required three or four months of time to be spent there. This was just right for them to recuperate and to be ready for the streets again. This wasn't such a bad place to do time.

Preston even had its own jail. A jail within a jail, it was called "lockup." Prisoners were sent there if they got into some kind of trouble, such as having drugs or getting caught with a shank [a homemade knife]. If we got in a fight with someone of another race, this could start a riot. The guards would then call up front to have a car pick us up and take us to lockup. If those fighting were of the same race, it was no big deal to the guards. At times they would put the two inmates in the large shower room and let them continue fighting.

They had their own special police in Preston. When they made their call, within minutes a Preston car would be there to pick us up. If a riot started, one phone call was made; and the riot cops were there. I always wondered where those riot cops stayed. When they were called, they arrived quickly. I wondered what they did when there wasn't a riot, which was most of the time. Sit around in their cars waiting? I never received an answer to my question.

When I was there, the buildings on the Loma were newer. The

rest of the buildings were probably built in the 1930s or 1940s.

Preston is in the small town of Ione, California. At times we received a special treat and had a live show; sometimes this included famous entertainers, sometimes not. The people from the town were invited and were seated upstairs in the balcony.

We had our big theater at Preston. Every week there were different movies shown, and the town's people also came.

Outside of Preston there was a company of inmates [part of Preston] who took care of the animals. Preston had its own farm. We drank fresh milk, and some of our other food was from the farm.

Preston also had its own graveyard. Inmates died every so often without a family or anyone else who wanted their bodies. They were buried at Preston.

There were 15 foot-high fences all around and a tower right in the middle of the grounds with one or two guards in the tower. If I was sent somewhere within Preston and I was going by myself, they made a phone call to the tower to notify the guards I would be out on the road.

My first day at receiving, things were cool; there were no big problems. I didn't know anyone there, not even the guys from Perkins. The guys who came with me were all from different companies at Perkins.

At lunch time they told us to get ready to go eat. We all lined up to use the washroom. The washrooms were big with the front wall made of glass, so we could be watched. In the middle of the restroom there was a big fountain with a ring on the floor around it. By stepping on the ring, you could turn the water on. This was the sink where we washed up, no privacy whatsoever. If someone was in the restroom taking care of business, the guard, from where he was sitting, could watch everything and everybody. There were no doors on the stalls.

The guards were also called counselors at Preston. I think it sounded better for us young guys. When we said counselor, it sounded as if they were someone we could talk to and trust. However, not all of them could be trusted. There were some good counselors who really tried to help us. To us, helping us was helping us to be released with good reports. When we appeared before the board to see if we would be released, it sure helped if we had good reports.

The giant cafeteria was very old and creepy looking. As we walked there, I remember the big, old doors and all the noise coming from inside. We were the last ones to enter. The place was full of guys from all over Preston. When we walked in, it was a strange feeling. Everybody in the place stopped talking and turned to look at us. When you're standing there against the wall in line, waiting to be served, and you have what seemed to be about 800 guys looking at you, it's not a good feeling. In a few seconds the noise went back up, and everybody went back to eating and talking. This would happen every time we went in to eat. Everyday new guys came into receiving, and some inmates left.

Later in my everyday life at Preston, I became part of the other guys' group and stopped eating to look at the new guys in receiving. We would all stop talking and stare at the new prisoner because in our company we heard stories about each new inmate. News traveled fast. Sometimes there were wild stories and sometimes gruesome ones about different guys who were arriving. Also we heard of our homeboys, so we'd look for them. If a prisoner entered Preston for rape or child molesting, we heard about it before he arrived. We then looked for him. Nobody liked guys sentenced for these crimes because it was thought the victim could have been our sister, mother, or little brothers who were raped or molested. For their safety, these prisoners were usually kept away from everybody else.

One day about two weeks after arriving at Preston, they told me I was classified as a CFM [follower]. Some guys were leaders, others manipulators. These prisoners were always trying to con us out of something! They grouped all the guys of one classification together in the same company. One can imagine how it would be if the officials were right in their classifications. If leaders were all put together and thought of the bad things to do, how could they lead the followers who were placed together in a separate company? I was a CFM. I don't remember what that stands for, but it means follower. If somebody would say "let's go rob a bank," I was supposed to say, "OK, let's go!" With all the aptitude tests I had to take, I never thought they had it right.

All the companies were named after a letter of the alphabet. In our company there were guys who were leaders and guys who were always trying to con us out of something. In Company "G" there were supposed to be leaders, but I saw some wimps who could never lead anyone. All of us always laughed when they told us what we were supposed to be. We all thought it was a big joke.

I was escorted to my new company, Company "I." We called it "Lampara" [lamp]. It was on the Loma or hilly part of Preston. The buildings were surrounded by grass and made of red brick. The floors of the building were concrete. It would seem they would be cold, but the heating system was built in the concrete. The building had pipes in the concrete slab on the floor, with hot steam traveling through them. Therefore, the place was warm.

I was checked into my new company and told what I could do and couldn't do. The guard took me to the lockers and assigned me one. I had never had a locker before with my own lock.

As I went over all these things with the guard and while being checked in, I saw the Locos. They kept looking at me; they wanted to know what kind of guy I was. I felt I'd better show them soon.

The day room resembled a big hall with tables and chairs that one might rent for a wedding reception. In one corner there were guys lifting weights on a platform. In the middle against the wall, there was a TV on a tall stand with all different colors of couches and chairs around it. The guard sat on a platform about two feet high to overlook the entire room. Around the platform there was a bar railing. We weren't supposed to enter the railing when talking to the guard. There were some guards who didn't care if we entered. They were with us twenty-four hours a day, seven days a week, and got to know us really well.

Once I was done being checked in, I looked around. Then I sat on a chair to watch TV. I was really checking things out. This place was going to be my home for a while.

I had to use the restroom. Getting up and walking away, I saw a Blood walk up to and sit on the chair I had just left. The restrooms were the same as in receiving, with a big fountain and a glass front wall.

Returning to my seat, I saw just how big the Blood was. He was a weight lifter and had to cut his sleeves, so his arms could fit through them. Looking over at the guard, I thought to myself, "The guard isn't too far, so the fight won't last too long." Walking up to the Blood, I thought, "I have to make this look good, so the Locos will know I'm tough."

"Hey, man, that's my chair!" I said loudly, so everybody would know I was starting the fight.

Staring at me he said, "Hey, ese, get another chair. There's a lot of empty seats here."

I gave him a hard look and said, "I don't want another seat. I want my chair!" I reached over and slapped his head, waiting for him to get up.

The other Bloods sitting around said, "Hey, Blood, don't let that ese do that to you!" He started to stand. I reached back and hit him as hard as I could, as I always did with my knockout punch. However, when it connected, nothing happened! This guy was too big, and I only weighed 150 pounds. He really had an angry look on his face. His eyebrows came down, and he took a deep breath and held it in. He came toward me, not moving too fast because of his size. When he grabbed me, I hit him again. Everybody was yelling and running over to us. We started to struggle. Well, I started to struggle but not him. He was grabbing me and had me by my neck in order to hit me with his other hand. All I could do was kick him. Just as he was going to give me his knockout punch, the guard came up through the crowd and made everybody get back; he stopped the fight. Saved by the guard! I had it well planned.

"Gee, Rodriguez, you just got here; and you're already in a fight!" the guard said. Talking to the Blood, he said, "You sit there! And, Rodriguez, you come with me!" He took me up to his platform. "You know I have to send you to lockup, don't you?"

"Why?" I wanted to know innocently.

Within just a few minutes, the riot crew arrived. Whenever there was a fight between races, the guard called to the front offices. The guard now looked at me, feeling sorry for me and thinking the other inmates started the fight with the new prisoner.

"How long will I be in lockup?" I asked.

"Oh, about three days," he answered.

One of the men who came in asked, "What's up?"

Just as on the outside, they frisked me and put handcuffs on me. They placed me in the back seat of the station wagon. We drove to the far corner of Preston. The fence was behind this building with the castle on the other side. The lockup facility looked almost as old as the castle. Lockup was a very old building with big, tall doors in front. There were some guys who worked on the outside taking care of the sheep at Preston. They told me they'd been inside of the castle. In the basement there were dungeons with locks on the walls where they would chain a prisoner if he didn't behave. If I were to be chained on the wall for three days, I probably wouldn't want to come back to lockup again. But compared to the Castle lockup, it wasn't that bad.

Walking into the building, I was reminded of the movies of a big prison, with walkways on top, cells on both sides, and cells on top in the back. Everything was made of red and white bricks. These weren't cells with bars; they were small rooms. On the bottom floor on one side of the court, there were about four padded rooms. If a prisoner made too much noise and didn't want to be in his cell, the guards would remove his clothes and put him in the padded room. A hole in the corner was the bathroom. The room was soundproof, so a prisoner could make all the noise he wanted. I never had to spend time there. I knew when to shut up.

All the rooms had a little door or slot in the door to allow our food to be served to us. I couldn't see the person serving the food, and I was not allowed to talk to him. If I was caught trying to speak to him, I would have to go to the hole for the day. For three days I didn't talk to anyone. My personal record was eight straight days in lockup.

Once in my room, I was reminded of Juvenile. There was nothing to do. At least in Juvenile if I were a good reader, I could have read. In lockup there was nothing to read, not even a magazine. I had a small window with nothing to see but a wall of the building next to our building. What I learned to do really well was to use my imagination. I could go anywhere I wanted and be anyone I wanted to be. Of course I thought of things I did when I was home and things I was going to do when I returned.

REBELLION

When we lived in the little house on Spencer Street, my mother worked nights at the cannery. She slept in the morning. When we kids were up, we would have breakfast and go to the park. I was five years old, and Eddie was seven years old. His job was to take care of us at the park. In those days it wasn't as dangerous as nowadays with kidnappers and child molesters. But this doesn't mean there weren't perverts out there.

On the way to the park on a particular morning, I was feeling rebellious. When crossing the streets, we had to hold hands, a rule from my parents. If we didn't and my father found out, I really got the belt.

We arrived at the corner where the store was located, on Virginia Street and Delmas. Reaching out so I could hold his hand to cross the street, Eddie said, "Come on, Arthur, hold hands."

"No!" I protested "I don't want to!"

"Come on! Hold my hand!" he demanded.

He was always telling me what to do, and I didn't want to be under his thumb. I replied, "I don't want to cross the street there. I want to cross here!" pointing to the street in front of me, which was Virginia. Ed was crossing on Delmas; and I wanted to cross on Virginia Street, a busy street with fast-moving traffic.

"No! You can't! Come over here and cross the street with us!" Eddie insisted.

"No!" I said.

"Arthur, you better come over here; or I'm going to tell Dad you're not minding me." If Eddie did that, I knew I was going to get the belt. But on this day, I just didn't care what he did. Waiting for me at the corner to cross the street and looking over at me, Eddie yelled, "Arthur, come over here!"

"No, I want to cross here!" I said.

Eddie, now fed up with me, said, "If you cross there, I hope you get hit by a car." I didn't hear him; and if I did, I didn't care. I was going to do things my way. I started to cross the street. Eddie turned and started to take a step to cross the street on Delmas. Just as he was going to start to cross, he heard a car's brakes and a loud thumping noise. Frightened, he turned to see what it was. The loud noise was the car's bumper on my head. I was flying through the air.

My poor brother really felt bad that he told me he hoped I'd get hit by a car. He probably thought I was dead. I had three big holes on my forehead. I was lying on the street with my head all swollen and completely unconscious. The man who hit me also felt really bad. He said I had walked out in front of him from nowhere. I probably didn't even look to see if any cars were coming. I had been looking at my brother because I was taunting him.

A neighbor lady heard all the commotion down the street and came out to see what had happened. She saw me lying on the street and people waiting for the emergency vehicles to arrive. She ran to our house where my mother was in the middle of washing her hair. She had long, brown hair; and it was hard to get the soap out quickly. The lady told my mother to drink a glass of water before she told her what had happened, thinking it would help calm her down.

The next thing I remember, I was having a dream. Rocks were rolling all around me, trying to crush me. It was like the Walt Disney movie when the brooms are chasing Mickey Mouse. I had hundreds of rocks trying to roll over me and couldn't get away. I think I was trapped by the rocks. No one could save me from being crushed. The rocks were closing in on me. I opened my eyes and realized I was in the hospital. Looking over toward the side of my bed, I saw my mother holding my hand, smiling at me. Now I felt safe.

I was in the hospital for a few days, and my mother didn't leave my side. Even the poor man who hit me came to see me. He felt really bad.

My brother Eddie recuperated from blaming himself. And me? Judge for yourself to decide if I stayed loco from that blow! At any rate, I think it helped me to mind my brother's orders to hold hands when crossing the street.

* * *

"Rodriguez! Rodriguez, wake up!"

I lifted my head from the mattress, "What?"

A guard standing at my doorway looked at me and said, "Come on! It's time to go back to your company."

"Man, those three days went by fast," I said, rubbing my eyes and waking up. I stood for a second, brushing my hair back with my hands and trying to get my thoughts together. I stepped toward the door and looked back at the room, thinking I may have forgotten something. Then I remembered there was nothing to take because I didn't bring anything with me.

Arriving back at my company, I found things went the way I thought they would. The Locos came and talked to me. They invited me to sit with them. They went on to tell me the things I should do and things I shouldn't do. There were no homeboys in the group at that time. When there was a homeboy in the group, we had a safer feeling. No matter whom you were fighting, the homeboy would back up your play.

The closest Loco I had to a homeboy was Danny from Hollister. We became really good friends. Danny had a homeboy with him who was being released in about a month.

As time went by, I got to know the guys well. When I went to YA, I entered with a year of continuance. We called it a bala [bullet]. A bala travels fast and goes a long way. A year was long, but the time was supposed to go by fast. That's what they said, but it sure didn't seem like it. With a year of continuance, I was supposed to do a year before I returned to the board; then I would probably get another year. A board is a committee the governor appoints to review our cases.

While I was in Preston, I saw a lot of guys come in with programs. A program was about three or four months. While I was there, some prisoners came in, got out, and then returned—some up to three times.

It's hard to explain how it felt to be locked up for so long and to be away from home. I was never happy, not for a minute. I longed for home every passing second. To some guys it wasn't bad; they were used to it. To them it was their home away from home. As for me, I couldn't wait for the day I was released. I awoke many mornings thinking it was a big nightmare.

I often asked myself, "What if in a year I go to board, and the board gives me another year? Can I take it?" I didn't think so. Maybe I'd run. Escape!

Every so often some guys tried to escape. Once in a while they made it all the way home, but they always were caught. Once three Stone Outs from our company tried to escape. Coming back from dinner, they hid in garbage cans. All of Preston was locked down. Nobody could go outside or do anything, not even in our day room could we move around. The guards thought we all knew about it. We had no idea what the Stone Outs were planning.

The escapees' plan was to hide out in the trash cans; after a while everybody would forget about them. At night they would climb the fence and go home. Very simple. The only problem was the people who managed Preston didn't forget about them. The escapees spent two days and nights in those garbage cans.

Preston had all the lights on, including the search lights, with men and dogs walking around the fence on the outside. It was a big thing for these prisoners to try to escape. For two days we couldn't do anything in our company because of those Stone Outs. Finally, they couldn't take it anymore—being there with the garbage—so they crawled out. They walked up to the door of our company and knocked to be allowed to enter. We looked out the windows; they sure looked bad, really bad! Two days in garbage cans, they must have smelled! Our guards told us to sit down and shut up, not to say a word. Within about three or four minutes, they had an army of guards around our building with the dogs. We never saw these guys again. They were sent to Tracy or somewhere else; therefore, escaping was out of the question. Everyday was a struggle for me to get a grip on myself and to accept what was coming. I needed to do my time.

Every so often the guards put up a list of all the prisoners who were apprehended within six months after being released. Almost everybody I knew in Preston was back in custody within those six months. I told myself that when I got out, I was not coming back. This was no country club—being away from home and dealing with the Straights, Bloods, and even the Locos. It wasn't too bad if I were getting along with everybody. But when I wasn't getting along, I had to watch my back all the time.

I was confined to Preston for many months. My good friend Danny was getting ready to be released. He was excited he was going to be home in Hollister soon. The day he left was a happy day for him but a sad one for me. We had become close homeboys. We spent all our time together then.

Today, thirty years later, when I meet people from his town, I ask if they know him or his family or someone else on a particular street. How did I know the streets where everybody lived? I helped Danny write letters to his friends and his young wife. He wouldn't write very many letters to his wife because he couldn't put his feelings into words. I told Danny I would help him. How could I do this if I couldn't even spell? Well, I wrote love letters my way, expressing feelings the way I thought he would have, if he could.

After I wrote his letter, Danny would sit next to me with his writing pen and paper and ask me what each word meant, since every word was spelled wrong. He really liked the way I wrote his letters: "My dearest love, I truly miss you. I remember how I used to look into your beautiful eyes and..." Not only did he like the letters, but his wife would write back telling him how much she loved his letters and how his writing had changed. I wrote back, or should I say, he wrote back, or was it I? One of us wrote back and told her he was taking classes on writing to express his feelings to others. She loved it.

As time went on, other guys wanted me to write their letters, "Hey, Art, would you write to my old lady?"

"Sure, ese, for the same price that everybody else pays," I would reply. Nothing's free. I charged them some cigarettes for each letter.

Danny had been my business partner, and now he was leaving. Lately we had been receiving some prisoners to our company from another part of the state. I didn't like them very much, and they didn't like me.

A few days after Danny left, one of the Locos whom I didn't like was getting wise with me. I didn't like it at all. He would tell a joke and use my name, and everybody would laugh at me. The Locos would say it in a way that I shouldn't get angry. It was supposed to be in fun. If I became angry, he made it seem as if I couldn't get along with the Locos. I knew if I was to fire on him right there on the spot, it was going to be trouble for me, since the Locos liked him. Lately I was being sent to lockup a lot for fighting. I had been in Preston for about four months now. It was time to slow down the fighting. I also knew if I fought him around his homeboys, they would probably jump in; therefore, I had to think this out. How was I going to do this so it would work out in my favor?

The next day the guard stood up and said he needed another Game Boy. Being Game Boy was usually handled by one of the Stone Outs. The Game Boy was in charge of all the games. He would check them out and check them back in at the end of the day or when the prisoners were done with them. The Game Boy didn't get paid for doing this job; it was just something to do.

Ernie was a Loco who thought he was tough. He had straight, short, black hair. He was like Bobby X, always combing his hair, a really conceited guy. In the mornings when he was washing up, Ernie spent the longest time in front of the mirror. He loved looking at himself.

Ernie was always the one who checked out the cards for his poker games. I thought I could be the Game Boy and make Ernie turn in his cards early. If he didn't, then I could fight him and not get into trouble. Whoever was Game Boy didn't get anything for it. I didn't like doing it for nothing, but I planned to get something for doing the job. I raised my hand and said, "I'll be Game Boy!"

Mr. Campbell, the guard, looked at me and replied, "I don't know, Rodriguez! I don't think . . . Well, we'll try it for a while, but you have to be fair with everybody."

Looking at him and nodding my head, I said, "I will, man! These guys will have it made with me as Game Boy!"

Mr. Campbell pointed his finger at me said, "We don't want you to be too nice now."

The guys always try to talk the Game Boy into keeping the cards overnight. That way they could play all night in the dorm.

Mr. Campbell let me be Game Boy but not for long. That very

night at 9:30, I was to start checking in the games. The Game Boy usually left the tough guys for last, or he might get into trouble with them. I walked straight over to Ernie's table where he was sitting with his homeboy next to him.

"Hey, Ernie, give me the cards, man!" I said.

"Get out of here, Game Boy!" he laughed.

I thought to myself, "I'm going to nail this guy, but first I'm going to fix myself up!" I went back to where the guard was standing and asked him something I already knew.

"Hey, Mr. Campbell, if somebody doesn't want to turn in the cards, am I supposed to insist on it?" I asked.

"Sure, Rodriguez, that's your job. If they don't want to turn in their cards, tell them they don't have any choice. They have to."

"Yes, sir," I said. This was the answer I wanted to hear.

I returned to the other side of the day room where Ernie was playing cards. As I approached his table, I turned to make sure Mr. Campbell wasn't looking to see what I was going to do. This time I didn't want the guard to get to us right away. I wanted a chance to get this vato [guy] Ernie. I just didn't like him, and he didn't like me. Showdown time.

"Hey, Ernie!" Ernie turned around to see who called him. I was waiting for him to turn toward me a little to let him have it. I wasn't going to let him get out of his seat as I usually did, just in case his homeboy wanted to jump in. The first few seconds of a fight are critical.

Ernie looked at me, and it seemed for a second he knew what was going to happen. BOOM! I slammed him right in the face as hard as I could. He bent backwards, falling out of his chair. As he was falling, he held his jaw. His homeboy stood up with both of his hands clenched, ready to start fighting.

Just then Richard ran from the next table where he was playing cards and told Ernie's homeboy, "Hey, ese, if you jump in, then it's you and me!"

I had never expected this from Richard.

Ernie got up right away and started fighting. I had never seen Ernie fight before. I thought he was just a talker and had a good act. He was at Preston before I arrived, but he sure talked tough and thought of himself as a good fighter. But it was all talk; he was not a fighter. Every time I hit him, the punch connected; and he felt it. He was doing a lot of swinging, but nothing was hitting me. He was hitting the air. Within a few minutes the guards were there breaking us up.

They took Ernie and me up by the platform. The guard told me to sit on a chair away from the platform and had Ernie go up to the platform and have a seat. He told them the story. I could hear one of the guards, Mr. Campbell, telling him that whenever the Game Boy asks for the cards, you're supposed to return them. They ordered him to sit in front of the TV for a while. It was then my turn.

"Rodriguez, come up here!" I went to the platform and sat on the same chair Ernie had been using. "Rodriguez, what happened? This is your first day as Game Boy, and you're already in a fight! I knew I shouldn't have let you be a Game Boy!"

Looking up at him with a bewildered look, I said, "What was I supposed to do? He didn't want to turn in his cards!"

"You should have told me," he said. Just what I wanted to hear.

"I did, and you sent me back."

Now Mr. Campbell was scratching the back of his head.

"Yeah, you're right; I should never have sent you back. It's really my fault." Hey, this was what I really wanted to hear.

He told me I would no longer be the Game Boy. Cool with me. I was a Game Boy as long as I wanted to be.

Richard was all right. He was from the LA area. He came in about a month before this happened. Most of the guys in company "I," my company, were in for assault or some kind of fighting. Richard said he was in for assault also. He was a tall guy with a thin frame and a thin face. He had one of those noses that was long and pointed. A really easy going guy, it didn't seem as if he could be there for being a gangbanger as he described himself to everybody.

One day we were sitting outside on the grass. We were talking about things back home—how it was in our hometown. Richard looked at me and said, "Art, can I tell you something?"

"Sure, Richard," I answered.

"If I tell you, you can't tell anybody, OK?"

"Sure, no problem," I answered again. I loved hearing secrets.

"Well," he started, "I told my lawyer how it is in here, and he fixed my papers to say I am here for assault."

"Oh no!" I thought to myself. "I hope he doesn't tell me he's here for rape or something like that." I sat there for awhile, waiting for him to start talking.

Finally he said, "Well, I'm not here for assault but for being an arsonist."

"What do you mean arsonist? Did you burn things down?" I asked. He looked at me, wondering what I was thinking, because the inmates didn't like those who were in for these crimes. The other inmates thought these criminals were crazy. Richard didn't seem crazy at all. He was an all-right Loco.

Richard answered my question, "Yeah, I burned a lot of things down."

"Why?" I asked.

"I love to watch things burn. You know, when you're standing there and a building is burning and all the firemen are trying to put it out it, it's so exciting!" His eyes were opening up wide.

Richard continued, "It's so exciting with all the lights from the fire trucks and police cars."

I cut in, "But what if someone gets hurt, or a kid dies? Then what?"

Richard sat there not knowing how to answer me. "Nobody died, Art! Just a few buildings got burned down."

No wonder he didn't want to tell anyone. He really looked crazy when he was talking about it. Richard looked at me with a weird expression and said, "You know how it is, Art. It's so much fun!"

"Was it so much fun?" I thought. Most little kids got into trouble for playing with matches or something similar.

THE FIRE

I was in the fifth grade and went to Lee Matson School. I should have been attending Mayfair Elementary, but Mayfair had too many kids at the time. The fifth and sixth graders were sent to Lee Matson.

Behind Lee Matson there were no freeways, houses, or anything else. It was all fields. Some of the Story Book homes were being built. In between Mayfair and Lee Matson, there was a big, empty field. Shortly after this time some homes were built there. Today they look old.

We used to walk home the back way. Behind the school was a dirt road. The man who owned the field used the road for his vehicles, to harvest whatever he planted in the field. A dirt road was behind Mayfair School where there was a playing field where the kids played ball. Behind this field was another one with tall, dry weeds. Next to this field were the fences to the houses that were on La Vonne Street.

Around the month of September, the tall weeds were really dry. We made a trail as we walked through them everyday to get home.

I was in my class when the bell rang. On the playground one of the kids I hung around with was Billy. Billy called me to the field. He wanted to show me something. Once I was on the field, he looked around, reached in his pocket, and pulled out three books of matches.

"Hey, Art, want to burn the school?" he asked. Billy and I had been going to school together since we were in the first grade. We always did dumb things together.

When he showed me all the matches, I said, "Billy, I don't want to burn down the school. That's crazy!"

"Na, I probably won't do that; but I thought it was a good idea," he replied.

"Let me have a book of matches," I said, wondering how it would feel to burn down the school.

After school I got a cigarette from one of the kids who smoked. At this time I experimented with cigarettes once in a while, but I really hadn't started smoking yet.

I was late leaving school. Most of the kids had already gone home. I had a book of matches and a cigarette. Should I start a fire? I stopped behind Mayfair School at the field with the tall, dry weeds. I glanced around to make sure nobody was watching me. I pulled the cigarette out and put it in my mouth. I took out a paper, wadded it up, and threw it on the ground. Next I took the cigarette and cut a slit on the side of it. I took the book of matches and stuck one in the cigarette, with the other matches leaning against it. Next I placed them on the paper. I thought that when I lit the cigarette, it would take time to burn down to the matches and to start the paper on fire before igniting the grass.

Walking away through the playing field of Mayfair School, I looked back as I went through the fence on the other side. No smoke yet. As I walked down the street toward King Road, I glanced back again to see if there was any smoke. At this point I started to worry. I began to think, "What if it's not a little fire, and it gets big. What if it burns one of the houses down? What if it burns Mayfair School down?" I started to turn around and run back to stop the fire. Just as I started to run, I heard all the sirens. FIRE TRUCKS! I ran the next few houses to King Road. Just as I reached King to cross the street, in a hurry to get home, I heard all the fire trucks coming my way. The first big truck went screaming by me. Then another one went by with all its lights flashing and with the firefighter hanging on the back of the truck. The third fire truck also passed, screaming in front of me. As this truck passed, one of the firefighters who was standing on the back of the truck looked straight at me. I looked at him. He wouldn't take his eyes off me. He knew I started the fire! Guilt was written all over my face. Even as the big, red truck, with lights flashing and sirens sounding, turned the corner, the firefighter kept staring at me. He turned his whole body in order to keep his eyes on me. I shot off across the street, scared, and was almost hit by a car.

Once I reached home, I stayed in my room, worried they were going to knock on the front door to take me. They knew I set the fire. If my father found out I started a fire, he would kill me. Everyone at home wanted to know what was wrong with me that evening. I didn't even eat supper.

No one came to my house. No one ever found out I started a fire. The next day I walked to school as I usually did. When I reached the field, from far away I could see it was all black. Only the dry grass burned, no houses, no school, and no kids. What a relief. I had worried all night and didn't even tell my friends. I was embarrassed and ashamed to say anything.

* * *

While Richard was telling me how much fun it was, I knew better and disagreed with his thinking. I told Richard, "Don't start any fires here, please. You'll kill us all!"

"Oh no, I wouldn't do that. I'm not that crazy."

"Yeah, right!" I thought to myself.

A few days later we heard a Loco was coming from San Jose. I had hopes he would be placed in my company because I needed the help. Since I had the fight with Ernie, things hadn't been going too well. Ernie knew a lot of guys from all over Preston, and they gave me hard looks. I would walk to the cafeteria, and a Loco who was his homeboy would ask, "Ese, how's Ernie?"

I looked at him and answered, "What do I look like, ese, his keeper? He's around here somewhere; you ask him." I would get smart with him and his friends because I knew why they were asking. Ernie and his homeboys were going to be fighting us in a few days. We all knew it.

During one of our meals, the inmates from receiving came in. I looked at them as I always did. I wanted to see if there was anybody I might know. Sometimes we saw guys who left a few months before. They returned to Preston because they loved it so much. There was this short Loco who looked tough. When he was in line, the guys eating would say, "Orale, Chuco. How you doing, ese?"

Others would say, "Orale, Chuco!"

I thought to myself, "That Chuco knows a lot of people."

Then the guy sitting next to me said, "Hey, Art, that guy Chuco, he's your homeboy from San Jo."

Looking at him standing in line, I thought, "That's him!" I felt as if I knew him. No matter where I went in Preston, I saw his name, "Chuco de San Jo," written all over the place—in the books, on games, and also carved on the benches. All right, my homeboy. As I sat and looked, I hoped he was being sent to my company. At that time there were only four of us who hung around together and about seven of the other Locos in our company.

The time was getting close to have my big fight with Ernie again. Richard and the other two guys said that when it happened, they wanted to fight too. When he was talking to his homeboys about something, Ernie was the kind of guy who would turn his head, look at me, and start laughing as if he were talking about me. Twice I stood up from my card game and walked over to his table, asking, "What did you say, ese?"

Both times he looked up at me and said, "Nothing, ese. I didn't say anything." I knew he didn't want to fight me again, but his homeboys did. I didn't care. I was ready when they were.

Time went by slowly. Everybody told me it should be going by fast, but it wasn't. I received letters from home all the time. My mother would be coming to see me soon. My poor mother wanted to see me every week, but money was the problem. Later on I learned my mother paid half of the lawyer's fee; my father the other half. She came to visit every few months, not too often. I didn't realize it then, but it was better that way. Guys who had a lot of visits had a harder time. They saw their families often and missed home even more. Some guys received packages every week, full of cartons of cigarettes and canned foods.

Not only did I get letters from home but also from friends. I had three girlfriends to whom I wrote love letters. The girlfriend I had while I was in the county jail found another boyfriend later. She was my girlfriend before I was sent up. I really cared for her, but she couldn't wait for me. She found another guy who she ended up marrying.

My girlfriends to whom I wrote love letters were Alice, Yolanda, and Sally. I never met Sally in person; she was Andy's sister. Andy was one of the two guys who wanted to fight Ernie and his homeboys with me. He told me his sister was really good looking, and he had told her about me. After that, she wanted to write to me. After writing a few times, I thought that if she looked as good as she wrote, I'd go to see her in Stockton when I was released. I received a picture from her one day, and I couldn't believe it! She looked just like her brother, like a gorilla wearing lipstick!

Alice was Dennis' girlfriend before I was locked up. Every few days she called me for advice about Dennis and her. I talked to her about Dennis. I liked Alice as a good friend and didn't think of moving in on her. When I was in Preston, I received a letter from Alice asking how I was and how things were. I wrote back and told her all about prison life and how I was looking forward to getting out and seeing her and all my other friends. In just a few days, she wrote a strong letter telling me how much she liked me. She said she had these feelings when she called me to talk about Dennis, and she wanted to be my girlfriend. "Why not?" I thought. I probably had a year-and-a-half to go before I was released from Preston. I kept busy writing letters to all my girlfriends.

In Preston we had school along with a number of shops: arts and crafts, wood, metal, and leather. Some of the shops were part of the school at Preston; some were to teach the inmates different trades. One of the classes I took was a leather shop, making nice women's leather purses. The school building was about the same age as the buildings on the Loma. It had a few different classrooms, and the teachers were cool. They had a hard time putting up with unruly guys. They didn't want to get us into any more trouble than we were in already. These classes reminded me of the good times we had in grammar school.

THE SHOWER ROOM

When I started going to Lee Matson, we were there with all the big kids. Lee Matson School had PE classes and a big gym. Billy and I didn't like dressing down for PE. One day we talked each other into cutting the class, but where would we hide?

"Let's go behind the gym. If anyone comes, we'll pretend we're walking somewhere else. They'll never know," Billy said.

I remember not hesitating and saying, "OK." We took off behind the gym. Back in those days Lee Matson was a brand new school. From behind the gym no one could see us.

Half an hour later from the windows over our heads, we could hear all the girls in the shower room. We both looked up at the same time.

I looked at Billy, and he looked at me. I said, "Want to?"

"You know it!" he said.

"Me first!" I exclaimed. The windows were the kind the older buildings had that pull down from the top. The bottom of the window had about an inch-wide crack. Billy helped me up on his shoulders. I was just tall enough to see through the window.

"Wow! I never saw anything like this before!" I whispered to myself.

"OK, Art, it's my turn!" Billy yelled anxiously. I couldn't believe I was looking at all the girls taking showers.

"Hurry, my shoulders are going to give out. You're too heavy!" he yelled. I knew I wasn't too heavy. He just wanted to get up there to see what I was looking at.

After a while I got tired of Billy crying about his shoulders. "OK, OK, hold your horses; let me down." The girls were almost done with their showers anyway.

He put one foot on the wall pushing himself up. I put my hands together so I could help him, and then stood on my shoulders—first one foot, then the other one. Billy wore big clod-hopper shoes. They were hard and hurt my shoulders. Just as he was up and looking in, through the corner of my eye, I saw the coach walk around the corner. The coach didn't know I saw him walk around the building. I turned a little, and now my back was toward him.

Just as I turned, I saw he was standing there with his arms crossed. "Hey, Billy, I don't think we should be doing this!"

"What? What do you mean?" Billy answered.

"Yeah, what's in there?" I asked innocently.

"What do you mean?" he asked.

"Billy, I think you better come down. I don't think this is a good idea you had!" I was almost falling from the weight of Billy. I was surprised the coach hadn't said anything yet.

"Come on, Billy, you better come down now. This just isn't right!" I said, hoping the coach would think I was the innocent one.

"What are you talking about?"

"OK, boys! Get down from there!" the coach barked at us. I was glad he finally said something; my shoulders were getting tired. Billy almost fell off my shoulders when he heard the coach's voice.

Getting down and facing the coach, Billy whispered, "Why didn't you tell me?"

I looked at Billy and shrugged my shoulders. The coach wasn't really angry at us. He told me to go to my PE class and not to ever look in the window again. Billy, well, he had to go to the office.

* * *

One day in Preston I received a notice that one of my teachers had moved somewhere out of Preston. They were moving me to Mr. Williams' class. I had heard stories about Mr. Williams. He was a very old man, maybe in his eighties. He had retired from his job; and since he was such a good teacher, the state gave him a job at Preston.

The inmates said the students would run his class. He couldn't hear; he was going deaf. Some said he just didn't care. I knew I was just going to be wasting my time in his class. I had more important things to do, like play poker at my company.

As I walked into Mr. Williams' class, everybody was talking and playing around. Mr. Williams was in his chair at his desk. It looked as if he had been doing something and just fallen asleep. I wondered if he was dead.

I saw some guys I knew sitting at the back of the class. I sat with them, not waking the teacher.

"Hey, ese, how you doing?" I asked.

"All right, are you going to be coming to class here?" he asked.

"Yeah, I didn't know if I should wake him," I replied, lifting my chin toward the teacher.

He looked over at Mr. Williams and said, "He doesn't know. If you tell him anything, he won't remember anyway. So if I were you, I wouldn't even tell him you're here. He'll get a paper saying you're in his class anyway, but he probably won't even read it. So it doesn't even matter."

After school I went back to my company, wondering how I could use this situation to my advantage. I was always thinking of ways I could make things better for me at Preston. There was no one else there who would take care of me. Even if someone wanted to, there was not much they could do. If I had a teacher who couldn't remember, maybe I would be able to do what I was planning. I didn't think it would work, but the next day I was going to try it anyway.

The next morning I walked into class. Passing by Mr. Williams' desk, I said, "Good morning, Mr. Williams."

"Huh," he looked up at me, with his glasses on the end of his nose. Looking over the frame, "Good morning," he acknowledged. I think I surprised him because nobody said "good morning" to the teachers. Some Stone Outs did once in a while but not very often. When I greeted Mr. Williams, he looked at me and didn't notice I was a new student. I think, to him, we all looked alike. I sat where I had the day before and waited.

Mr. Williams stood up from his chair, went to the blackboard, turned, faced us, and said, "Listen up, everybody has to read these pages in your books." He pointed to some writing on the board.

One of the Locos in the class had his feet up on the desk next to me. He taunted, "Yeah, yeah, yeah, yeah!" Everyone in the room started laughing. I didn't know if the teacher heard him. It didn't seem as if he did. Mr. Williams went back to his desk with his work done for the day. Within a few minutes he was in a deep sleep.

Getting up from my seat, I approached his desk. "Mr. Williams, Mr. Williams!" I said. The second time a little louder. "Mr. Williams, Mr. Williams!"

"Yeah," startled, sitting up on his chair, he focused on me. "Yeah, what is it?" I wondered if he recognized me.

"Is it OK with you if I go to the office to check something out?"

"Sure, go ahead," he answered.

Walking out of his class into the hallway, I headed for the office which was at the end of the long hallway with classrooms on both sides. At the end of the hallway were big, glass doors with a counter and a man working on a typewriter.

Turning as I walked into the office, the man looked at me and asked, "What do you need?"

"I want to see how many credits I need to graduate," I answered.

"Sure, what is your name?"

"Arthur Rodriguez."

"Let's see if I can find it."

He walked over to a cabinet and opened it. It had small drawers. He pulled open one of the drawers which contained a lot of small index cards. "Here you are, Arthur Wiggins Rodriguez," he said.

All my legal papers had my middle name as Wiggins. Since I don't have a middle name and that's my mother's maiden name, Wiggins was what they used.

He handed the card to me without looking at the contents. I looked at it and asked how many credits I needed to graduate.

Sitting back in his chair with his hands on the typewriter, he said, "The State of California requires 190 credits."

"Can I take this back to class to my teacher? I'll bring it right back."

"Sure, let me write this down just in case you don't come back." He jotted a note, looked at me, and said, "There, you are all set."

As I walked out of the office and back down the hall to my classroom, I knew I'd find Mr. Williams sleeping. I hoped his memory was as bad as everybody said it was.

When I was home and going to school, I was an "F" student. Even if I went to school the rest of the time I was at Preston, I couldn't have graduated; I was so far behind in credits.

I entered the classroom. There was Mr. Williams, just as I thought, sleeping. There was so much noise in the room, I didn't know how he could sleep.

"Mr. Williams! Mr. Williams!" Putting my hand on his shoulder, I shook him a little, "Mr. Williams, wake up!"

Shaking his head again to regain his senses, he asked, "What is it?" He looked up at me. He was a little irritated that I kept waking him up during his morning sleep.

"Mr. Williams, I have a big problem," I said anxiously. Mr. Williams was now wide awake, and he sat up in his chair.

"What is it?"

"Well, look at this. I went to the office to check out how long I have to keep going to school. I asked for my card with all my credits, and look what they showed me!" I said rudely. I placed the card down in front of him on his desk. He looked at it as if he were confused. I don't think he could make heads or tails of it.

"Yeah, what is it?" Mr. Williams asked.

"Well, Mr. Williams, I think you're just too old for this job!" I insisted. "You forgot to give me my credits for last year. Look!" I pointed to one row of empty blocks on the card. The reason they were empty was because I wasn't in Preston at that time, and Mr. Williams didn't know that. "Right there!" I pointed again to another row of empty blocks. "I feel like I've been coming here all this time for nothing, Mr. Williams," I sighed. He picked up the card and took a better look at it. He studied it for a few seconds. Then he put it down on the desk in front of him and started to fill in the first block with a five. In the next block, he wrote another five; in the next, five again. My heart was pounding. It worked! He went down the row with 5 fives!

"Now, that's better," he said.

"Yeah, but what about the first semester?" I asked, suddenly becoming greedy.

"Oh, yeah, all right." Now the next row five, five, five. He finished the row with another set of fives. I thought to myself, "This teacher is really old for this job. He doesn't even know who I am!"

"There you go," he said with a smile.

"Should I push it, or should I stop while I'm ahead?" I thought to myself. During this time of my life, I loved to gamble. "What the heck, all or nothing!" I thought.

"What about the beginning of this semester, Mr. Williams? You didn't give me any credits for this semester." He did the same thing, wrote all fives. When he finished, I had him write his initials on all the fives. I took my card from him, so he could go back to his morning sleep as I headed back to the office. In the hallway I counted the fives he gave me plus the credits I already had on the card from high school. There were 195. "All right!" I yelled in an undertone. I happily jumped to touch the ceiling! "I can't believe it worked!"

Walking into the office, I stood by the counter until the clerk finished his typing. He looked up at me.

"All done with it?"

"Yep, I'm done. How long am I supposed to go to school if I've got all my credits?" I asked.

"What, you got your credits?" he questioned. He took the card out of my hand. Taking the pencil from his ear, he added up the numbers on the card to see how many I had.

He finally said, "You don't even have to be here. You have enough credits; you've graduated." He went on to tell me I didn't have to go back to class.

"Can I go to my arts and crafts' class if I want to?" I liked the leather class because I was allowed to make things to send home to my family and friends.

"Sure you can."

What a good student I was!

About two weeks after I finished the classes, I saw some big wheels from Preston enter our building at our company. The men were all wearing suits, and I had only seen them in passing on the road or at special events. They entered the day room and headed in the direction of the platform where a guard was sitting. As soon as the guard caught sight of them walking toward him, he rose from his seat. I wondered what they wanted. I had never seen them come into our company before. The guard came down from the platform and met them on the floor. When they met, they were huddled in a circle for a few minutes. The guard looked up from the huddle and scanned the day room very slowly, squinting his eyes and looking for someone. I watched him to see what this was all about. I wanted to see where his eyes were going to stop. Whomever he was looking for, he missed him. He scanned the room again very carefully. All the big shots were waiting for him to find whomever he was looking for. His eyes were getting closer to where I was sitting. His eyes met mine, and he stopped looking. He was looking for me! He bent his head over to the other man and pointed his finger in my direction. I looked around to make sure he was looking at me.

"Oh no! What did I do?" I thought.

The guard raised his hands, and he yelled, "MAY I HAVE YOUR ATTENTION! May I have your attention?" All these men with their big-shot suits looked my way with smiles on their faces.

I thought, "If they're looking for me, I must have done something good for once."

"May I have your attention everyone? I want it quiet! Completely quiet!" the guard yelled out. When the noise level dropped totally, he continued. "I want everybody to go to the sides and stand against the walls. These gentlemen want to make an announcement!"

"An announcement!" I wondered. "An announcement, and they're all looking at me." One of the professional, business-type men with the suits wouldn't take his eyes off me. "What do these people want, man?" I thought, feeling irritated.

The warden of Preston moved to the middle of the day room with papers in his hand. He started to speak, "I have a very special announcement to make. Here at Preston we do not have this happen very often. When it does, we think it's special. It might encourage the rest of you to work very hard for your future. One of you has worked really hard on his studies, and my staff and all of Preston would like to congratulate him on his achievement at Preston School of Industries! I would..." Lifting the paper to eye level and putting on his glasses, he continued, "I would like to congratulate this person for graduating from our school! You have helped in making it a success!" Now he read the paper, "Arthur, and, let's see, Arthur, and, and." He was having a difficult time reading my middle name. "Arthur Wiggles

Rodriguez!" he said confidently.

"Not Wiggles! Wiggins!" I exclaimed to myself.

Instead of clapping, the inmates all started laughing. "Hey, Wiggles! Someone yelled out. "Orale, Wiggles!"

This man didn't know the damage he had done to me. As time went on, I had to fight that name off! I didn't mind their teasing me with the name, "Wiggles"; but I became angry when the inmates tried to make it stick as my nickname.

After a few days Chuco, my homeboy from San Jose, went into our day room. We all looked at him, and I thought to myself that my wish had come true. Once he was checked in, he didn't wait for us to go to him; he'd been through this a few times before.

"Orale, Chuco de San Jo," he said as he started on one side of the Locos and walked toward me. He shook everybody's hands. "Chuco de San Jo," he repeated to whomever he'd introduce himself to. Each Loco told him where they were from.

"Art de San Jo," I answered back.

"Art, hey, homeboy! I heard I had a homeboy in this compania."

After this day Chuco became one of us. Ernie and his homeboys didn't like it. When we'd go to eat and as we walked down the road, everybody from the other companies knew Chuco. Chuco was a short guy who looked and acted like a chuco. We weren't really together that long before he was released, maybe less than a year.

On one side of our company was the day room. In the middle of the building was a hallway that went into the dorm. The dorm was as big as the day room with wall-to-wall bunk beds. We had at least two guards watching us at all times. In the day room there was a guard on his platform watching us, and in the dorm there was another platform overlooking the large night room.

Once the lights were turned off, the guard was on the platform reading our mail. Everything was read before it was delivered to us. My bed wasn't too far from the platform. Some guards opened the mail with their letter opener and put it on the pile that was supposed to be read. Once all the mail was opened, the guard pulled out his own book to read. Therefore, not all our mail was being censored.

Some nights were crazy. When the lights went off and everything was quiet, some guys fixed up their beds as if they were sleeping in them. They would get on the floor and crawl all the way to the back corner. Once there, they would play cards or just whisper. When the guard made his rounds every hour or two, the inmates hid under the beds until the guard passed. They were never caught, but they had some close calls.

I never played this game. I always thought there was enough time during the day to play cards and talk. Nights were for sleeping. I would close my eyes and dream, drifting to summers back home.

BLOW YOUR HORN

San Jose was a small town in the fifties. Virginia Place was at the end of town, and behind our house we had barbed-wire fences and ranches. The ranches were mostly dairy farms with a lot of milking cows. Traveling farther down King Road, you would find fields with nothing much on the land. Some new tracts of homes were starting to spring up here and there. Once in a while you saw a ranch house just as you would see if you were traveling down a country road.

On some hot summer mornings, my mother would get us out of bed and tell us, "I'm going to take you kids to "Blow Your Horn" today!" We would get excited because we loved going to "Blow Your Horn," and she always let us take our friends with us. "Blow Your Horn" was a swimming area we went to on Coyote Creek.

My mother drove an old 1935 Plymouth. The car had a big front seat with standing room only behind the seat, but the standing room was connected to a huge trunk. It was one of those old cars that looked as if the trunk was sticking up in the air. It held about fifteen kids or more. All of our friends would come over and wait around until we were ready to leave for "Blow Your Horn."

We went to "Blow Your Horn" often. When we were ready to leave, we piled into the trunk and behind the seat. Kids also sat in the front seat. It seemed as if it would take a while to drive there. The name "Blow Your Horn" was made up by the people who lived on the east side of the city during that time.

On this particular hot summer day, we were traveling down King Road to an area we called the sticks. These were country roads where there was not too much of anything. Traveling all the way down King Road where it started to turn, we turned off on another small road heading west. This took us to Singleton Road, not far from Senter.

From the trunk with a crowd of other kids, I yelled out, "Mom, are we almost there?" We couldn't wait to arrive. It was so neat to go to "Blow Your Horn" in the summer. The water was clean and fresh, and in a couple of places the water was deep. It was like a park nobody maintained. Arriving on a small country road, we found parking on the banks of the flowing creek.

The trunk opened, and we all piled out of the car. We ran down the hill next to the road. Instead of a bridge going over the creek, the road went down into the creek. The water flowed under the road through two big pipes, and it headed back up the other side of the creek bank. In the winter during the heavy rains, the road was covered with water. The two big pipes underneath were big enough for us to go through them with our inner tubes.

As water gushed through the pipes. I jumped in the pool next to the road, I found it refreshing and pleasant. The water came up to my chest at this spot, clear and fresh. I was ready for my first run through the pipe. The water was being sucked into it, and it turned into white water until it came out on the other side of the road. There it splashed into a pool.

It was so exciting waiting for my turn to enter the pipe. One of the bigger guys went first. As I approached, I could feel the current starting to draw me in. There I went! I was drawn inside as I held onto my inner tube. It was a natural, raging water!

Everything was green and clean around the creek. Every so often a few cows came down to have a drink of water. At that time it was no big thing for a cow to approach us. There were many friendly cows in the valley.

Once through the pipe we ran across the road, over the street, and jumped in the pool to go through the pipe again. We did this over and over. We really had a good time when we visited "Blow Your Horn." My mother had fun just watching us.

Taking my tube, I climbed the bank of the road and got ready to run across the road. A car blew its horn as if it were saying, "Watch out, kid!"

When it was time to go, my mother sounded the alarm, "OK, kids, last dive, we're leaving!" Some kids took their last dive; some wanted to change their clothes behind a tree; and others swam until the last possible minute. In a little while my mother yelled again, "Time to go!" Walking up to the car, she opened the trunk so all the kids could get in. Now came the hot ride back home.

On this particular afternoon at "Blow Your Horn," my brother Eddie went to change his wet pants. My mother had not noticed he wasn't with us. Since she had so many kids, she drove away and left Eddie. Ed came out with only his cutoffs and a wet shirt, probably thinking we would return for him in a little while.

When we arrived home, all the kids piled out of the car and they thanked my mother for being so nice. I went inside to take my shower. Eddie wasn't there. Since he always wanted to be with his friends, I thought he was with them rather than take his shower.

My mother was fixing supper, since it was time for my father to arrive home from work soon. His shift at the American Can Company ended at 3:30. The company was on Fifth and Martha, so it took him about a half hour to get home after he washed up at work.

At 3:45 my mother asked, "Arthur, where's your brother Eddie?"

"I think he went to Freddie and Robert's house," I answered.

"Call him. Your father will be getting home soon."

I walked out the front door, stood in front of the house, and placed my hands to both sides of my mouth, "EDDIE! EDDIE!" Moving my head a little so the call would go in all directions, I yelled "COME HOME! EDDIE, COME HOME!" I felt this should have done it.

I walked back into the house, and my mother asked, "Is he coming?"

"I don't know, Mom. I called him," I replied.

Robert and Freddie lived across the street about six houses down. In those days in our small city, noise traveled far. It's not like today in a big city, however. If you wake up at 3:00 a.m., everything's quiet. If you yell out in the street, you can be heard three blocks away. But try that during the day to see if you can be heard.

"Arthur, go look for your brother. Supper's almost ready," my mother said.

Heading toward Freddie's house, I asked some kids playing on the street if they had seen my brother Eddie.

"No, we haven't," they answered.

I knocked on the front door of Freddie's house. His mother told me all the boys were in the backyard. I headed around the side of the house and saw Robert, Freddie, Donald, and Genedale—but no Eddie.

"They probably saw me coming, and Eddie's hiding," I thought.

"Hey, you guys, where's Eddie?" I asked.

Robert answered, "We haven't seen him since we were at "Blow Your Horn."

"Come on! I know he's with you guys!" I insisted.

"No, he's not with us. We thought he was home. We were going to go over to your house right now," Freddie said.

Not believing them, I walked over a few feet to a nearby shed and looked inside to make sure Eddie wasn't in there.

"Well, if you guys see him, tell him my father's coming home right now. If he's not there, my father's going to be mad!" They all looked at me with worried expressions, knowing how it was when my father became furious. Walking away, I turned and walked backwards a few steps, still not believing them. I said with a loud voice, "Eddie, if you're here, you better come home!"

When I walked into the house through the back door, my mother asked, "Did you find him, Arthur? Where is he?" She looked behind me, expecting to see him.

"I couldn't find him, Mom. He wasn't with Robert or Freddie. Maybe he's with someone else."

"Ay, ay, ay, that Eddie! Your father's going to be home in a few minutes. I hope he gets home before your father!"

Later in the evening all the guys who were at Robert's came around the back door to our house and knocked. I went to see who it was.

"Hey, you guys." I said, when I saw Robert and all the other guys at the door. I looked around to see if Eddie was with them, thinking they were playing with me.

"Is Eddie here?" asked Freddie.

I thought these guys were still trying to trick me. I knew they were. I was sure of it.

"You guys know he's not here. Where is he? He's already in trouble," I said.

"He's not with us. We haven't seen him since we got back from "Blow Your Horn," one of them shot back.

I told them he wasn't home, so they left thinking Eddie was there and that I was just telling them he wasn't. I still thought they were tricking me.

The sun was going down, and we were waiting for Eddie to come home. By this time he was in big trouble. Everybody thought he was in one of the houses on Virginia Place. I was on the street playing with the kids when I saw someone who looked like Eddie walking toward us from a distance. Eddie had a walk nobody could copy. When he walked, he swung his body back and forth. As he walked closer, I stopped playing because I thought it sure looked like him.

"Where was he?" I thought. As he neared me, I noticed he still had his cut-offs and wet shirt on from "Blow Your Horn." I ran into the house to tell everybody about Eddie coming down the street.

He finally made it back. My brother had walked most of the way. Some teenagers in a car picked him up on King Road and took him to Virginia Place. He was tired and cold when he arrived home.

My mother felt really bad that she forgot one of us at "Blow Your Horn." After this happened she counted all the kids, so it wouldn't happen again.

* * *

I received a letter from my mother. She wrote that the family would be moving to another house on Emory Street. The good news was they were coming to visit me soon. I really looked forward to a visit since they didn't visit very often. I hadn't seen my mother for a long time. It would sure be nice to see my sister too. The last few years she and I had grown closer and hung around together with our friends on Virginia Place. I also missed my kid brother Victor. I hoped he wouldn't turn out like me and end up in Preston.

Two weeks later I dressed in my good clothes and was waiting for my visit. When they arrived, I was called and taken to the front part of Preston to the visiting center. My mother was really happy to see me. She looked much older and had dark circles around her eyes. I thought she was sick. My brother Victor told me my mother cried and wailed every night for Eddie and me. He said he often went to her bedroom to try to comfort her. I was very selfish back then. I told Victor, "I don't know why she's crying. I'm the one locked up, not her!"

A few months later I was called again for a visit. As I walked to the visiting center, I wondered who was visiting me this time. If it were my mother again, I would have known about it. They would have written and let me know they were coming. Maybe it was a surprise visit.

Walking into the visiting center, I looked around for my mother. She was nowhere to be found. At first I thought it had to be a mistake; no one was there to visit me. The visiting center was a very large room, like a big hall with a lot of people. As I stood there trying to see if I recognized anyone before turning around and walking back, I saw my father stand up. I couldn't believe it. My father was there! I didn't think he would come all the way to Ione, California, to see little old me. I didn't think I was that important since I didn't think my father cared much for me. He and I had experienced a lot of problems before he left to Mexico.

RUNAWAY

When I was about fifteen years old, my father's plant, American Can Company, was about to close. My father had said for a long time that when his plant closed, he was going back to Mexico. He had been saying this for such a long time, we really didn't believe it. We looked forward to his leaving, if it were true. Life would be much easier, we thought.

One morning after I spent the night at my second cousin's house, we got up early in the morning. I hadn't asked my father if I could spend the night; if he woke up before I arrived home, he would have a fit. This was if he arrived home before I did. Lately my father had been staying out all weekend. After work he'd go straight to Ralph's Bar on Keyes Street and come back late at night. He was always angry about one thing or another during those days.

My second cousin's nickname is Chico. His real name is Fermen. He lived behind the North Side Market on the corner of Thirteenth and Hedding streets. His backyard faced Hedding. On the other side at the front of the house was a small street. We never used the front street but always walked through the back over the railroad tracks. On this particular morning, we walked over the tracks on Hedding Street. It was 6:30 a.m., and there were no cars on the road. From a distance I saw a car coming from the direction of Tenth Street. It was moving fast and looked like my father's tan Cadillac. I felt it couldn't be him because a woman with long, dark black hair was sitting close to the man driving. As the car flew by me, I saw my father and the woman laughing. She had one arm around my father, facing him as her hair blew in the wind. My heart sank to my stomach. I couldn't imagine my father with another woman besides my mother. He probably was going out all the time with other women; but as one of his children, it was hard to accept.

When I arrived home, I told my mother what I saw. They were having a lot of problems at the time, and she seemed as if she already knew about the other woman. My father didn't come home that day or night. He came back on Sunday, and he slept most of the day.

Unknown to me, my mother had found a phone number in one of my father's pockets. My mother and Eddie looked through the entire phone book for the number which matched, thinking it was his girlfriend's number. I don't know how my father heard about it, but he got the story wrong. He probably mixed it up with my telling my mother about the other woman. He thought it was I who looked through the phone book with my mother.

At this point in my life, I was having a very difficult time with him. I felt he didn't care for me. There was a lot of animosity built up between him and me. I didn't talk to him, and he would only talk to me when he was angry. I still did what he told me to do, such as working from sun up to sun down on the yard on Saturdays and finishing all my chores around the house. When my father didn't come home on Saturdays, we would wake up and look out front to see if his car was home. If it wasn't, then we didn't have to get up and work at sun rise. Sadly, it seemed my mother didn't love him; and he didn't love her anymore.

About two weeks after I saw my father with the other woman, I called my girlfriend and asked her if she and her sister wanted to go to the show with my friend Tony and me. We all went and had a really good time. We took the bus to Willow Glen, went to the Garden Theater, and watched a Beatle's movie. The Beatles were a big thing during that time. I wasn't really a fan, but I went to see what the big deal was all about.

Arriving home after walking my girlfriend from the bus stop and walking to my house on Virginia Place from the Capitol and Story Road area, I saw my father's car in the driveway. I hoped he was sleeping after a heavy day of partying. Walking into the back door quietly, I went into the kitchen to get something to eat. I was starving. The house was very quiet. No one was home except my father. I walked into the kitchen and noticed him sitting in the living room with his dark glasses on, drinking a tall, 16-ounce can of Olympia beer.

"Hi, Dad," I said.

It was a rule in our house that whenever we saw our father or mother we had to say good morning, hi, or something. If we didn't, it meant trouble. My father didn't say anything. He just sat there. He had been waiting for me. My father usually didn't sit in the living room by himself. As I opened the refrigerator door, I knew something was up.

I removed the carton of milk, put it on the counter, and reached for a glass. My father said, "Arthur, come here!" I walked over to the arch of the living room and stood there to see what my father was going to say. I knew it wasn't going to be good because I knew my father was a little drunk.

"What, Dad?"

My father took a puff of his cigarette, exhaled the smoke, and said, "Arturo, I despise you!"

I yelled out, "I CAN'T TAKE IT ANYMORE! I HATE YOU! I HATE YOU!"

My father stood up, very angry. I turned and ran out the back door. As I was going out the door, I yelled out one more time, "I HATE YOU!" I had never talked to my father this way in my entire life. I yelled out again, "I'M NOT COMING BACK!"

I went to one of my friend's house and spent the night. I called my mother every day to let her know where I was, so she wouldn't worry about me. My mother told me my father thought I tried to find out the identity of his girlfriend. I stayed away for a few days. She told me my father said I could come home, and he wasn't going to tell me anything.

I finally went home, and everything went all right for a while. But we still didn't get along.

Now my father was visiting me in YA. I was shocked!

* * *

My father gave me a hug and said, "Hello, Arturo."

"Hi, Dad." I said, still in shock, not knowing what to say.

"Did he come to give me bad news or something?" I wondered.

He told me to follow him to a small room on the side of the large room. One of the guards standing there looked at my father and smiled at him as we entered the small room. I always wondered if my father paid them to get that small private room, or if he told them he was an official or someone important. My father often used some slick moves.

We sat on the chairs next to the table. "Mijo, I can only stay for about an hour to visit with you. I have important business in Los Angeles. My people are waiting for me outside."

In Mexico my father and his family were well-known. His brother, my tio [Uncle] Pancho, was a judge in Mexico City. He also was an advisor to the President of Mexico, so he had a lot of pull in the country. When we went to court, my father presented an official letter from the President of Mexico. It stated that if we were released to my father, we would be taken care of and educated in Mexico. My other tio, Jorge, lived in Mexicali. He was a doctor and later became Surgeon General of Baja California. My father spent a lot of time with Tio Jorge.

"Arturo, how have you been?" my father asked. He wore his dark glasses inside the building. He also had on a gray suit with a tie. It was extremely hot to wear a suit; it was a hot summer day. My father started to tell me about the business deals he had in the making and how much money he had made.

As he was telling me this, I was thinking to myself, "If you have so much money, why don't you leave some here?"

My father meant well. He was just going through a time in his life when he thought money was everything. His visit only lasted about an hour. This was the only time he came to see me; my mother came every few months. My father's visit ended, and that was it.

One day I was sitting in the day room watching TV when one of the Locos came and sat next to me. One thing to say at this point is that although some of us Locos didn't get along, we still hung around in the same group. We just didn't like each other. On this particular day on the platform, there was a young guard who was working. His name was Mr. Gorman.

The Loco looked over at him and told me, "You know, ese, that Mr. Gorman is really religious."

Looking over at the guard, I said, "Is that right?"

The Loco continued, "Hey, man, if you let him preach to you, they say he'll get you a time cut."

"Really, ese? I'm going to see what I can do about this."

I didn't waste any time. In about five minutes I stood up from my seat and headed to the platform. I put my foot on the platform, hung onto the bars, and said, "Hey, Mr. Gorman, how you doing?" Mr. Gorman was busy doing something at the time.

Glancing over at me but not paying too much attention, he replied, "I'm all right, Rodriguez."

"Mr. Gorman, I hear you are a religious person." That got his attention right away. He dropped what he was doing and turned to face me.

"Yes, that's right. I am. What about you, Rodriguez?"

"Sure. I like learning about all religions." I was lying. I didn't know about religions. My father wouldn't let us kids learn about any religion as we were growing up. He felt we could make our choice when we became adults.

I hung around the platform for a while letting him preach to me.

Later when I sat down, the Loco who told me about Mr. Gorman came over and asked jokingly, "Ese, are you getting out?"

"Hey, ese, I'll do anything I can to get out of this place. If the guy wants to preach to me, he can preach to me!"

Between Juvenile Hall, Preston, and being with Isaac and Phil, I picked up the Loco slang—"ese"—and all the Loco words. Before I was sentenced to Preston, I didn't speak this way. When I finally went home, my friends really thought I'd changed from the way I spoke. I became so used to it, it became my language.

My pastime in Preston was playing cards, usually poker. I started a little business. On one game I was playing a Straight and was winning. I already had about three packs of the Straight's cigarettes. He was running out but didn't want to stop playing. He wanted the cigarettes back that he lost and borrowed some from his friends. Those were lost too. He asked me if I would lend him some of my winnings to play against me.

"You want me to play with my cigarettes?"

"Yeah, man, why not?" he asked with a friendly look.

I propositioned him. "Look, man, here's what I'll do. If you want to borrow cigarettes to play against me to win your cigarettes back, then I'll lend you one for two."

"What do you mean one for two?"

"Well," I explained, "I'll lend you one cigarette, and you can pay me back two. How does that sound?"

"Yeah, that sounds good," he said. So that was what I did.

The very next day he received a package in the mail, and he paid me back my cigarettes. Everybody was always trying to bum them from everyone else. If we didn't have any cigarettes, we had to smoke the ones the state gave us, and their tobacco was like smoking sawdust with a bad taste. It came in little bags, and we rolled our own.

"Hey, Art, would you lend me a cigarette?" an inmate would ask.

"Sure, two for one." I would take out my note paper and write it down, so I knew who owed me cigarettes. If someone wanted to borrow one and didn't receive a package or was never sent any money, he would have to go out and get a co-signer, someone to vouch for him.

As time went by, I had my locker full of cigarettes. Cigarettes served as money in the correctional system. We weren't allowed to have any cash. It was the same as in jail; we had money in an account and could buy personal things we needed. I had to have two lockers to store all my cigarettes and the other things I bought with the earnings from my new business. We were only allowed one locker each, but I rented one from a guy who had to have cigarettes.

Mr. Gorman came back the next day with some religious literature. I looked his way, and he motioned for me to go to the platform. He gave me the literature and told me about it. I told him I liked to read materials like this and would read it. I was a big liar. I didn't like to read religious material, and I wasn't going to read it because I couldn't. I took the literature and went to sit in front of the TV, lying on one of the big chairs facing Mr. Gorman with the TV to the side of me. I opened one of the magazines and pretended to read. Although I had the magazine open, I was really watching TV. Every so often I turned my head and acted as if I were turning the pages. I saw Mr. Gorman look at me. Sometimes the same Loco would come over and tease me about what I was doing.

"Hey, ese, I think you're going to get out pretty soon. You got him going!"

Mr. Gorman kept bringing me literature, and I kept acting as if I were reading it. I thought I was so cool.

When I arrived at Preston, I didn't weigh much. I didn't gain a whole lot of weight in that place. Shortly after I reached my company, I was told that when we went to the cafeteria not to eat the rice.

"What do you mean, don't eat the rice?" I asked.

One of the Locos went on and explained the situation to me. He said the Locos who worked in the cafeteria messed with the rice, and they let us know not to eat it.

I couldn't understand. "Why would they want to mess with the rice?"

"This way we can burn the Bloods and the Straights, and they won't even know it!" he said as he started laughing.

I thought this was silly, getting someone and they didn't even know it. If I were going to do someone in, I would want them to know I was getting them.

When we went out to eat, we asked the Bloods, "Hey, Blood, do you want to trade my rice for your beans?" The Bloods answered, "Sure, ese, I love rice!" They even asked us first if we wanted to trade our rice for their beans.

I thought these Bloods weren't very smart. Then one day I was in line behind a Blood as we were getting our food. As we walked down the serving line, we saw only the server's hands. There was a shield over the top of the serving line, so we couldn't see the guys on the other side. The servers knew who we were by the color of our hands. That day, the server of the beans was a Blood. When he served the Blood in front of me, I was a little closer than usual. I heard the server tell him, "Hey, Blood, don't eat the beans!"

"What!" I thought. All this time we thought the beans were clean. If the Bloods were messing with the beans and the Locos were messing with the rice, what were the Straights messing with? After that day I started losing weight.

THE ANTS

When I was about five years old, we lived on Spencer Street. At that time my parents needed extra help around the house and someone to help take care of us kids. They hired a lady to help my mother. Inesita was nice to us when our parents were home; but when they left, a transformation took place. She didn't speak English very well, having just arrived from Costa Rica in Central America. Once we were outside playing in our boat in the backyard when she called us into the house. I wondered what she wanted. She sounded angry. As we went into the house, she told us to sit down on the chairs and shut up.

"Who stole the bread?" she demanded.

"Who what?" I said, not understanding what her beef was.

"Who stole the bread?" she repeated. She said one of us stole a slice of bread from the bread box, and she wanted to know who it was. I didn't know who it was. I looked at Eddie; he said he didn't know. Little Tita, well, she wouldn't have stolen a slice of bread. If she wanted a slice, she would have just taken one; she didn't have to steal it. Inesita had us crying. She told us that if she didn't find out who stole the slice of bread, she was going to tell my father when he arrived home. We all knew what that meant. I couldn't believe I was probably going to be killed over a slice of bread. Inesita marched back and forth in the kitchen trying to make us confess. She held us there until my father came home.

As we heard my father's car drive in the driveway, we were really worried. He walked into the kitchen and saw all of us sitting there being interrogated. Inesita looked at my father and thought he was going to approve of her methods. At first I thought he was going to take her side and spank us for stealing a slice of bread. "Que pasa aqui?" [What's happening here] he wanted to know.

Inesita went on to tell him she saw that the loaf of bread was smaller, and there was a slice missing. She knew one of us came into the kitchen and stole it. My father became angry—really furious, not at us, but at her! My father had his bad qualities, but he also had his good qualities. He told Inesita the bread was ours to eat when we wanted to eat it. It couldn't be stolen by us because it was ours. Then there was the matter of our lying about taking the bread. My father sent Eddie to buy the same kind of bread from the store at the corner of Virginia and Delmas. When Eddie returned, they opened the loaf and counted the slices, not to see if we were lying but to show her we were not lying. How did my father know we weren't lying? He was pretty good about looking at his kids and knowing if we were telling the truth, not all the time, but most of the time.

During the time Inesita was taking care of us, we got up early one morning to go to the park. We sat at the table to have our breakfast. Usually we liked to have a banana in our cereal. This morning we were going to have something quite different. Ready with our bowls and spoons, Inesita served our cereal. Out of it came ants, a lot of ants! Our cereal was covered with them.

Eddie screamed, "Inesita, this is crawling with ants!"

Expecting her to say, "Oh, I'm sorry. Let me give you something else," instead she said something quite different. "Eat them. They're good for you!"

Why would she want us to eat them? Maybe in her country they ate ants or even rode them, but not here. She became really angry with us. When we refused to eat the cereal, she told us my father was going to spank us when he returned from work. She sat at the table, put the spoon in her hand, and fed the cereal to us. I think Eddie and I are the only humans to have ever eaten live ants. They tasted like chili. Every time I crunched down on an ant, it tasted HOT like a hot chili!

Why did we let Inesita feed them to us? I was about four, and Eddie was about five or six. We were powerless. We put up a good fight, but in the end we ate live ants.

During this time Inesita was in love with my father. My mother had no idea until Inesita left. Once in a while she needed a ride to San Francisco; my father would take her. My mother didn't go because she was tired and wanted to stay with us.

She told my father, "You go, Joe. I'll stay here." That was a big mistake.

The day Inesita left, she left behind a letter telling my father she had to leave because she was in love with him and couldn't take it anymore. What did that mean for us kids? It meant there would be no more accusations of stealing bread and no more ants for breakfast!

* * *

The big fight with Ernie finally took place. The guards heard through the grapevine that there was going to be a riot. They thought it was going to be a race riot. That evening the guards had the riot crew sitting outside in their cars waiting. We had to spend the day sitting in the day room without making any noise. This alone almost caused a riot among the races.

One of the Bloods kept playing around, yelling out, "Come on, ese, let's get down!" The other Bloods kept telling him to shut up.

"The eses are going to start a riot because of you, man." Even though the Locos were outnumbered, the other races had to be careful with the Locos because we were more likely to stick someone with a shank. This was why we were called Locos.

Two days later we had our big fight. One of the Straights came over and told me we shouldn't fight with Ernie. He and Ernie were good friends. If we started fighting, he was going to break it up right away. I told him he'd better stay out of it because this involved only the Locos and had nothing to do with the Straights. When the fight started by the lockers, it was Richard and Ernie's homeboy who started going at it first. I was close by; and as soon as it started, the Straight tried to break it up. The Straight grabbed Richard by the arms; Ernie's homeboy was hitting him. We all started fighting, and within seconds everybody was involved. Guys who had nothing to do with it started fighting. It turned out to be a brawl. It looked like an old cowboy movie with a riot at the bar. Looking back, I have to say, it was fun.

The riot squad charged in, and we were all taken to lockup. This was the longest time I had to spend in lockup. If they had found out why it started, that I wanted to beat up Ernie, I would have been sent to prison in Tracy. They never knew what happened, or who started it.

Later on I had other fights but not as many as in the beginning. I started to slow down. It was just as Isaac had said back in jail, "After you start fighting everybody, in time they'll respect you and will leave you alone."

Mr. Gorman kept bringing me literature, and I kept pretending to read it. Sometimes I put the literature in my locker and told him I was going to read it later, which I didn't. I let him preach to me for hours at a time. One day he asked me if I wanted to sit down with him and have a religious discussion on a regular basis.

"Sure, for only one hour a week? Could some of the other guys come and sit in on the discussion too?"

"The more the better," he said. I went around the day room asking everybody if they wanted a time cut. I told them they had to give up only one hour a week. Four guys wanted to get out of Preston early and ended up accepting my offer.

Sure enough we had our discussions with Mr. Gorman, and I received a time cut. However, it was not exactly a time cut. Mr. Gorman sent a recommendation to the board that I go before them three months early.

"I'll be getting out early. Thirty days after I go to board, I'll be released," I told my homeboys.

The morning I was to go to board, I woke up really excited and was very nervous. Later that morning I sat outside in the waiting room where the hearings were taking place. All the guys who went in came out of the room happy. I thought for sure I was going to be released early.

I walked into the room to see five, stone-faced men and women. Sitting behind what looked like a big desk big enough for all of them, they were all really quiet, looking down at the papers in front of them. One of the men was the one who went to my company, gave the diploma announcement, and called me Wiggles. I thought once he looked at me, he'd recognize me and give a good word.

A lady who was not looking at me but studying the papers said, "I don't know why you're here early. You're in here for murder. You can't be released."

I felt like telling them, "I'm not here for murder. I'm here for assault. Not murder!"

They all marked something on their papers, looked up, and said, "All right, next."

"That's it?" I asked.

"Yes, Rodriguez. Next."

Walking out of the board room, I felt like dropping on the floor. I thought for sure I was going to be released. All the hours I studied with Mr. Gorman were for nothing.

When I walked into the day room, I saw Mr. Gorman sitting on the platform. He called me over.

"What happened?" he asked. I told him what the board had said. He told me not to worry. He was going to try to get me a sixty-day time cut, and it would probably work the next time.

"Not to worry," he said.

"How can I not worry? The board didn't sound very promising," I said, walking away in disgust.

In another month I went back to board. It was an exact repeat of the first time. I then went for a thirty-day time cut. Again it was the same thing.

After ninety days I went to board on the date I was originally supposed to go. I thought for sure I was going to be released. I entered the room and sat down. One of the board members looked up at me and said, "Murder is a very serious crime. We're going to give you another year." I almost fell off my chair. I didn't know if I could take another year in Preston. I wanted to go home right then!

I still studied with Mr. Gorman because I felt it would pay off later. When this year was up, Mr. Gorman would give me my time cut again. Maybe I'd get out.

Time started to go by a little faster during the second year. Most of my pastime was spent playing cards and writing letters.

During the second year I received letters from either my family or my girlfriends. In a letter to one of my girlfriends, I told her I was almost done with the purse I was making for her. I wrote to her earlier, at least I thought I did. She wrote back in about a week and told me she didn't know I was making a purse for her. This was when I realized this purse was for my other girlfriend. I told the wrong girl about the purse. Now I had to make the other girlfriend one. I sent two nice purses out on the same day.

About two weeks later I received letters from both girls on the same day. They were furious. They both went shopping at a store downtown, and both saw a girl they knew. As they were talking, my name came up. They both had a boyfriend by the name of Art who was in Preston. What a coincidence. They both were sent the same purses recently; and they looked the same, from the same manufacturer. Both girls were really steaming. Each thought they were my only girlfriend. Alice told me she had another boyfriend; but now, because of this, I wasn't first anymore. Now her other boyfriend was first. What could I say? The other girl forgave me for "cheating" on her and for not being the only one who received a purse.

Mr. Gorman told me he was going to have me see the board ninety days early again, and the time was getting close. I had about six months left for the big day. I hoped the board would release me this time.

In Preston we had our own hospital. If anything was wrong with us, we put our name on a list. Every morning the list had about 15 or 20 names on it. The guys who had to go to school were always on the list. If they faked it well enough, they didn't have to go to school. For a while I was getting really bad headaches, and I wrote my name on the list every morning.

The hospital was an old building. If you have ever seen old black and white movies that show old hospitals built in the thirties, that's what the hospital at Preston looked like. It had old doors, old windows, old everything. Even though we were now in the 60s, everything at Preston was from the 30s. However, the hospital was kept clean.

When it was my turn to see the doctor, he looked at me and asked me about my headaches. He said the medicine he gave me was really strong and that it should help. I told him it seemed to help. Every morning the doctor told the nurse to give me two spoonfuls of the stuff that looked like green syrup. One morning when I went into the examining room, a new nurse joined the doctor. He asked me as usual how I was, and he told the new nurse to give me the same medication.

Surprised, the nurse looked at the doctor and said, "But, Doctor, that's not going to do anything for him." I looked up at the new nurse to see the expression on her face; then I looked over at the doctor and saw the expression on his face.

He looked irritated at the nurse and said with a stern voice, "It depends on what I'm curing."

"Oh," she said, embarrassed. She did what the doctor told her to do. In other words, it was all in my head. On that day I stopped putting my name on the list to go to the hospital.

In my leather shop the instructor put me in charge of the storage room. I was the one with the longest time in his class. I did my work in the storage room. If anyone needed anything from the room, such as a piece of leather, glue, thread, dye, or other stuff, they came to the counter and asked me for it.

One day one of the Locos came over to the counter and said, "Ese, Art." He handed me a small jar. "Fill this up with some of that glue, man." I took the jar and looked over at the instructor to make sure he wasn't looking.

"OK, go sit down; I'll have it filled in a little while," I said. I went back to where I was doing my work. The instructor was at his desk. He hadn't looked over at me because he trusted me. He'd known me for a long time, and I hadn't messed up in his class yet. I liked being in this leather class, making things to send home.

In a little while I had the jar filled and walked back to the counter. The Loco came over and took it. I put it in his hand, covering it so no one would see what I passed to him.

He looked at the teacher and said, "Come over with us, ese. We're going to get loaded."

I told him I might do that, but he knew I had to think this one out. I only had six months to do before going back to the board. If I were caught sniffing glue, I'd get another six months automatically. Then when I appeared before the board, I would probably be given another year. During this time I was trying to think and reason things out before I made my decisions.

What the heck? I hadn't been loaded for about two weeks or so. I felt we wouldn't get caught anyway; we never did in the past.

Sometimes we sniffed glue in our company. Sometimes we got beer and got drunk. The Locos made beer from potatoes in the kitchen and would send us some. We'd pay for it with cigarettes. Once in a while one of the guys would get a joint.

In a little while I told the instructor I was finished in the storage room. Class was going to end in about ten minutes.

"No problem," he said.

I walked out of the storage room and went to sit with the guys with the glue. They looked up at me and started to laugh, already loaded from the glue.

"Let me have some, ese!" I said.

I sniffed the glue for about ten minutes, but the other guys had been sniffing for about twenty. The glue was strong and didn't leave the same aftertaste on my breath as the other kind we had in our company. This glue was different; it was for leather products.

It was 11 a.m., time to go back to our company and to get ready for lunch. Leaving the room, I felt so loaded I bumped into the door. The instructor looked up at me to make sure I was OK.

"I hope he doesn't think I'm loaded," I thought as I stepped out of the door.

I started to laugh with the other guys. We were all loaded. I felt as if I talked with a loud speaker inside my head. When I reached the outside of the building, I stood leaning on the wall and closed my eyes. I was really spinning inside of my head.

As soon as I closed my eyes, I was somewhere else. I was trapped in a big, round room, as if I were inside a big ball. The ball had a hole in the bottom, and I started to fall into the hole. I hung onto this small thing on the side of the wall, inside of the ball. Whenever I swallowed, the walls of the ball would move; and I'd fall a little deeper. I had the urge to swallow really badly; my throat was so dry. Every time I swallowed, I started to fall in the hole. I didn't know what was in the hole at the bottom of the round room, but I knew it wasn't good. My throat was dry, and I had to swallow. If I swallowed one more time, I would be in the hole. What would I do?

HEY, MAN! ART! ART! ARE YOU OK?"

I opened my eyes.

"Where am I?"

A Blood from my class was standing in front of me. "Are you OK, man? You really look loaded! You better cool it, or you're going to get caught!"

"Man, you're right." I grabbed my head and pulled my hair back, trying to snap myself out of it.

As I walked back on the road to my company, I started to come down from the high. Usually it took only a couple of minutes to come down with the other glue. This one took about ten to fifteen minutes. It was some strong stuff.

By the time I walked in the door of my company, I felt like dropping on the floor. I was so tired. I went over to one of the couches and lay down to go to sleep.

"It's 11:30!" someone yelled out. "Time to eat."

One of the guys asked, "Hey, Art, are you going to eat?"

"No, I'm going to stay here and go to sleep." Within thirty seconds I was in a deep sleep.

Two hours later I woke up because of all the commotion.

"What's up, man?" I asked one of the Bloods sitting next to me.

"I don't know, ese. Something happened in company 'H' next door. They have an ambulance over there."

Maybe someone got in a fight and was cut. I looked at the clock; it was already 2:30. I didn't feel hungry. This was not like me. I was always hungry. In fact, I felt a little nauseated. Maybe it was something I ate earlier. But I hadn't eaten anything since that morning. "Oh well," I thought. "It will probably go away when I am up and around the day room."

I stood up and went to the restroom. While I was there, I heard someone who was really sick, even moaning, as he was throwing up. It sounded terrible—must have been that lunch. Someone messed with the beans.

I walked over to the table where the Locos were playing cards and sat on an empty chair.

"You want to play, Art?" one of the Locos asked.

"No, I don't feel too good right now—my stomach," I said.

"Oh, yeah. Neither does Freddie; he's in the bathroom throwing up," one of the Locos said.

Freddie! Freddie was one of the guys who sniffed the glue with me. I didn't think it was the glue, but my stomach was getting worse by the minute.

One of the guys picked up his cards after they were dealt to him and said, "I hope Nacho's not sick, ese!"

"You mean Nacho in company 'H'?" I asked.

"Yeah, ese. They had to come and get him in an ambulance a few minutes ago."

Oh man, Nacho was the other guy who sniffed the glue with us. I looked at the guy who knew about it and asked, "What happened to him?"

"They don't know. My homeboy over there just came to bring something for the guard and told me Nacho was throwing up green stuff. He passed out as he was throwing up. He said it was gross; his face was in it. It was bad, ese. I hope we're not catching some kind of plague or something. Hey, man, when Freddie comes back over here, I'm going to tell him not to sit over here. I don't want to catch no plague."

Just as the words came out of his mouth, we all turned around. Everybody was running to the front of the day room. Something had happened right next to the platform. We all stood up to see if it was a fight or something else.

In a few seconds one of the Straights walked past us, back to his table, and said, "It's Freddie, man! He looks bad. I don't know what he took, but it doesn't look good!" Within a few minutes Preston's ambulance arrived to take Freddie away.

In a little while I started to feel a little worse. I thought to myself, "I hope it's not the glue. If it is, I'm going to get sick like those guys." I kept trying to convince myself I wasn't going to get sick. All of a sudden my head started to hurt badly.

One of the Locos looked at me and asked, "Are you all right, Art?"

When he asked me, I stood and said, "Something's happening to me. I don't know what it is!"

Taking a few steps toward the front of the day room, I felt my stomach turning. Out came this green stuff, shooting out of my mouth. I felt as if I were going to pass out; my body felt very weak. I dropped to my knees and didn't know if I should hold my stomach or my head. I dropped the rest of the way down.

The next thing I knew, everybody was around me. The guard was yelling at everybody, "GET BACK! EVERYBODY GET BACK!" His arms extended out to keep everyone back. The last thing I remember was the guard asking somebody something. He didn't want anybody to touch anything at the table, thinking it might be contagious.

"RODRIGUEZ, RODRIGUEZ, WAKE UP!" I opened my eyes. I was in a white room. The doctor was standing on one side of me, and a nurse was on the other side. "How do you feel?" he asked. Just as he asked me, I answered by throwing up. They tried to get me a pan, but it was too late. The nurse put a towel around my neck.

"Do you remember eating anything different? Did someone give you something to eat that you normally don't eat?" the doctor asked. I tried to nod my head, but the next thing I remember was everything going black.

In a haze I remember someone trying to clean me up, changing the towels around my neck. "How do you feel?" the nurse asked. "Hang on, kid. We're bringing an ambulance in, and in a little while you'll be on your way to Perkins where the best doctors are."

The room was dark. I didn't know what time it was or how long I'd been there. In the hallway I saw two doctors talking. They were looking at what looked like a chart or something.

I woke up again, and things looked scary. I picked up my head a little to see if anybody was around me. I remember thinking I didn't want to die alone. The doctor was leaning against the wall in the hallway with his hand covering his head; he was in deep thought or trying to rest his eyes. I heard a voice. The doctor stood straight up and spoke to someone walking toward him. When the person who was speaking walked up to the doctor, I could then see him. He was an older man dressed in black. He had a little, black derby hat; a black shirt with black pants; and a long, black trench coat. He was carrying a bag that looked like a doctor's black bag.

The doctor pointed to my room. The old man looked over at me, and his eyes caught mine. He walked into the room slowly, staring at me. I didn't like this old man. He tried to be nice and had a friendly smile. He stepped to the side of my bed, picked up my hand, and held it.

"Almost time, Arthur!" Feeling my hand with his other hand, he continued "Not just yet. I'll be back in a little while for you." He gave me a smile. I saw a nurse walk by and tried to yell to stop her. I wanted her to help me; so this ugly, old man wouldn't take me. However, I couldn't yell.

163

Months after all this was over, I put my name on the list to go back to this hospital. I asked about the old man, but no one knew whom I was talking about.

I woke up about two more times. The next time I woke up, they were cleaning me again. They had put fresh towels around my neck and wanted to know how I felt. I couldn't talk. Every time I tried, I started to throw up ugly bile.

The next time I woke up, I was moving down the road in an ambulance with the lights flashing. I think they thought I wasn't going to make it. I was only awake for a few minutes, and again they tried to ask me some questions. "What hurts? What did you eat? Did anyone else eat what you ate?" I still couldn't talk. Towels were still around my neck.

The next time I regained consciousness, I was in a hospital room at Perkins. A nurse was sitting next to me. Another nurse came in and said, "You can take him back to his room now; his X-rays came out negative." They took X-rays, and I didn't even know it. I was semi-conscious.

When I returned to my room, the nurse saw I had my eyes open. She asked, "How are you doing, guy? We'll have you in surgery very soon now. The doctors are getting ready."

This was the first time I could talk. I looked at her and asked, "What are they going to do?" I wanted to know if they found out what was wrong with me.

"They're going to see if they can find out what's wrong with you—exploratory surgery. Do you feel any better?" the nurse asked. I started to black out again. I don't know if I answered her or not.

I do remember thinking, "I can't tell them what I did because that will mean I can be sent to Tracy and get another six months added to my time. I would rather die then get another six months."

The next time I woke up, the nurse said the doctors wanted to wait for surgery because I talked the last time I regained consciousness. That was a good sign. Directly in front of my bed, there was a big clock on the wall above the door. I saw the time each time I woke up. I was staying awake longer as time went by. Another nurse came into my room and told me I was going into surgery in one hour. I told the nurse I felt better now. She rushed out and told the doctors. They all came in to see me and told me I gave everybody a big scare.

They didn't think I was going to survive, and they had no idea what was wrong with me.

I felt better as time passed. I found out later that what seemed like one day of being out of it was really about five days. As the days went by, I got better and regained my strength. Every so often someone came into my room and asked if I had any idea what happened. Even some men with suits came to see me and wanted to interview me, to see if they could figure out what happened. I told them I didn't know. They said they didn't know either.

I was in Perkins for about two week and was kept in a small room, locked up, never sent to a company. Then one day they took me back to Preston to my original company. All my friends wanted to know what happened. I didn't tell them what really occurred, just in case it would get back to the guards.

We heard the first guy, Nacho, had died. We never heard from Freddie, the other guy, again. We didn't know if he died, recovered, was sent home, or went to another prison; but we did know he wasn't in Preston anymore. Even his homeboys didn't know what happened to him. They had sniffed the glue twice as long as I had. Maybe they were visited by the old man with the trench coat and derby, just as I was.

It was time to go to board. Mr. Gorman came through with his ninety-day time cut as he said he would. The day I went to board, I was nervous just as I was the year before.

I walked into the board room as I did the last time. I told myself I needed to start talking as soon as I entered the room—to impress them. "I would like to thank all of you for not letting me out earlier; staying here has really helped me." And so on. I hoped they would be easy with me. I'd been there a long time, and I wanted out.

"All right, Arthur Rodriguez. In reviewing your record, we see you have made some big improvements."

I really wanted to hear the next few words.

"We're going to grant your release!"

FREEDOM!

Thirty days had passed since I appeared in the board room. I woke up in my bed not believing it was finally here, the big day! Today I was going home. Those last thirty days seemed the slowest of all the time I was confined at Preston. Every day I looked at the clock and watched the hours go by, even the minutes. It was finally here!

Getting all my things out of my locker to see what I was going to take home and what I was going to leave was a hard job. Some things I had no use for now that I was going home. I was going to take home a few things, such as picture frames made of cigarette packages, leather goods from my leather class, and my personal photographs. Everything else I gave away to my friends.

I now had to say good-bye to all my friends and also the day room, which was my home for two years. Just like jail, it was hard to leave my cell after more than six months. All my friends came and stood around me. They told me they would come to San Jose to visit me when they were released. They asked if I could get some beautiful girls to write to them. They asked me not to forget about them. I said I wouldn't forget them, and to this day I haven't.

Mr. Gorman was on the platform getting ready to come down to say good-bye to me. Before he stepped down, I walked over to him, wishing to be alone with him for a second.

"Mr. Gorman, thank you for being so kind to me while I was here."

He put his arm around my shoulder and said, "Make sure when you go home to behave yourself, Rodriguez. All right?"

"I will, for sure."

I walked out of the day room; and everybody waved and yelled out their good-byes, even the Bloods and the Straights. During that last year I got along with everybody, which made my time easier. Driving through Preston, I looked around and hoped I would never return as so many of the other guys had done.

The Preston car took me all the way into the little town of Ione to the Greyhound bus station. As I stepped out of the car, the driver from Preston gave me an envelope with my bus ticket home and $5.00 for food. As he drove away, I really felt free.

I boarded the bus and sat by a window. As I left the town of Ione, I thought about the saying related to the castle. I could see the castle from the corner of my eye as the bus moved parallel to Preston, but I didn't dare turn my head to look at it. I didn't get out of my seat or move until we left the area. I didn't want a round-trip ticket back to Preston.

As the bus driver drove into San Jose, I remembered the day I left the city. That was the last time I saw Phil. Isaac was in Preston with me. He was over on the other side of my company, in "J" company. I talked to him a few times but not too often. It seemed as if he had a hard time at Preston. As time went by, I didn't see Isaac anymore. I don't know if he messed up or was sent somewhere else in Preston.

In one of Tita's letters, she wrote me that my brother Eddie was being released. This made it about a month that Eddie had been home. I still couldn't believe I was soon to be home.

The bus parked in the Greyhound parking lot, and I picked up my box and two bags of belongings. Walking into the Greyhound building, I looked around to see if my mother was there or if she had sent someone else.

Ed waved at me, "Hey, Art!" We embraced each other.

"Eddie, when did you get out?" I asked.

"About a month ago," he said.

"How's Mom doing?" I asked as we walked out the front doors of the bus station.

"She's doing good."

We walked up to the car that Eddie drove to pick me up in. "Hey, this is nice. Whose is it?"

"Mine," Eddie answered. It was a 1960 Chevy Impala, lowered, almost touching the ground, and with chrome wheels. It was gray and red pinstripped. Pinstripping was the latest thing in those days. How could Eddie buy this car after only one month of freedom? It turned out he had found a job right away, and my mother co-signed to purchase the car.

As Eddie drove, I asked him how things were at home. "Things are OK. Mom has a boyfriend, and he seems to be cool."

Arriving at the house on Emory Street, the car came to a stop at the front curb. I got out and stood in front of the house reminiscing. This was the house my grandparents lived in. I remember when we were kids and when we arrived. Aunt Maryann and Aunt Connie came running out to greet us kids. Those were nice times. Later, when I was older and my father and mother owned the house, Eddie and I went there to pull weeds and to help our father with fixing things, jobs the renters were supposed to do. "Those weren't good days!" I thought. "It was hard working with my father."

I never lived on Emory Street before this. My mother moved there about a year before I returned because she was getting some threatening phone calls on Virginia Place. She worried about what those calls could lead to and moved to her other house on Emory. Now she didn't have to worry. Eddie and I were home!

I walked into the house. The first thing I noticed was the small living room. "How could people live in a small place like this?" I wondered. Actually it wasn't that small; it's just that in Preston everything was so big. Here our living room seemed as small as a matchbox. As a matter of fact, everything seemed small to me that day, even the bathroom. In the kitchen when we sat down to eat, the utensils seemed too small to use. In Preston and Perkins everything was extra large.

As soon as I entered the house, my family welcomed me back, giving me hugs and kisses. They were all happy to see me. There were so many things I wanted to do. "In time," I thought. "In time."

My friends, Art and Dennis, came to see me that evening. They said they were going to take me out to have a good time. Alice, my ex-girlfriend, also came to see me. She already had another boyfriend, whom she eventually married; but it was nice that she came anyway.

The house on Emory Street was built around the 1940s, about three houses away from Coleman Street between Hedding and Taylor streets. It was right across from a company called "Master Metal Products," a big silver building.

My grandparents lived in this house years before. When we were kids, the house had a garage. When we visited my grandmother, my uncles and aunts had parties in the garage. We used to peek in; it looked like "American Band Stand," a show from the 50s and 60s. Everybody was dancing. When we got out of jail, my mother let my grandfather and grandmother live in the garage. It was fixed into a small apartment with a bedroom which also served as the living room and a kitchen. There was no bathroom; they had to go into the house to use the facilities. Later on when my grandparents moved out, Eddie and I moved to the back house. From this point we didn't call it the garage; it was the back house.

During the time we were locked up, things had really changed. The hippie days were in full swing. Everything was flower children and free love. Some of our friends were not the same. They were hippies with long hair, beards, and headbands. At times they wore shirts that looked like nightgowns.

During the first week after my release, I started to look for a job. I also checked in with my parole officer. At first I was supposed to see him every week. I made up my mind I wasn't going to get caught for doing anything bad and be sent back to jail. However, I wasn't planing to keep out of trouble; I was planning not to get caught for doing anything bad. Big difference.

After the first few days I was home, I already knew we, Eddie and I, were going to have trouble. I felt my mother's boyfriend who lived with us didn't like me, and I wasn't too sure how I felt about him. My little brother Victor got along with him OK. Tita, not as well, but she got along with him all right too.

One night Eddie was working swing shift at a job he found at a chrome-plating shop. I was home in my room when I heard my mother and Bob arguing in the kitchen. I got up to see what was going on. Bob was a little drunk, and he was yelling at my mother.

"HEY, MAN, what do you think you're doing yelling at my mother!"

He looked at me and said at the same time he was waving his hand, "Go away, boy. Go back to bed. This is none of your business!" He looked at my mother and started yelling at her again, moving closer to her.

I was getting angrier as the seconds passed. This was my business.

Then I yelled, "Hey, man, you better shut up; or I'm going to knock you out!"

Bob pointed at my chest and yelled something. I didn't hear him. I was ready to take my first swing. I knew I was going to have a hard time because Bob was a good-sized man, and I was just a youngster. Just then Eddie walked in. As he closed the door behind him, he saw what was happening.

"What's going on?"

"This guy is giving Mom a bad time, man; and I'm going to knock him out!" At the same time Bob was yelling out something, and my mother was yelling at Bob. It was difficult to hear everybody at the same time.

"Art, be quiet! Mom, Bob, calm down! Quiet!" Eddie yelled.

I started to scream something at Bob again; Bob was yelling back at me.

Eddie demanded, "Art, wait, listen! Bob, if you want to talk to my mother, that's OK; but don't call her any bad words!"

Bob looked at my mother and said, "You this and you that, and you're a —————." Eddie's eyes met mine, and we both let go at the same time—punch after punch from both of us. Bob didn't know what hit him. As we were hitting him, he made his way to the front door. We opened the door and kicked him out. He rolled out on the front porch. I thought he'd had enough, so I closed the door and left him lying on the porch.

My mother was upset. Eddie was also upset, since he had been living with Bob for over a month. And me? Well, I felt good. I thought we did our duty.

We looked out the front window every so often to see if we could see what Bob was doing. He wasn't around anymore. But we knew he didn't leave because his Chevy Corvair was still out front. In a little while I looked outside again; I thought I heard something in the front. Sure enough it was Bob.

Man, this guy was a slow learner.

This time he had some kind of tool in his hand, something like a big pick for digging holes. This was why it took him so long to come back. He was going around the block looking for something to use to fight us. The pick didn't help him much. I opened the door and ran toward him, hitting him before he could take a swing. Eddie was right behind me also swinging.

Bob wasn't hurt too badly. The next day he had two black eyes and was all bruised up. I think what hurt him the most was his ego, because two boys beat him up. After that day he was careful and quiet. He never called my mother bad words around us again, and he was careful not to argue too loudly with her. He continued to live at the house for a while.

From the day I was released from Preston, I partied heavily. At first it was on the weekends only; but as time went by, it was every day of the week. Not too long after I got out of jail, Art and Dennis asked me if I wanted to go partying with them.

"Sure I will."

They came by to pick me up at my house. "Hey, where are we going?" I asked.

"It's still early, so we'll just cruise around for a while. Later we'll look around for a party and pick up some girls," Art said.

We went back to the east side of town. We stopped at Tico's Tacos on Alum Rock Avenue, next to Highway 101. In those days at this particular Tico's Tacos, a girl came out to your car to take your order. They brought out your food to the car and hung a tray on the window.

We stayed at Tico's Tacos for a while, where I told stories about Preston. After a while we left and stopped at Dennis' house; he had to pick up something. When we left Dennis' house, we stopped to buy a case of beer. Dennis was in the driver's seat, Art was on the passenger side, and I was in the back seat. At the store I took out some money. Art said to put my money back into my pocket because they were buying. We cruised around the east side since it was still too early to go to parties.

We drove into a gas station to get some gas for Dennis' car. When he finished, he pulled the car over to a phone booth. At first I thought they were going to make a phone call. Art stepped out of the car and walked over to the booth. I couldn't make out what he was doing, but he wasn't calling anyone. He turned around and walked back to the car with a smile.

Something was up with him. I knew that smile anywhere, the one he used when we did things we weren't supposed to do when we were younger. It was the same smile he showed when we embarked on an adventure.

"I got it!" Art said, as he was getting in the car.

"Got what?"

He had his T-shirt pulled up and full of coins he had taken from the phone booth.

"What the heck!" I said. "How did you get all that money? What did you do, break open the phone booth?"

"No," Art said. "What we do is cut these little plastics the size of the slot where the money falls out. We came here a couple of days ago and stuck them up into the slot. Everybody who uses the phone doesn't get back their change. We do!"

He picked up a thin, long wire and showed it to me. "When we come back, we stick this up in the slot and pull the plastic that's holding the change up in the phone. It's like winning a jackpot, man! Don't worry; we'll split it with you."

I thought about it for a second then took a drink of my beer. After swallowing, I said, "I don't want any money, Art. I don't want to go back to jail. Hey, man, if you guys want to break into phone booths and get the money, go ahead. I'm happy here with my beer. We can go to a party later."

"Are you sure? Because there's enough for all of us." Dennis said.

"Yeah, I'm sure. I want to stay clean at least for a while. I'm on parole, man. If I mess up for any little thing, I'll get sent back just like that," I said, snapping my fingers. "Hey, if my parole officer knew I was here drinking beer, he would send me back right now!"

We stopped at three or four more phone booths. By now they had a bag full of money. I told them they should buy some more beer.

We pulled into a store by Thirty-Second Street and Alum Rock. Art and Dennis got out of the car and entered the store to buy the beer. When they walked out, they walked over to another phone booth. These guys had set up phone booths all over the place. I saw Art's hands move up by the phone to catch the money that came out as if it were from a slot machine. As Art turned around, I saw his T-shirt pulled over with all the coins. It was hard to believe people put all that money in a phone booth in just one or two days.

They got into the car. Art looked at me and asked, "Are you sure you don't want any money? There's plenty for all of us."

"Like I said, Art, I'm happy with my beer. If you guys want to do your thing with the phone booths, go ahead."

We put the beer on the back floor next to my feet. As we pulled out of the driveway and made a right turn down a residential street, a cop drove by us, moving in the opposite direction. Art and Dennis turned around to see if he noticed us. That's the worst thing you can do, turn and look at a cop. I turned my head, and I saw his brake lights illuminate.

"Oh no!" Art said. Dennis made another right turn and stepped on the gas. His 1964 Chevy Impala moved out fast. We made another right and then a left on Alum Rock Avenue. Dennis looked in his rear-view mirror.

"No sign of the cop," Dennis said. We zipped along the street and moved into the turning lane to enter the freeway on Alum Rock. Once on the freeway Dennis stepped on the gas; he put his pedal to the floor. The engine was really picking up speed. We got away from the cop. We passed the McKee exit and were still picking up speed. All of a sudden there were red lights all over the car. Now we could hear the sirens screaming at us. There was a cop car behind us and another one next to us. As we were pulling over, Art told me to put the money, wire, and plastic under the seat. Just as we came to a stop, I shoved it all underneath.

One cop ran toward us. The other cop parked in front, jumped out of his car, and ran toward us. He opened my door and said, "GET OUT!" Not even a half second went by. "I SAID GET OUT!" he yelled.

"OK, OK, I'm getting out! What's the big deal?" I asked, wondering why they were so excited.

When they had Dennis and Art out, the cop asked, "OK, what are you guys up to?" He held Art and Dennis against the car with one hand, frisking them with the other. As one cop started to frisk me, the other finished frisking Art and Dennis. He crawled in the back seat of the car. From where I was standing next to the car, I saw him reaching under the seat.

He pulled out the wire and plastic and said, "I got it!" It sounded as if he knew what he was looking for in his search. He put the wire and plastic on top of the car. "What's this?" he asked. I really didn't think he knew what it was. I sure wouldn't have known. "Possession of burglary tools," he declared as he pulled out the bag of coins and slammed it down on top of the car. "You guys are under arrest for burglary!"

I didn't want this. I didn't want to go back to jail. The cop started to push me toward the back of the car to get me away from Dennis and Art. I looked over at my friends. On both of their faces were such sad expressions as they watched the cop push me in the other direction away from where they were standing.

On the way to the police station, I told the officer I didn't have anything to do with the burglary. I was drinking beer, but that was it.

"We know you were part of it. We were waiting for you to come back for the money. We saw you the other night, but you got away," the cop said.

"You didn't see me the other night because I wasn't here. I don't know what you're talking about," I said sadly. I didn't want to go back to jail.

We arrived at the police station. It was the same as the last time I was there. The same lobby where Art, the Redhead, said, "Wrong place at the wrong time." We walked down the same hallway to the same small rooms. Walking toward the rooms, I shook my head. I couldn't believe it. I couldn't believe I was back at the same place again. I never wanted this. I really didn't.

Once we were in the room, the cop came in and wanted to know what happened. Again I repeated my story.

"If my friends were robbing phone booths, I didn't know."

The cop sat on the table next to where I was sitting and said, "If you didn't know, what did you think when they kept stopping at the phone booths?"

I looked at the cop as if I were concentrating and trying to think back. I replied, "I thought they were calling girls to get set up for tonight. I didn't know anything about the phone booths."

"What about the bag of money? Where do you think it came from?" he asked.

"I thought they had the money all along. If they were taking it, I sure didn't know," I answered again. The cop asked to see my wallet. I took it out of my back pocket and handed it to him. The cop browsed through it and suddenly stopped.

His eyes looked up at me. He pulled out my parole officer's card and asked, "What were you locked up for?" I thought they had called my name in and knew I was locked up in the past.

"Murder, I mean assault with a deadly weapon."

He then stood up, walked toward the front of the table, stopped, put one foot on a chair, and said, "If you tell us what really happened, we'll give your parole officer a good report and tell him you cooperated with us. How does that sound?"

I put my head down and brought my hands up to my face, rubbing it with open hands and taking a deep breath.

"I told you, man. I told you everything! Give me a break. If I tell you anything else, I'll be lying!"

He took his foot off the chair, walked toward the door, and opened it. "OK, if that's the way you want it!"

When he left the room, everything was quiet—very still. If I had dropped a cigarette ash, I would have been able to hear it. I could hear mumbling from somewhere. It wasn't in the hallway; it was farther away. I was in the room for about forty-five minutes before he returned with another cop. Now they played bad cop, good cop. One wanted to be my friend and help me, and the other cop wanted to put me away for life.

I remembered thinking back then, "Do they send these guys to school for this good cop, bad cop routine? They do it so well. Pure theater."

We arrived there about 7 p.m., and I was held until about 2 a.m.

Back and forth, the question and answers remained the same. "You knew!"

"I didn't know!"

"Yes, you knew!"

"No, I didn't!"

"We know because Dennis and Art told us."

"I don't know what they told you, but I didn't know!"

After leaving the room and returning, one of them finally said, "OK, Arthur, let's go to jail!"

He put handcuffs on me, placed me in the car, and drove me around the building to the jail's entrance, the same place where I left Isaac and Phil. I was booked and placed in a holding cell. Once booking was complete, I was taken upstairs. I hated the smell of that place. It smelled like Pine Sol and body odor at the same time.

Everything looked the same as when I left it almost three years before; even the people looked the same. Once we were upstairs, we headed toward a hallway where big bar doors appeared. Things started to look familiar. It couldn't be. Not again! Mini Row! As we walked through the big, open bar doors, I looked in at the big cell where Phil, Isaac, and I had spent so much time together. There were two inmates sleeping there, all wrapped up in their blankets. Walking past that room and heading toward the small cells, the sheriff grabbed the door of one of them and said, "This is your cell."

As I stepped in, I just couldn't believe it. Again! I looked up at the ceiling, and what did I see up there etched in the wall? "ART WAS HERE." It sent a chill up my back! Bringing my hands up to my face, once again rubbing them against it and feeling frustrated, I sat on the bottom bunk. I couldn't believe I was back for some dumb crime. I stood up and looked at the top bunk to see if anyone else was there. I thought I heard somebody breathing. Someone was sleeping all wrapped up in his blanket.

I lay on the bottom bunk thinking how I was going to miss my family again. I had just arrived home, and my mother was happy with her two boys. And my sister, well, I was going to miss her. Tita had been a good sister these last few years.

CURLY HAIR BRAT

I thought back to the sixth grade. I was very mean with Tita. I thought I was tough, and I didn't want her to walk to school with me. I remembered how she hurried out of the front door of our house on Virginia Place to catch up with me.

I thought to myself, "Oh no!" Then, I'd yell out to her, "WALK ACROSS THE STREET. DON'T COME OVER HERE!" I thought if she walked with me, it would make me look bad, my having to take my little sister to school. I picked up rocks and threw them at her.

"Don't walk with me, I said!"

She still tried to follow me, but she stayed about two houses away. Why did I treat her like this when we were kids? I remembered. Tita was a spoiled, little girl. It wasn't her fault. My father spoiled her. When it was her birthday, my father went all out with parties. Eddie, Victor, and I never had any birthday parties. Why? Because we were boys. For my father parties were meant for girls only. Also when my mother and father went out to eat, Tita went with them because she was a girl. Victor went because he was the baby. Eddie and I? Well, the food was too rich for our blood, my father would tell us.

I remember once I was in Tita's room playing with her. I did something to get her angry. My father was in the living room resting on the couch and watching TV. Tita gave me this threatening look. She stood up; and she walked to the door of the bedroom, crying out, "Dad! Dad! Arthur's hitting me!" I sat there not believing she did such a thing. My father jumped from the couch and walked to the room.

"Arturo, come out here! What's wrong with you hitting your little sister?" My father was now taking off his belt, "Turn around!"

"DAD, I DIDN'T HIT HER. SHE'S LYING!" I yelled.

Well, this didn't do any good. My father didn't believe me because I am a boy and Tita is a girl. To my father girls were special. Crying, I went back into the room. Again Tita told me I better watch out, or I was going to get it.

"I'm not going to get it," I contended.

"DAD, ARTHUR'S HITTING ME AGAIN!"

My father came back to the room, and he beat me again.

"Dad, I didn't hit her! I didn't hit her the first time she said I hit her!" My father looked at me as if he believed me.

"Look, when I was a little boy, my mother whipped me because my sister said I hit her. She only did it one time because the next time she said it, I really hit her. After that she only told on me when I really did it. So if you're not really hitting her, you might as well do it before I get to the room because you're going to get whipped anyway."

I went back into the room with Tita. I told her if she told my father I hit her, I was really going to let her have it. I don't think she believed me because in just a little while she yelled out, "DAD, ARTHUR'S HITTING ME!" I jumped on top of her and started really hitting her as hard as I could. I didn't stop until my father entered the room. Tita was really crying by now. I was hit again, but that was the last time. Tita never did this to me again.

Tita was a pretty, little girl with little, black curls. When we had company, my father would call her out. Tita, with her little curls and her pretty dress, came out to show off. My father would put a record on that Tita liked, and she would dance for everybody. When she was done, she took a bow; and everybody clapped for her. She was a pretty, little, spoiled girl.

There I was thinking of my family and maybe going to be sent up again. I was going to really miss them. I dozed off to sleep.

* * *

"RODRIGUEZ! ROLL'EM UP!" I jumped out of my bunk and put on my pants. I was going somewhere. Man, I wondered where. I looked over at the guy on the top bunk; he was still sleeping. I didn't even get to talk to him. The door made a loud, clanging noise as it did when it was being unlocked. It was about 6:30 a.m. It looked as if it was getting light outside.

I walked down the hall. Everybody in the cells was still sleeping. I wondered if they were just changing my room or what. When I reached the end of the hall, the sheriff was waiting for me. He turned around as I walked up to him, so I could follow him. He took me to the small rooms where I once talked to my lawyer. Inside sat a detective with some papers in front of him. He examined me as I walked into the room.

"Arthur, how are you this morning?"

"I'm all right. I'm still waking up."

"First of all I would like to know if you have anything new to tell me?"

Wondering why he came so early to ask me that, I answered, "Not really, just the same thing I said last night."

He looked at me with a friendly look, then he said, "Well, the arresting officers last night wanted you to sleep on it. In their report they said the other two boys went along with your story. So the detectives wanted us to release you this morning." I was so happy. I couldn't believe it! I wasn't going to be sent back!

The detective continued, "And as far as your parole officer is concerned, you don't have to tell him anything because we're not going to notify him. Your two buddies told us what went down." He stood up from his chair. I also stood up and shook his hand, thanking him for the break. I also asked him to thank the other cops for releasing me. Before walking out, he told me to keep out of trouble. "That is a hard thing for me to do," I said to myself.

Not too long after almost being sent up for the telephone booths, I bought my first car. My mother tried to co-sign for me as she did with Eddie, but my mother's credit was overextended. I needed a car desperately in order to find a job and to get around. My favorite uncle Frank came to my rescue. He told me he would loan me some cash to buy a car. With this money I bought a 1959 Pontiac. My uncle Frank told me not to worry about the money. He said I could pay him back sometime in the future.

When I was released from Preston, I started to look for employment right away. I woke up at daybreak and spent all day looking for a job. I went to an industrial area, started on one corner, and went from one door to the next submitting applications. One morning I got out of bed, looked out of the window wanting to see what kind of day it was going to be, and I noticed the company across the street. It had been there all along, but I never saw it as a place to find a job. It was Master Metal Products. The company had a lot of people waiting to go to work by the front door. Once I was dressed, I walked over and submitted an application. The manager wanted to have an interview with me right away. After the interview he told me, "You have a job, and you can start tomorrow."

The workers at Master Metal Products got a kick out of me. In the mornings my mother would tell me to move my car out to the street. She didn't want me to block the driveway with my car while I was across the street working. So I had to move it out in the street before I went to work. In the morning all the guys across the street waited in front of the building for the manager to open up. As they stood there, they watched me walk out of the house and start up my car. I let it warm up before moving it, backed it out of the driveway, and parked it in front of the house or across the street where all the guys were standing. I stepped out of the car, locked it up, and walked over to them.

"Why do you do that, Art? Why do you drive to work?"

"Hey, man, if I didn't drive to work like everybody else, I wouldn't feel right," I joked. I did this every morning, and they thought I was crazy.

Living across the street from my place of employment had its advantages and disadvantages. It was difficult to call in sick when I really wasn't sick. At times I had other things to do, such as cruising around with my friends.

Once I even planned how and what I was going to do the day before. I parked my car around the corner the night before calling in sick. If I didn't park the car there, the bosses would see me drive away and know I wasn't really ill. The next morning when I called in, I made myself sound very sick, hung up the telephone, went out the back, and jumped over the fence. I think I must have made the manager feel sorry for me because he came over to see how I was doing. He left his business card on the door because the sick guy was so sick he couldn't get out of bed. That's what I told him the next day. "I was too sick to come to the door."

One day shortly after getting my new job, the painter started to train me to be a sheet-metal painter. I worked really hard my first couple of months. The most difficult day was Mondays because I partied heavily from Friday until late at night on Sunday and came to work with a hangover.

One day I came home from work. My mother told us my father called from LA and wanted all four of us kids to go see him. I didn't know if we should go, since we hadn't seen our father for a long time. My mother never talked unfavorably about him and never taught us to hate him. Then again, she didn't talk about him favorably either. We were all home that day sitting in the living room.

I looked at Eddie and asked, "What do you think, Eddie? Should we go?"

Since Eddie was the oldest and we looked up to him, we let him call the shot on this one.

"Yeah, let's go." So that's what we did. Eddie, Tita, Victor, and I drove in Eddie's Chevy to San Gabriel, California. My father was dealing in different types of businesses, and he was staying with a rich friend. I don't really know how rich he was, but we thought he was wealthy. He even had a driver and a phone in his car. Back in those days not too many people had phones in their cars.

We all sat with my father and talked. He was happy to see us and wanted to be close to us. We didn't blame him for the experiences we went through when we were young. We were just glad we were able to see him and to get to know him better. My father was the same as when I saw him in Preston, talking about all the money he was making and bragging about his wheeling and dealing.

Making this trip to see my father opened a way to get close to him, which we were never able to do when we were growing up. Before leaving, we all went to the front sidewalk and took a picture with him in front of his friend's house.

One day after work at Master Metal Products, I walked home across the street. When I arrived at the back house, I noticed the door open a little. A guy was sitting in the room talking to Eddie. As I walked in and saw who it was, I thought, "Man! What is this guy doing here?"

Richard Para stood up and said, "Hey, man, how's it going?" He didn't extend his hand to me because he didn't know how I would react. I stood there and thought of the last time I saw Richard. It wasn't a good thought.

LOVER'S LANE

Not long before we went to jail, we were cruising around town. I was in a car with Eddie and a few of the guys. Our other friends were following us in a second car. In a third car were Richard, Rudy, and others. I didn't like Richard and Rudy, and they didn't like me. I saw Rudy and Richard quite often at Overfelt High School. They thought they were tough, and I thought I was tough. We gave each other hard looks. Richard hung out with my brother and his friends once in a while but not too often. We knew that some day we were going to throw blows.

The other car pulled up next to us, and one of the guys said, "Hey, man. Rudy wants to fight Art!" I told the driver to pull over right there. I was ready, and I didn't want to wait.

"Hey, man, pull over. I'll get that chump right now!" I yelled, trying to climb over everyone. I wanted to get out of the car. Eddie told me to cool it.

He said, "Calm down, Art. You can fight him later, man!" As they drove by us again, I saw Rudy trying to climb over everybody in his car. He wanted to fight with me right there in the street. I saw Richard trying to hold him back.

In a little while someone said, "Hey, let's take them to Lover's Lane." Lover's Lane was a nice quiet street with a big, dirt parking area. Back in those days it was a place to take your girlfriend to talk and to smooch. It was part of Williams Street Park. The actual

Lover's Lane was on Sixteenth Street next to the park, starting at Williams.

Eddie continued, "There won't be anyone there right now; it's too late. They can fight all they want."

"Hey, man, I'm ready. Let's go!" I said, burning up inside and ready for a fight.

We motioned to one of the other cars to move next to us. When they were next to us, one of the guys said to the others in the other car, "Lover's Lane, man. They can fight there."

By this time it was late, and all the parties were over. Nobody would be at Lover's Lane.

We were on our way to Lovers Lane, but this wasn't over love! I really didn't know how good a fighter Rudy was, but I did know at school he acted tough. I really wanted to fight Richard because I had heard he was a good fighter, and I liked a challenge. This fight was going to be just Rudy and me because all the guys there were friends. Sometimes even as friends we got into fights with one another. The difference was that the next day we were friends again.

When we arrived at Lover's Lane, I was ready to find out what kind of fighter Rudy was. We parked the cars and walked quietly into the park; we didn't want to wake the people in the nearby houses. It wasn't that we cared about them; we just didn't want them to call the cops. We all walked out under some big trees and were ready to go at it. Rudy took his first swing and missed. I then took mine.

"This guy can't fight," I thought as we started throwing blows. When it was over, I had beat up Rudy pretty badly. He had two black eyes the next day. According to everybody, I was the unanimous winner.

We left the park. Richard was really angry because I had beaten up his good friend.

"Hey, Art, it's going to be you and me next!" he said.

"I'm ready right now, man." I said, angrily walking toward Richard.

Eddie grabbed my arm, "Cool it, Art. Not right now. If you want to fight Richard, wait for another time!" I was tired and covered with Rudy's blood, but I didn't care. Richard was the one I really wanted to fight. As the next few days went by, we let each other know we were both game to fight at the next opportunity. That opportunity never came. We took on the "big fight" and were sent up.

Now Richard was here in my house talking to Eddie.

* * *

"How you doing?" I answered Richard as I looked over at Eddie. When Eddie looked at me, I motioned with my head, moving it up and over, signaling him to go outside with me.

Ed told Richard, "I'll be right back." He stepped outside with me. As we were leaving the room, Richard stood up and put his hands in his pockets, as he really didn't know what to make of this. Outside, Ed had a look on his face as if he knew exactly what I was going to say.

"Hey, Eddie, what's this? Why is this guy here?" I asked. During the time I was locked up, I dreamed about taking care of unfinished business with different people. Richard was one of them.

Eddie, hands at his sides and bringing them up with his palms up, said, "Cool down, Art! You're mad at something that happened a long time ago! Richard doesn't want to fight you anymore. He's all right now."

I looked at Eddie with doubt and went into the back house where we talked to Richard for a few minutes. I felt uncomfortable and decided to go into the front house. It turned out Richard lived around the corner; this made him our neighbor. It also turned out Richard and I later became the best of friends.

Living in the back house during this time gave us a lot of freedom to come and go as we pleased. My mother didn't like us to go out at night. She worried so much for us, thinking we might end up in jail again. She said she hated to wait for our cars to arrive home late at night.

There was no let up for our mother. Between dealing with my father and us as we were growing up, she had a difficult life.

A KID'S NIGHT LIFE

My father was always out with his friends and probably his girl-friends. My mother was left alone a lot. Things were just not going well for my parents. When things don't go well with parents, things just do not go well with the children. My father was still strict with us during the time he was home. Eddie hung out with his friends, and I hung out with mine. Sometimes we hung out together.

When I was between thirteen and fifteen years old, my night life consisted of fixing my bed as if I were sleeping, although I was sneaking out the window. My friend Art and I had this thing about drinking. We loved it. At this time Tropicana homes were built, as was Newberry's department store and the grocery store on King and Story. Art and I walked down King Road to Newberrys. The park and the freeway weren't there, just barbed-wire fences, fields, and dairy farms.

We read in the paper one day that Mrs. Prush, who owned all the land behind our house, was going to donate her house and prop-erty to the city for a park for the kids. All she wanted in return was for the city to paint her house once a year for the rest of her life. I remember we kids were excited because we were going to have a park by our house. My father laughed and said, "That park isn't going to be for you kids; it's going to be for your kids!"

Art and I walked down King Road to Tropicana. We talked about what we were going to do that night after we got drunk.

Walking into Tropicana Foods, we checked things out. The liquor department was right next to the candy. We walked by the cheap liquor. It was always in the same place. I grabbed a bottle of whiskey, walked to the candy counter, and left it there. This was our regular routine. We'd walk through the store to make sure no one saw us. Once the coast was clear, we'd return and pretend we were looking for candy. Before entering the store, I loosened my belt. If no one was looking, I'd stick the fifth of cheap whiskey inside my belt and hang my shirt over it. I'd grab some candy and go to pay for it.

Once we were back at Virginia Place, we sold the bottle to the older guys for $2.00. With the $2.00 we went to stand by the Pink Elephant store at the end of the street. We waited in front of the store until someone came along ready to help a kid out. We asked if they could buy us some beer. Some men simply said, "Sorry, kid!" and kept walking. Others put their finger up, wagged it, and said, "No, no!" Finally someone said, "Sure, what do you want?" We drank the beer from straws and got drunk. Not until we were a little older did we start drinking the whiskey instead of selling it to the older guys.

At the corner of Virginia Place and King Road was an empty lot. One day some trucks brought in a burger bar. I say they brought it in because it was built somewhere else. It was pre-fabricated. We young teenagers made the burger bar our hangout. We ordered our food from outside or in the dining room.

This was our alternative hangout for a while. Our regular hangout was at the Lopez girls' house; but when their father was home, the burger bar was our hangout.

Once I snuck out of my window as usual. Art and I went and got our bottle at Tropicana as we always did, stealing it. By this time we were keeping it for ourselves. I became so drunk that night that I could hardly stand. We were at the burger bar that evening because Fred, the girls' father, was home.

The guys who worked at the burger bar were in their twenties. They liked having us teenagers around late at night; it wasn't so boring for them with us there. On this particular night, I could hardly stand up. I drank way too much. I had my bottle in my belt and was standing by the counter by the dining-room-order window, talking to the guy who worked there. He was telling stories of his youth when he was a youngster like us.

Then he said, "Ese, your mother's here!"

"What did you say?"

"Your mother's here," he repeated a little louder.

My mother couldn't be! She was at home sleeping. I knew she wasn't there at the burger bar. This guy was pulling my leg. My mother wouldn't leave my house with my father there. He would have a fit.

"Hey, ese, you'd better turn around because your mother looks mad!" he said. This time he didn't sound as if he were joking.

"My mother isn't here, ese! Ha, ha, ha," I laughed with a drunk voice.

"Your mother just got madder." The guy looked as if he were embarrassed.

"What? What do you mean my mother is here? If she's here, I'll give you a drink of my bottle," I said as I turned around laughing. "Ha, ha, ha." I stopped laughing really fast.

My mother was standing there. She stood about two feet from me, wearing her big coat, with her arms folded, not saying a word, staring, and expressing a very angry look on her face. All the kids who were in the burger bar dining area quieted down and watched, wondering what was going to happen. "Ah-h-h, hi, Mom!" My mother didn't respond; she just stood there looking at me. I didn't know what to say. I was so drunk. My mother knew it. I had done this so often and had never been caught.

My mother finally said, "Come with me!" She took me by the arm and out the door, while all my friends watched. It felt as if she had me by my ear, holding it up, as we walked out the door.

As we walked out, I turned in the direction of our house. My mother pulled me in the other direction toward King Road. Before we went home, we had to go to the store. That's what she told my father she was going to do in order to leave the house. She found my bed made up as if I were sleeping in it and had to come out to look for me. As we walked out of the burger bar and across the street, my mother scolded me.

"What will your father do if he checks your bed? What are you doing drinking? Where did you get the alcohol? What's wrong with you?"

I was trying to think about what she was asking me and also

trying to walk in a straight line at the same time. We walked into the Pink Elephant market and bought a loaf of bread. I forgot about the big bottle under my shirt. The clerks at the Pink Elephant market knew my parents through the years. Once we stepped up to the counter, a clerk stared at my shirt. He knew I had something under it but didn't know what. I thought for sure the security guard was going to stop us on the way out, thinking I had stolen something from their store. As we walked out, the security guard looked at my shirt and then looked up at me. I think he knew I was drunk. He looked at my mother. My mother looked at him and gave him a friendly smile. She wasn't worried about my being drunk anymore. She was in a trance, worried, thinking about my father and what he would do if he found out I was drunk.

Once back home she took me in through the back door, trying to keep me quiet. My father and I were having a lot of trouble as it was. Before going to bed, I became really sick. Usually I would vomit before I went into the house, so I wouldn't wake anyone. My mother was trying to keep me quiet, so I wouldn't wake my father.

When did I start drinking? I think back to when I spent time in the LA area, when I was a young guy who wanted to be like my uncles.

LOS ANGELES

When I was young, my grandparents moved to the LA area. They lived in the projects in Harbor City. When I was about thirteen, my grandparents moved to a house in San Pedro, California. Aunt Connie; Aunt Maryann and her husband, Uncle Alfred; and Uncle Joe all lived with my grandparents.

During this time Aunt Connie wasn't married to Uncle Ray. Ray was her boyfriend, and she was going out with him. Aunt Connie was Eddie's age. Maryann was about two years older than Connie. Uncle Joe was about two years older than Maryann. When we visited my grandparents, Aunt Maryann talked my father and my mother into letting me stay a few weeks longer.

Maryann was a very good aunt to us, even though she was close in age to us kids. She was about four years older than I was. I remember when we were small kids, she loved to bite us, but not to be mean. I think she felt she loved us more if she bit us. No, she wasn't crazy. She was just a very loving aunt. That was her way of kissing and hugging us. My parents let me stay longer with enough persuasion from her. I came home later on a Greyhound bus.

Aunt Maryann was married to Uncle Alfred who was a wild guy even though he was a married man. He still liked to drink and go out to parties. Uncle Joe was also a very wild guy. At this time he wasn't married. He had a nickname in the streets, Guero [whitie]. He had light skin, light brown hair, and was a Loco from Harbor City.

When I was about thirteen years old, I stayed with my grandmother for an extra three weeks after my parents left. At my grandfather and grandmother's house, they let me do whatever I wanted. During this time I started to smoke regularly.

I remember Aunt Connie, my mother's youngest sister, telling me, "Arthur, you can smoke when you're here. My father and mother don't care."

If this were true, it would be cool if I could smoke without having to hide. I tried it. I sat on the front porch and smoked to see if they told me anything. Not a word. I smoked so much those first few days that I became sick to my stomach. The Camels and Pall Malls were so strong, I'd even throw up.

One day my Uncle Joe asked me, "Art, do you want to come with me? I'm going to Harbor City." Harbor City wasn't that far away, only a few miles.

"Sure, Uncle Joe," I answered.

"If you come with me, you have to back me up if there's any trouble."

I thought he was kidding, so I asked, "What kind of trouble?"

"Come on, you'll see!" My uncle was a Loco and well known throughout the neighborhood.

Here I was with Uncle Joe, who was a Loco, cruising around town. I was having fun. I felt like a tough guy sitting with him in the front seat, low riding in Harbor City. When we came around the corner of one part of the strip that had cruisers at all times of the day, we moved behind another low rider.

"Hang on!" Uncle Joe exclaimed.

The car in front of us was an older low rider with the back window so high it was hard to see who was in the car. I noticed Uncle Joe shifted the transmission to low gear, making the car jump and jerk a little. He then let the clutch out. We hit the car in front of us, bumping it, just enough to get their attention. I saw a bunch of heads pop up, looking out of the back window. The clean, fixed-up low rider was full of Locos. There were probably about four heads in the back seat alone. Uncle Joe said again, "Hang on tight this time!"

He stepped on the clutch. The car was still in first gear as the car in front of us came to a red light. Our car jerked as my uncle let out the clutch.

We were not stopping behind the low rider but were hitting it. When he hit it, I turned and looked at my uncle. He had a smile on his face as if he knew those guys. Our car came to a stop, and for the third time my uncle let out the clutch again. This time I knew the guys weren't his friends. He hit the car hard! "What the heck," I thought. I wanted to tell my uncle there were too many guys in the car, but things were happening too fast! All four doors of the car in front of us flew open. Eight mean-looking Locos jumped out of the car in the middle of the street. They looked angry.

Not looking my way but starting to open his door, my uncle said, "Come on, let's get them!"

What? Did I hear right? I heard my uncle was a bad Loco in the streets, but I didn't know he was this bad!

Uncle Joe jumped out of the car and started running toward the guys. As he approached them, he put his fists up and started dancing in a boxing posture.

I got out of the car on my side and thought, "Oh well, I guess I'm going to get beat up today!" My uncle encountered five guys as I was still getting out of the car. He started to dance around them. I remember thinking, "Man, my uncle is really tough! I want to be just like him! He sure looks good fighting all these guys!" While I thought this, three guys came running up to me. I put my hands up and started to dance like Uncle Joe. Here I go!

Suddenly someone yelled out, "Hey, Guero!" Guys who were standing on the corner in front of the liquor store came running toward us. At the same time cars that were moving in the other direction were stopping in the middle of the street. Guys were jumping out of their cars to help Uncle Joe with the fight, since those guys in the low rider in front of us were from another town.

Not one of them threw a punch at me. Saved by the Locos of Harbor City! Those Locos were in the wrong town. They were beat up and didn't stand a chance. While they were trying to leave, after being beat up, my uncle was still trying to pull one of the guys out of their car to hit him.

Some of Uncle Joe's friends were telling him, "Orale, Guero. Let them go; they had enough!" They felt sorry for them. The others finally drove off, and we started to walk back to our car.

We heard a roaring engine and turned to see a cop car flying around the corner with its red lights flashing. As we were getting into our car, which was in the middle of the street, the cop pulled up behind us.

"What does he want?" Uncle Joe said.

The cop stepped out of his car and asked my uncle, "What's wrong? What happened here?"

Uncle Joe looked at the cop and sarcastically answered, "What does it look like, man?" I thought we were going to get into trouble because of the way my uncle talked to the cop. Looking back at this incident, I think these cops were used to it. This cop let us leave since he couldn't see any sign of trouble.

I went back and told my other uncles we had been in a fight with eight guys. Uncle Joe laughed and said that wasn't a fight. If I wanted to see a real one, then they were going to take me out the next night where they would show me what a real fight was.

A few nights later they tried to find someone. I went out with them, and they tried to start a fight with some guys. Even though it didn't happen, they did get me so drunk that the next day I spent all morning washing Uncle Alfred's car. I made a mess of it from being so sick. I don't know why I liked getting drunk so much. It seemed as if I always became sick.

Uncle Joe shot himself in the head a few years later, having become depressed with life. Later on Aunt Maryann divorced Uncle Alfred. A few years after that, Uncle Alfred died from a bad liver, the result of living a wild life. Uncle Ray died years later, also from the same illness, a bad liver.

My poor uncles, I loved them so much. They lived hard and died hard.

My uncles

Uncles Joe, Alfred, and Ray were really fun to be around. I remember when I got older, after I was released from jail, I went to see them. They lived in Wilmington at the time. I went out drinking with them, and we went to some of their friends' houses. On the way home we stopped to eat at a decent restaurant about 3 a.m., one that was packed with people. We were the only Chicanos in the whole place. My uncles were still a little high from drinking but were in cheerful moods. The hostess found us a table in the middle of the restaurant. It was crowded, and everybody was making a lot of noise. People kept turning and looking at us. I thought it was because we were the only Chicanos in the restaurant.

Uncle Ray always came up with the good ideas. This time I don't think he asked me because I wasn't that drunk. My other uncles usually went along with what was happening in order to have fun. By this time in my life, I was becoming smarter.

"Hey, Joe and Alfred, let's see who can give the loudest Mexican grito [yell]," Uncle Ray said, laughing.

I looked around and saw all the gavachos [Anglos]. They were well-dressed from a night of partying. We were wearing our Pendleton shirts, Levis, and khaki pants.

I thought to myself, "Oh no! This is going to be really embarrassing."

Uncle Alfred said, "No, No, Ray, you want us to give a Mexican grito with all of these gavachos here?"

Uncle Ray answered, "No! I don't want only you guys to do it. I'm going to yell with you."

"Yeah, right," I thought.

"Hey, Ray, why don't you yell first. If we think it is a good Mexican grito, then we'll yell too," Uncle Joe said.

"Good idea," I thought.

Uncle Ray didn't give up so easily. "Come on you guys. Don't tell me you're scared of all these gavachos? Are you? I'll yell with you, and I'm not scared. Come on. We'll all yell together, OK?" That did it. My uncles had to prove they weren't scared.

"OK," Uncle Joe said, "we'll all do it together. You too, Art."

"Hey, man, leave me out of this. I'm not going to give a Mexican grito. I don't know how anyway," I said.

"OK, OK, you guys," Uncle Ray replied. "I'll count to three, and we'll all do it together. Ready?" I looked at Uncle Alfred and Uncle Joe. They had a look of anticipation, waiting for Ray to start counting.

"OK, one," Ray started counting, waiting in between numbers. Uncle Ray was having fun with this; he was giggling as he always did when he was having fun. "Two!" Uncle Joe and Uncle Alfred had their mouths open a little, ready to give their Mexican grito as loud as they could. "All of us NOW! THREE!" "AYYY, AYYYYY, AYYY!" Uncle Ray didn't yell. He took a deep breath as if he were going to yell but didn't. My other two uncles didn't realize it until it was too late. Uncle Ray tricked them.

I remember this night well because it was one of the most embarrassing nights in my whole life. And fun! It was so noisy before the grito, you could hardly hear yourself think. Right after the grito the 200 or so in the large restaurant were quiet, looking over at us. Even the manager came out to look at us crazy Mexicans. It looked as if he wanted us to leave. I'm glad they didn't ask us to. My uncles would have had a fit and would have wanted to fight.

Not too long after that incident, Uncle Ben, my mother's other brother, was also visiting from San Jose. One of my uncles had been to New Mexico, and one of his cousins told him our side of the family had more Indian blood in us than we thought. In fact they gave him a record with Indian music. It was drum music and also sounded like rain or a war dance.

I spent the night at Uncle Ray and Aunt Connie's apartment. In the morning I was asked if I was going to go to my grandmother's house. Everybody was there visiting before Uncle Ben was to return home.

"Sure, I'll go see him, even though I see him all the time in San Jose."

Uncle Joe lived about two blocks away. The apartments where my grandfather lived were single-story; there were about six apartments to a building, all in a row. The small complex had about three or four buildings of apartments. The landscape was decent, green with trees and flowers, although the apartment where he lived was small. The layout had the living room as part of the dining area.

Walking up the walkway as I entered the gate to my grandfather's apartment, I heard the Indian drums. Someone was having a pow wow. My family lived about three doors from the gate. As I walked in, I heard the wild music coming from my grandfather's home. It was 1 p.m.

As I walked into the apartment, someone said, "Art's here!" Uncle Joe was sitting in a chair at the kitchen table. Uncle Alfred was next to him along with Uncle Ben. My grandmother was in the kitchen with Aunt Maryann. Everybody was drinking.

"Hey, Art, want a beer?" someone asked.

It was kind of early but what the heck. "Yeah, I'll have one," I answered.

I really didn't like the music that was playing, but my grandfather loved it. He was singing along with the music, high from the beer he had already drank. During this time my grandfather was a heavy drinker.

I drank about three beers. There was a knock on the screen door. I was sitting on the couch talking to Aunt Maryann when I looked over to see who was at the door. A cop! It was about 2 p.m. by then. What did he want? My grandfather went over and turned down the stereo. He looked over at the cop.

"Whatsa matter?" my grandfather asked. My grandfather's everyday talk was English and Spanish mixed, more so Spanish. His English wasn't very strong.

The cop looked around the apartment through the screen and said to everyone, "We received a complaint that your music is too loud. Turn it down, and keep it down!"

At this point Uncle Joe stood up and walked to the screen door but didn't open it. He was not scared of anybody or anything.

With a bottle of beer in his hand, he said, "Hey, man, why don't you go bother someone else. What's wrong with you bothering us? It's only 2 p.m."

The cop looked at him without saying anything. He scanned the room again and then said, "I don't want to hear any more complaints." He left, although he wasn't happy with Uncle Joe's attitude.

For about fifteen minutes the music stayed low. Then because my grandfather liked a certain song, he turned up the stereo again. We were sitting around talking. Suddenly there was a knock at the door once more. I looked, and the same cop had appeared. He stood there as if he wanted to enter. There were a lot of us in the apartment: my grandmother, aunts, uncles, and cousins. The officer put his hand on the screen door to try to open it, but the door was locked. Uncle Joe stood up from his seat. I was hoping the cop wouldn't enter. Uncle Joe had drank too many beers, and he was ready to fight. Once he drank more than three beers, he was ready to fight anyone, even the cops.

The cop stood at the door. My grandfather turned the stereo down again, and the cop stayed for a few seconds looking at us. Another cop was behind him waiting to see what the first cop was going to say. It looked as if the officer was waiting for someone to tell him to enter. If he did, my uncle was ready to fight. "What will I do then?" I thought. "I've only been out of Preston for a few months. If I get into trouble, I'll be sent back. I was supposed to let my parole officer know I was coming to LA, and I didn't. Well, what the heck. If this cop comes in and starts fighting, I'm going to back up my uncles and grandfather."

The cop who was standing at the door saw my uncle sitting at the table. He pointed at him and said, "I'd better not have to come back one more time. If I do, you're going in!"

Uncle Joe stood up from where he was sitting at the table. With his beer in his hand, he said, "Yeah, yeah, yeah!" The cops turned and left. After they walked away, my uncle said, "They think they're tough, man; but they're not!"

Everything went back to normal for a little while. In about fifteen minutes one of my cousins came into the apartment and said, "A whole bunch of cops are coming."

"Here we go!" I thought. I stood up and moved to the stereo, opposite where my uncles were sitting in the kitchen. I saw the cops walk up the small sidewalk in front of the apartment. They were walking fast. From where I was standing, I couldn't really tell how many there were. The cop who had kept returning to the apartment was the first to reach the door. Not stopping at the door as he did the other times, he reached for the knob and opened the door. He marched into the living room with another cop right behind him.

When he was right in the middle of the living room, he stopped and looked at Uncle Joe, pointing at him with his billy club. He said, "You . . ." As the words came out of his mouth, Uncle Joe stood up from behind the table. With his bottle of beer in his hand, he reached back and threw it as hard as he could. The bottle went flying across the room and struck the cop right in the head! He fell like a bowling pin, and Uncle Joe leaped over the table to attack him. My other uncles who were there also started fighting with the cops. As my other uncles entered the fight, one cop turned around. I slugged him in the face as hard as I could. I knew this was going to send me back to jail anyway, so I thought I might as well go for it and help my family.

I started swinging at all the cops, left and right, not really knowing which one I was hitting. I only remember aiming for the blue uniforms. All of this happened in a matter of seconds. The door to the apartment was crowded with blue uniforms. They were lined up outside waiting to enter. The cops who were by the front door started taking everybody outside.

I thought about what was going to take place. I knew this was going to send me back to jail, and I didn't want it to happen. There had to be a way out.

By now there were a lot of police in the apartment, standing room only. I backed up a foot or two to the wall by the stereo and saw the door to the apartment had a little standing room behind it. I was about four feet from the door. Most of the cops' backs were in front of me trying to get Uncle Joe handcuffed, trying to remove him from the cop at whom he threw the bottle. I stepped behind the door and held the knob tightly against me. Through the crack of the door, I could see cops coming in, one after another. There were so many, I didn't know how they could all fit in the small apartment.

Within seconds the cops started to take my uncles out of the apartment, handcuffed. I could see them through the crack by the hinges. Once everyone was out, I felt the door move. I thought if a cop pulls the door and finds me, I'm going to hit him hard and run. I thought if I ran, I would get shot in the back. However, if I ran fast enough, I might make it around the corner of the apartment building.

No one pulled on the door. In fact the apartment was really quiet. Everyone was outside. I stood very still without moving a muscle. Should I get out now? I thought I better wait a few more minutes.

Just then I heard cops returning to the apartment. One went in to check the apartment one last time. The other stood at the threshold of the door. The crack by the door hinges was no more then five or six inches from my eye. The cop who was standing there waiting was inches from me, but I didn't move. It even seemed as if he looked through the crack once and saw me. If he did see me, he was going to have a fight on his hands. I wondered where the other cop went. The cop's eyes again looked as if they were looking at me through the crack. Holding my breath, I waited to see what was going to happen.

At that moment, the other cop said, "Nope, no one is left in here. Let's go."

A close call. I waited a few minutes just in case one of them was standing outside. Everything was quiet inside and outside; the coast was clear. I peeked around the door, stepped out, and peeked out of the front door. No cops. I looked out toward the street and saw everybody by the gate and on the sidewalk. I fixed my shirt and combed my hair, so I wouldn't look as if I had just been in a fight. I walked out.

Everybody was yelling and telling the cops to leave my uncles alone. I hoped none of the cops would recognize me. There were about three officers standing in front of the police cars, so none of the spectators could approach. Uncle Ben was in the back seat of the police car, and cops were on both sides. The doors were open, and they were hitting him with their clubs.

I was angry and ready to run over to help him. By then there were about 20 cops standing around, waiting and talking.

"HEY! HEY, MAN, LEAVE HIM ALONE!" I yelled.

One cop who was standing in front of the cars had his hands on his hips as if he were guarding the police car. When I yelled, he looked at me. I caught his attention. Dropping his hands and grabbing his billy club from his belt, he walked over to me, staring and with a frown. Pointing the club at me, he yelled, "Hey! You were one of the guys inside of the apartment!"

"In what apartment? I live over there." I pointed to one of the other units across from where my grandparents lived. He stayed there looking at me, wondering if I was lying. For a minute I thought he was going to arrest me.

Another officer walked up to us and asked the first cop, "What's the problem?"

"I think this guy was in the apartment with the rest of them!"

The second cop had a little blood on his forehead. He looked at me really hard and said, "No, I don't think he was one of them. We went back and checked, and he wasn't in there."

My grandmother was an old, sweet lady. She always treated everyone with respect and was a very kind woman. When she was younger, she was a school teacher. She taught at an old school house in San Jose, the Horsemen School, an old-fashioned school house with all grades taught in one room. It was next to the Farmer's Market on Story Road.

My grandmother kept begging the cops, "Please stop beating my sons! Please leave them alone!"

One cop walked up to my grandmother and said, "Lady, if you don't shut up, I'm going to take you to jail too!"

The first cop who came into the apartment was beaten up pretty badly. The bottle Uncle Joe threw at him cut his head. The other cops were banged up also. My uncles were ruffed up a little in front of the apartments, but this was nothing compared to what happened to them on the way to jail. They were beaten up pretty badly. I think they knew it was going to happen from the expressions they had on their faces when they were taken away.

They didn't take me in, but they did take all my uncles. It was no light matter. My uncles had to go to court many times, for months. They had to hire lawyers, and it cost them a lot of money. Finally the court process was over. They all had to pay fines and go to jail for a while. It sure wasn't worth it, beating up the cops and having to pay so much. My life didn't look very promising. I was having a difficult time staying out of trouble. Would I straighten out my life? If I did, when? Would I get caught for some of the things I was doing and be sent back to jail? Would I end up dead like a lot of my old friends? Some of my friends were living on the streets. Others overdosed on drugs. Still others were killed. How was I going to end up?

BACK TO SAN JOSE

Back in San Jose, Eddie, our friends, and I were making a change from drinking and getting drunk to drinking and drugs. At first it was marijuana. In those days medical science was reporting that nothing was wrong with marijuana. Experts claimed it wouldn't do any damage. We bought it in sandwich bags called lids. At times we went to San Francisco to the Haight-Ashbury district and bought a kilo at a time.

Haight and Ashbury is where Haight and Ashbury streets intersect. When we went to San Francisco to this area, we parked our car and walked down the sidewalk. It wasn't a normal area. Hippies were dancing in the street. The street and sidewalk were filled with hippies, walking and standing around on the sidewalks.

To buy whatever we wanted, we merely walked down the sidewalk. Whenever people walked in our direction, we listened to see if they had what we wanted. Just as they passed next to us, they stopped whatever they were saying and slipped in the word for whatever they were selling. Then they continued with their conversation.

We walked farther down the sidewalk. Someone walking by would say, "Coke?" Someone else would walk by us and say, "Acid?" When they said the name of the drug we wanted to hear, we called them back to make the deal, if the price was right.

My mother never had any idea we were buying marijuana. She never knew we smoked it in the back house. It reminded me about the famous gangster of the 1930s, Al Capone. His mother was asked what she thought about her son. Her answer? "My Al is a good boy!" Mothers always think their boys are good.

We had a pool table in our back house. One day our friends Richard, Ventura, and the other guys were hanging out. We decided to go to San Francisco to get our kilo. When we arrived back at our house, we all worked to clean out the seeds. We had it in little bunches all over the pool table. At the same time everybody was smoking it.

Through the door my mother burst into the room. We all stopped what we were doing and looked at her. Busted!

My mother looked around the room and then at me. She said, "Arthur, the telephone." She cheerfully closed the door and went back to the front house. We couldn't believe she didn't know what we were doing. Smoking marijuana and possession of it were something that would send us to jail for a long time. If we were caught selling it, we could get twenty years in prison. We had no regard for the consequences. Fortunately, we were never caught.

Later on the same night when my mother had barged into the back house, I received a call from my friend Dennis. He wanted me to go pick him up at his house. He couldn't come in his car because he was repairing it.

"No problem, Dennis. I'll leave right now. Be ready because we bought a kilo, and we're all here cleaning out the seeds right now." I hung up the telephone.

"Hey, you guys. I have to go pick up my friend Dennis on Virginia Place. I'll be back in a little while."

During this time we got loaded on marijuana a lot, all day long: in the morning, afternoon, and evening.

As I opened the door to leave, Ventura said, "Hey, Art, I made these for you, so you can smoke them on the way back." He handed me three giant marijuana bombers.

"Ventura, I can't take these, man. There's too many cops out there. Today is Saturday. The streets are crawling with cops."

"Come on, Art, you're not going to get caught, man. Take them," Ventura insisted, still with his hand extended with the three giant bombers.

Almost reaching for them, I said, "No, I better not, Ventura."

Ventura was the kind of guy who didn't like to give up. He wanted to do me a favor. He said, "Take them. Smoke them on the way back."

I let out a big sigh and put my hand out, still thinking, "What if I get caught?" Usually if I had one or two small joints and was stopped as I had been so many times before, I placed them in my mouth and swallowed them. No problem. But these big giants? I didn't think I would be able to swallow them.

I walked out the door, closed it behind me, and put the big bombers in my shirt pocket. Walking out to the street, I stepped into my car and started driving down Emory Street. It was a dark, quiet night; no other cars were driving on the street. At the corner I made a right turn on Walnut Street. Just as I approached the intersection of Walnut and Ashbury at the next street ahead [Taylor Street], a police car turned around the corner, burning rubber and with red lights flashing. Another police car was right behind him. They caught me, man!

I reached for my pocket, looking for the three giant joints. On my right side another cop was racing toward me. From my left two more police cars were closing in fast with their red lights and their sirens screaming! I placed two giant joints in my mouth and started chewing as fast as I could, not knowing if this was going to work.

The cop car in front of me was the first to reach me. It was skidding sideways up to my car. I was at a complete stop by now and swallowed what I had in my mouth, knowing I had to get the other one down in time. The other police cars that were coming down both sides of the streets came to a screeching halt! Cops were running everywhere. I stuck the last, giant joint in my mouth; at the same time I was trying to swallow the other two. They didn't want to go down, and they were stuck halfway down my throat. The police got out of their cars, hid behind them, and drew their guns, pointing them at me. Seven or eight police cars surrounded my car with their spotlights aiming in my direction.

One cop yelled out, "DON'T MOVE! FREEZE!" I couldn't move anyway. I was choking! I felt like yelling back, "Help!" However, I couldn't.

One cop was pointing his gun at me from about 15 feet away. Another one ran to my front tire and placed his open hand on it, feeling the tire to see if it had any heat. Whoever they were chasing must have really been moving and would have hot tires.

After about two seconds the cop yelled out, "NO, IT'S NOT HIM. LET'S GO!" All the cops ran back to their cars, jumped in, and took off. All of a sudden I was left alone in the middle of the street, choking, and all by myself. I stayed there for about ten minutes, thinking I was going to die. Finally I coughed up a big glob of weed! Stepping out of my car, I couldn't believe what almost happened to me. What would the newspapers say the next day? "Youngster Chokes to Death on Marijuana!" I walked around the car a couple of times, trying to recover. I returned home, feeling sick and not wanting to pick up Dennis or party that night.

From marijuana we graduated to LSD. I remember Art and I went to the Rainbow Dance Hall. I thought I looked cool and was talking to all the girls, trying to dance with them. However, none of the girls wanted to dance with me. Some who didn't know me looked at me as though I was crazy for asking them to dance.

When I went to the restroom, I looked in the mirror and jumped back a foot. I scared myself when I realized I looked as if I had just awaken from a three-day sleep. My hair was all messy. I looked like a First Street wino. As soon as I stepped out of the restroom, I forgot how I looked and thought I was Don Juan again. That's what LSD does to you.

That night I couldn't fight anyone. I felt as if everyone was my brother and sister. We were standing by some tables, and I saw a crowd of guys walking toward us. It was Noah, the one who Eddie and I had a fight with once before—Tita's old boyfriend. He came up to me and asked me something, with his partners all around him. He said, "Ese, . . ."

I couldn't make out what he said; the music was blaring from all sides. My friend Art put his arm around me and tried to whisper something, but I couldn't make out what he was saying either. Being so loaded on LSD, I felt this guy was my friend. What happened had taken place a long time ago. I was willing to forgive him for making me angry.

I remember stepping toward him and squeezing his arm as if I cared about him. I told him, "That song they're playing is my song. I have to go find some beautiful girl to dance with." I left everybody standing there.

The next morning my friend Art told me Noah had a knife about eight inches long. He had been holding it under his shirt. Art told me he thought I was going to be stabbed. I became really upset. "Today I'm not loaded. I don't like that guy anyway. I'm going to get him for pulling a knife on me!" I went looking for Noah in the neighborhood and was planning to fight him. Later we met, but nothing happened. We both felt everything was over between us, and that's where it stayed.

About this time at Master Metal Products, I was called into the office a few times about my poor work habits. I missed a lot of work on Mondays because of hangovers. I had a hard time staying awake, and I often went in late. The manager had had enough. He called me into the office and told me he was firing me. I was relieved. I knew I had not been giving a hard-day's work. My father had brought me up with strong work ethics. My conscience bothered me because I wasn't working productively, and I knew my time was coming. Plus, I wanted to stay home for a while; so I could sleep late because of my late-night activities.

It took about a week to catch up on my sleep. My mother became upset with me. She wanted me to wake up early to find a job and said she wasn't going to put up with a lazy bum living in her house.

One day I got out of bed about 11 and left the house, hoping my mother would think I went to seek employment. Upon arriving home late that evening, I noticed a bunch of boxes and bags on the front porch. I walked up to them and wondered, "What is this stuff?" I thought someone had come by and left them. I reached for the front door knob. Locked. That was odd. I knew my mother was home. As I thought about this, I looked back at the boxes behind me and saw something in one of the bags that looked as if it belonged to me. I reached down and pulled one of my shirts out. "What the heck! This is my shirt!" I looked in one of the other boxes and saw my other clothes. "What's going on here?" I wondered. Stepping up to the door again, I knocked rather hard. "Mom, are you in there?"

My mother cracked the door open and said, "What do you want?"

"Mom, what's going on here?" I asked in a worried tone, anticipating the answer.

Not opening the door fully but leaving it cracked and peaking out, she said, "If you don't want to work, then you have to go live somewhere else! I don't want any bums here! Come back when you have a job!"

Now I had to find a work. For a few nights I slept in my car. My mother didn't mess around!

During this time I worked at different jobs. I even went into an apprenticeship as a painter, but it didn't last too long. I was working at one of the tall college buildings on South Tenth Street that had just been built. We were painting the rooms in the dormitory. The old men I worked with were all alcoholics. They told me, "Hey, boy, do you like what you see in front of you? That's what you're going to see the rest of your life. You'll get out of this trade if you're smart. All the colors are going to look the same in a few years." With all that discouragement, I had to find another job.

My friend Art and I met two sisters. He married one, and I married the other one. Despite being married, I still liked to get loaded on marijuana and go out with my friends. I was hard to get along with when I was young, had a bad temper, and became angry very easily. It was difficult being married when I still needed to grow up. I still loved doing things I shouldn't have been doing, even though I was a married man. Or should I say, a married boy?

I couldn't keep away from my friends and was having a very hard time. We lived off of Thirteenth Street, a block away from Hedding by the North Side Market. It was a street called Horning, a small place where we only paid $18 dollars a week. The living room was the bedroom; one hardly had room to get around the bed. The kitchen was very small. The largest room in the place was the bathroom. I think ten people could take a shower at once.

At that time I found a job at Owens-Illinois on Campbell Avenue off of Newhall Street. I worked as a lineman at Owens-Illinois for three months. The pay wasn't that great, like all the other jobs I was getting at that time. The company made plastic bottles for businesses like Clorox. I made sure the people who worked at their machines had everything they needed: bottle caps, labels, and boxes.

On one line there was a girl whom I supplied. Cathy was pretty and had a good shape. I never talked to her on a personal level. She yelled out like everybody else and asked for whatever she needed. Or if she ran short of something on her line, I made sure she received it. She never spoke to me more than she had to because a few of the guys and I gave her a hard time during lunch.

At lunch the other guys and I liked to hold up the big outside wall, standing there trying to look bad. The company had some picnic tables outside for the employees. We stood up against the wall, waiting for the girls to walk by. When everybody was out, we sat on the tables to eat our lunch. We loved it when Cathy walked by us. She walked as if she were moving her body parts on purpose. I learned later it was just her natural movement.

"Hey, man," one of the guys said. "Here she comes!" All of us prepared to watch her walk by us. As she started to approach, we began, "Hey, baby! Come over here! Chula, honey! Mama, Mama baby! Come over here, baby!" We were slobs, but we didn't care. We loved it! This went on whenever she came out for lunch, and we also waited for her to return after lunch. It looked as if Cathy didn't care what we did. Cathy always ignored us anyway.

One day after eating our lunch, we were waiting to go back to work, holding up the wall. She was in her car. All of the guys were standing there, watching to see when she was going to start approaching. We saw her get out of her car and start walking our way. One of the guys said, "Here comes the chula!"

Another responded, "Hey, man, did you guys know she is a very religious person?" I felt my heart fall to my feet.

"What?" I asked shamefully. Instantly I thought back to somebody I had cared about, Mr. Gorman.

"Yeah, man, she's really devoted to her religion. She was talking to one of the other girls about it the other day."

I couldn't believe my ears. All this time I was mocking someone who was devoted to her religion. I looked over in Cathy's direction, and there she was walking toward us. I now viewed her in a different light.

"Hey, man." I took a step away from the wall and looked at all the guys in a very serious way. "Nobody tells her anything, man!"

"Hey, Art, what's wrong with you?" onc of the guys questioned.

"Hey, if anybody tells her anything, whoever says anything, I'm going to get down with him!" They all looked at me as if I were crazy. She walked down the sidewalk, and no one said anything. Everybody was quiet. I think she thought it strange no one made any comments to her.

We went back to work. I worked really hard to catch up with all the lines, so I could go talk with Cathy a few minutes. I wanted to find out who she was and wanted to apologize for the way I always made comments to her. I finally talked to her. She was a really pleasant person, and she accepted my apology. She said she and her husband wanted to come by my house to talk to me.

In a few days they came over and talked about their religion for a while. It all sounded good. The last time I really talked about religious subjects was in Preston with Mr. Gorman. I really didn't listen to what he was teaching me, but I knew he was sharing information that was good for me.

Cathy and her husband made arrangements to return to talk with me again, but things didn't work out.

Two nights later I went out with my friends. We were at a gas station and ended up in a fight with some guy who thought he was tough because he had just returned from Vietnam. We beat him up. The next day the newspaper turned the facts around; they said we beat him up for nothing. He was the one who started swinging first. Now the police were looking for us. In addition to this I had a big fight with my wife. It was time to leave San Jose; therefore, I moved to Wilmington with my uncles. This was the only way I'd keep out of trouble.

I did a little better upon moving to Wilmington. I found a job at American Can Company. My father had worked for this company for twenty years in San Jose. Even though I was working and I was with my uncles, drugs were still a big problem in my life. There wasn't a boring day in Wilmington.

REDONDO BEACH

One day Uncle Ray asked me, "Art, do you want to go to the beach with us?"

"Who's going, Uncle Ray?" My uncles and aunts were only about four or five years older than I was. We were close in age, but I always showed them respect and called them uncle and aunt.

"Just your aunt Connie, our kids, and me."

"Sure, I haven't been to the beach for a long time."

This was in late spring, and the weather was just starting to get warm. We arrived at Redondo Beach about 1:00 p.m. As I was getting out of the car, I stood on the sidewalk next to the beach thinking back to the last time I was at Redondo. I went swimming far out into the ocean and was almost swept away. I now realized I'd better be careful.

It was getting warmer as the afternoon passed. The beach was crowded with people. I walked out on the sand with no shoes; it burned my feet. We put our blankets out and made ourselves comfortable.

After sitting there for a while, my nieces were playing in the sand. Uncle Ray asked me, "Hey, Art, are you going in the water?" I had my swimming trunks on and was ready for my first swim. I was well-built and wore a goatee. I loved to go in the water to swim, often swimming out in the ocean until no one could see me. As I sat there and looked at all the pretty girls, I thought about what I had to do to make this look cool.

"Yeah, Uncle Ray. I'll be back in a little while."

As I was walking away, Aunt Connie called out, "Art, don't go out so far!" I didn't know why she told me that. She knew I could swim.

The water looked refreshing. I saw a big wave coming in from far away and wanted to catch it; therefore, I picked up my pace, running a little faster toward the water. The wave was picking up speed. As I a jogged toward the breaking waves, I passed some pretty girls sitting near the water and threw them my cool smile. The wave was almost at the beach. When I was a good 20 feet away from the water, I ran hard the rest of the way. "I'll catch that wave!"

I picked up a little more speed. My feet hit the water. The water was cool. The wave became higher as it was nearing the shore. It looked as if it were about 5 feet high. I imagined diving into the cool water, and how refreshing it was going to feel. Now was the time. I jumped from the sand and dove into the wave. At that instant the wave came over, down, and fell on the sand! Within a half second it went from 5 feet to 1 foot high. My dive was like one you would take into a pool, head first, 1 foot deep. My head smashed on the sand.

I found myself sitting on the beach, seeing stars and little lights all around. The waves were banging against me as I sat there trying to recover. People were all around, and none of them noticed I hit the sand the way I did. None of them came over to see how I was. They must have thought I was sitting there having fun as the waves were hitting me. They didn't know I took a crash dive!

Five minutes later the stars and lights stopped. I stood up, still feeling a little dizzy. I touched the top of my head, and it felt numb. I walked back up to where Uncle Ray and Aunt Connie were and sat on the blanket.

"Hey, Art, that was a quick swim. What happened; you didn't like the water?" Uncle Ray asked.

"No, I crashed into the sand," I explained.

"What do you mean you crashed in the sand?" My uncle sat up to hear the story.

"Yeah, I ran and dove into a big wave. When the wave came in, I dove; but there was no water. You know, like they show in the cartoons. Except I didn't get stuck upside down in the sand!" Uncle Ray couldn't stop laughing. I couldn't laugh because it started to hurt right on the top of my head.

"Art, tell me again how it happened?" Ray continued to laugh. I still didn't think it was that funny.

I lay on the blanket for about an hour with a headache. Finally I sat up. As I felt the top of my head, I said, "Hey, Uncle Ray, feel this." I took his hand and lifted it up, moving it back and forth on the top of my head.

"Wow, Art, I think you broke your head. It feels soft." The top of my head felt spongy. "We better take you to the doctor right away," my uncle said. I looked at my aunt as she woke from her nap.

"What do you think, Aunt Connie?" I asked.

My uncle turned to my aunt and said, "Feel his head, Connie. What do you think?"

My aunt stood up and extended her hand to my head and felt, "Art! How did you say you did that?"

I explained once more.

We picked up all of our things. They thought it was important to take me to the hospital right away. They didn't want anything to happen to me, fearing I might die on the beach or on the way home. In the little time it took for us to prepare to leave, my head pain became worse.

Arriving at the hospital, we had to wait for a little while to see the doctor. We waited in the small examining room. "What happened?" he asked, looking down at his chart. "It looks as if you had an injury on the beach."

"Yeah, I dove in the water at the beach, my head hit the sand, and my head feels like it's swelling up."

"Yes, we will make sure everything is all right," the doctor said, raising his hand and feeling my neck.

I thought to myself, "Why is he feeling my neck?"

"Well," the doctor said, "we are going to take X-rays of your neck."

Now I thought to myself, "This dumb doctor didn't even look at my head!"

"Hey, doctor," I said as he was leaving the room, "my neck is OK." I moved my neck around. "It's my head. There's something wrong with it. Look." I brought my head down and pointed to it.

The doctor stepped back in the room to explain it to me, "Well, you see, most accidents that happen at the beach, such as yours, cause injury to the spinal cord, not to your head. So we want to make sure your spinal cord isn't injured." He left the room, not letting me tell him again that my neck was all right. The doctor took my X-ray, and it came out fine. We went home feeling we had wasted our time.

When I arrived home at my uncle and aunt's house, I went to bed hoping I'd be all right. I woke up the next morning and felt odd. Something wasn't right. I sat up on my bed and felt my head. "Wow!" I said in low voice as I jumped out of bed and walked toward the bathroom. As I entered the bathroom, I looked in the mirror and couldn't believe what I saw. Right at my hair line, my scalp rose one-and-a-half inches. Not in a gradual way—there was a ridge. It looked as if I were wearing a hat.

I walked into the kitchen where I heard my uncle and aunt. "Hey, Uncle Ray!" I didn't have to say another word.

When they looked up and saw me, they both said at the same time, "WOW!"

My aunt continued, "You'd better go to the hospital!"

Since I didn't have a doctor of my own and didn't know where to go, I went to the county hospital where I waited about four hours to see the doctor. Everybody who walked by me in the large waiting room stared at me. They probably thought I had cancer of the scalp. Finally the nurse called my name to see the doctor. She took me to the small examining room and asked what happened. "Oh, that sounds terrible," she said as she left the room. Shortly, the doctor entered the room.

"What happened to you?" Again I had to explain the story. I was getting tired of telling everybody the same details. The doctor looked at me, and guess what he did? That's right. He felt my neck.

"How does this feel?" he asked.

"It feels fine. Yesterday another doctor took X-rays of my neck, and he said it was all right," I told him.

"Well, we're going to take another X-ray of the same area just to make sure everything checks out."

"Look, Doctor, I already had an X-ray of my neck. My neck is OK. Look." I moved my head in all directions and stretched it up. I continued, "Nothing is wrong with my neck. It's my head. Look!" I pointed to my head once again.

"Well, I'd feel much safer if we had a picture of your neck."

I was starting to feel angry. "I don't want a picture of my neck. Do you understand? I want you to check out my head!"

The doctor stood and looked at me wondering why I was getting so upset. "Look, I'm the doctor; and you are the patient. OK?" he said as he walked out of the room.

He didn't even examine my head as I repeatedly requested. Forget this. I stepped off the examining table and walked out. On the way home I hoped the swelling on my head would go down by the next day since they didn't think anything was wrong.

I woke up the next morning and felt odd again. Jumping out of bed, I ran to the bathroom and looked in the mirror. I couldn't believe it. The ridge had moved down to my eyebrows. Man, I looked like a monster. My eyebrows were one-and-a-half inches higher than they were supposed to be. My whole head looked like a big beach ball.

My uncle decided to take me to a small clinic in Wilmington on the corner of Avalon and Anaheim. It was a private clinic that was supposed to cost more than my insurance would pay, but I didn't care. If they would take care of me, I was willing to pay whatever it cost. I walked into the waiting room and up to the counter. "What happened to you?" the receptionist asked.

Man, do I have to go through this another time? After explaining it to her, she took me to an examining room. I didn't have to wait at this place. As soon as the receptionist walked out and closed the door, there was a knock at the door. The doctor walked in. He must have been waiting for a patient.

"What happened?"

I was really getting tired of telling the same story. He was different from the other doctors, very young, almost my age.

"Look, Doctor, I want you to check my head. I've been to two other doctors, and both of them wanted to check my neck. There's nothing wrong with my neck."

"Well, you know, this is where injuries occur, in the neck. I want to see for myself, so I'm going to take some X-rays again," he said. I couldn't believe what I just heard.

"I don't want X-rays of my neck. I want you to check out my head! LOOK!" I pointed to it again.

"I'm sorry, but I have to . . ."

"Forget it, man!" I stood up and stormed out of the room. As I was walking out of the office, someone came in and stopped to look at me, "What happened to your head?" he asked.

The next morning when I woke up, I again went straight to the mirror. What did I see? A monster! That's right. I looked like a monster! The swelling came down my face. My nose was about two inches thick, and the swelling made my eyes look like a cross-eyed dragonfly.

During this time I would go to work and sit with the guys while having coffee and donuts. On this morning I walked into the large cafeteria at American Can Company. I saw the guys sitting at a table talking and having their coffee. I bought my coffee and donut, went to their table, sat on one of the chairs, and started to add sugar to my coffee.

One of the guys looked over at me and then at one of the other guys, nodding his head at the same time, as if he were asking who I was.

I looked over the table at him and said, "Hey, how's it going?" He just sat there and shook his head, acknowledging my remark. They were talking about something; I interrupted and gave my opinion. They all stopped talking and just sat there staring at me.

After awhile one of them said, "Art, is that you?"

"Yeah, it's me. What do you think?" They wanted to know what happened to me. When I told them, they all started laughing and wanted me to tell the story to everyone who entered the cafeteria. Most of the guys I worked with were a little older than I. After a little while I became angry and started my job fifteen minutes early.

It took forever for the swelling to come down, and my face stayed black and blue for months. I was never given a medical reason for the physical effects this injury caused to my head.

Changes

When I was living in LA away from my friends, things started to get better for me. It was helping me to get my life together. I still got loaded on marijuana every day, all day long; I was still having a hard time controlling my temper.

Some people came to my small apartment to visit me. They talked about their religion, and I let them preach all they wanted. I knew one day I was going to have to make some big changes in my life.

I smoked pot with Sal at work on a regular basis. I told him that when my children grow up, they were going to be able to get loaded on pot all they wanted.

One day I made up my mind it was time to make big changes in my life. I was wondering how I was going to do it. First I thought changes could be made gradually. Then I decided if I made these changes, I would to have to do it all at once.

The next day I was working on my line, forking cans. American Can Company was a noisy place. I worked in the warehouse. The cans were made in the factory and went through rail lines overhead, bouncing and hitting one another and making a lot of noise. The cans fell down a shoot to my line where I used a giant fork, to fork cans into boxes. I was forking when I saw Sal drive up on his forklift.

Parking his forklift not too far from where I was, he hopped off, walked to where I was working, and said, "Hey, Art, come to my car at lunch time, man. I have this good stuff from Columbia. Good stuff, man!" I stopped forking and turned toward Sal. I wondered what he would say when I gave him the bad news.

"Hey, Sal, I can't go to your car, man."

"Why not?"

"Well, man, I don't get loaded anymore."

He stood there trying to figure this out. He looked at me as if he didn't hear me right. He didn't say anything for a couple of seconds. Then he finally replied, "What do you mean you don't get loaded any more? You got loaded yesterday."

I thought, "He's right. He's probably wondering what happened to me this morning when I didn't show up to get loaded with him at six as we had planned."

Then I answered him, "Well, Sal, I decided I'm going to stop getting loaded. Hey, man, we get loaded in the morning, for lunch, when we go home, and then before going to bed. I know if I want my life to be a good life, I need to make some changes, man. So like I said, Sal, this is it."

Sal stood looking at me, putting his thoughts together. He asked, "What about your kids, ese. Aren't you going to let them get loaded?"

At this point in my life, things started changing. I had a full-time job, and I started to change my thinking about what was right and wrong. What a difference compared to my younger days. I still had a big problem with my temper. It took me a while to gain control of it. If I didn't take control of it soon, I was going to end up back in jail for knocking someone's head off. I might even be killed for blowing up and losing my temper so fast.

THE DEAL

    I lived in Long Beach, the next city over from Wilmington, in a nice apartment building on Chestnut Street, ten blocks from the beach. The American Can Company was about ten miles away. I could afford to live in these nice apartments because my pay was reasonable. I brought home, after taxes, $103 for forty hours of work a week. Actually $103 was good money in those days.

    One Saturday morning I got up early to take my battery for charging at the gas station down the street. The day before I had to have it jumped in the morning, and then one of the guys gave me a jump in order to get home. I figured my battery wasn't any good, since I had never bought one; but I wanted to give it one last full charge at the gas station.

    I had no one to give me a ride to the station, and the battery was too heavy to carry. An idea crossed my mind. I had a push-type lawn mower. Turning it around, I put the battery on its back. I started my walk to the gas station, pushing my mower with my battery on it. It was about 7:00 a.m., and nobody was up and about in the street at that time.

    As I was pushing my battery minding my own business, some guy pulled up next to me. I didn't stop but kept pushing. I had about six blocks to go before arriving at the gas station. He had his passenger window open and moved about two or three miles per hour, just enough to stay up with me.

"Hey, Buddy, come here. I have a deal for you!" he said with a Brooklyn accent.

At American Can Company I was paid once a wcck. After paying my bills for the week, I had about $40 in my pocket.

"I don't need anything, man," I said sarcastically. In the LA area everybody ran a scam, trying to sell watches, rings, or something.

He was driving his car next to the curb and leaned over my way. "Hey, buddy, I work for a high-priced store in LA; and I'm delivering these sweaters. They gave me too many, and I have to get rid of them before I go back. So just look at them. They're cheap!"

I stopped pushing and looked over at him. Putting the handle of the lawn mower down and walking up to his car, I reached for one of the boxes of sweaters.

"What do you have?" I asked. Then I thought, "What is it going to hurt to look?"

His car came to a halt, and he seemed delighted he had stopped me. He probably thought I was a fish and that he had me hooked. He wanted to sell me the sweaters for $80 each. It was strange that the price tag was inside the wrapped box. He said the sweaters were well made, and I was going to get a fantastic deal.

"You can keep or sell them and make a little money for yourself."

"How much do you want for them?"

I really didn't want the sweaters; but if I could make a buck from them, I didn't mind.

"I'll take $100, and you can have both of them!"

I put the box back in his car, turned, and walked back to my lawn mower.

"Hey, kid, come back here! You tell me what you want to pay for them. You have the advantage because I can't take them back with me!"

I was pushing the lawn mower again and reasoning at the same time. I thought, "If he's that desperate, he'll take what I want to give him. This guy's dumb, man! He shouldn't have told me he had to sell them!"

"Hey, I'll give you 20 bucks for both of them?"

"I can't do that. How about $80?"

"I don't even have $80," I answered.

He gave a sigh and said, "How much do you have?"

"I only have $40, but I need this money."

"Hey, kid," he continued with a convincing look on his face, "you can make money with these sweaters. You can sell them to one of your friends, and you'll come out doubling your money."

I thought to myself, "He's right. Those sweaters look nice, and they have a big price inside of the package." I stopped walking and put the lawn mower handle down on the ground again. I walked up to his car window.

"Let's see them. Are you sure they're good sweaters? They're not junk, are they?"

"Hey, buddy, just look at them. You can tell they're not junk." He had a good point. They sure looked like quality sweaters.

"Look, I have to get my battery charged; and I need a little gas. So I'll give you $35. Take it or leave it!"

"All right, kid. I'm going to do you a favor. I'll take the $35."

I bought the sweaters and took them to work. One friend at work liked them but didn't have enough money. He had an almost-new leather jacket he bought a few weeks before, which he brought to work to show off. I talked him into trading his jacket for my sweater. One week later he came to work and was steaming.

"Art, that sweater was junk," he said as he walked up to me.

"What do you mean 'was'?"

"Yeah. I washed it, and it disappeared," he said.

I looked at him as if he were crazy for washing it and replied, "You washed it in your washing machine?"

Shaking his head, he vented, "No, I washed it by hand; and it fell apart in a second."

"Hey, you weren't supposed to wash it."

He looked at me as if it was my fault and said, "What was I supposed to do? The label said, 'DO NOT MACHINE WASH, DO NOT DRY CLEAN, DO NOT VACUUM, DO NOT WET!'"

As I walked away from him, I replied, "That's your fault for not following instructions!"

I sold the other sweater to another guy at work for $45. He made the sweater last. He only wore it twice because he felt it was too nice to wear all the time.

One day I was sitting in my living room on a Saturday morning when the telephone rang. "Mijo, how are you?"

"Dad, where are you?"

"I'm here in San Gabriel." San Gabriel was about thirty-five minutes from Long Beach. "Come and see me, mijo. I'll only be here two or three days."

It was nice to hear my father's voice. It didn't sound the same as when I was a youngster and when he yelled at me, "ARTURO!"

When I was young, I remember wishing my father was like other fathers, someone I could talk to and be with, without getting into trouble. A natural love, I guess you'd call it.

"I'll go, Dad. Give me the address where you're at."

I went to see my father. He had married a girl from Mexico who was about the same age as my brother Eddie. Her name was Angelita, and she was the youngest of her family. Her mother lived there in San Gabriel with another daughter and a son-in-law. Angelita's mother had 23 kids, and all were alive and doing fine. She looked good for having so many children.

From this time on my father went to LA every three or four months. When he was in area, I traveled to where he stayed. Sometimes he visited me at my apartment. We started getting close.

When my father and mother were divorced, my father took his share of money from selling the little house; he went to Mexicali where he set up a drug store. Tio Jorge had his doctor's office next door. Tio would write prescriptions and send his patients to my father's drug store to have them filled.

Because my father liked to go on trips all over Mexico and spend money, he wasn't doing very well in his business. He also bought and sold diamonds. The man in charge of his store let the business go down; he wasn't taking care of it. My father thought he also stole some of his diamonds.

By the time my father went to the LA area to visit his wife's family and me, he had lost his store in a fire. He started selling other things. My father liked to spend money; he made it fast and spent it fast, by the thousands.

I received a call to pick up my father. He was in San Gabriel and wanted me to go along with him to handle some of his business. "OK, Dad, I'll be right over."

As time passed, I grew to know my father better. When I was young, I thought he didn't care for me. But now I knew he loved me. It was his hard personality that made him the way he was. My father, through the years, forgave us kids when we became upset with him or if he became upset with us. During those times he let it go over his head. And believe me, he didn't do that for everybody, not even his mother. About eight years before my grandmother Luzita in Mexico died from old age, my father became angry and stopped speaking to her. When she died, he went to her funeral and paid for everything. He cried for her very much. Again it was his hard personality. He loved his mother a lot. It was just the way my father was. Once his brother, the doctor, angered him; my father didn't speak to him for seven years.

I remember visiting my tio Jorge. When my father's name came up, he looked really sad and said of my father, "Ay, Jose. He's always been this way, even when he was a boy." My father's family in Mexico loved him and tried to understand him.

I found my father in San Gabriel. "Arthur, let's first go to LA and see if I can do business. I need money. I spent all my money in a little town in Mexico."

When my father said he spent all his money in a little town, I knew what he meant. He probably went to the little town, threw a party, bought drinks, and paid for mariachi music for everybody. He would spend hundreds in just a few minutes.

When we arrived in downtown LA, he told me which way to turn, since I didn't know my way around at the time. We were on a street that had nothing but wholesale stores. I stepped out of the car, noticing some of the stores had a guard standing outside to keep the public from entering.

"Dad, why do they have the guards standing there?" I asked. It seemed to me they would want people to enter and to buy all their merchandise.

"Because all the people will want to go in and want to buy things."

"Isn't that what they want, people to buy things?" I asked.

"These stores don't want to sell one thing at a time. People can go in only if they have a wholesale license. You have to buy not one thing at a time, but hundreds or thousands. Sometimes if they know you, you can buy a few things only."

As we walked down the sidewalk, my father pointed to the store we were going to enter. The first store we walked into, everybody knew my father. They knew him by the nickname Pepe.

"Hi, Pepe!" shouted a man who was helping someone else.

The man behind the counter said, "Pepe, how are you? I haven't seen you for a few weeks. Where have you been?"

My dad stood there with his hand pulling his hair back from his face as he said, "I was in Mexico doing business, John. How have you been?"

"I'm fine. Did you move all the merchandise you picked up the last time you were here?" the man asked curiously.

"Oh yes, the same day. What do you have now, John? Anything different?"

"No, the same things I had the last time you were here. I'll be getting some new things in, maybe in about a week. A ship will be coming in."

"OK, John, we'll be back then."

The other man waved at us as we walked out the door. Once outside my father said, "I only buy from him when I have to, only if he really has something good. Now we'll go and see my friend Max."

We entered the next store, and Max was really excited to see my father. He acted as if my father was his family. "Pepe! How good it is to see you," he said as he gave my father a hug and patted his back. Max continued, "When did you get in?"

While my father told Max what he had been doing and when he arrived from Mexico, I turned my head and looked around. There were racks and racks of clothes, as well as boxes and boxes of merchandise all over the place. To me it looked like a mess. Some things were set up very organized, and other things were stacked any old way.

"Max, this is my son Arthur. He lives in Long Beach."

I was going to shake Max's hand, but he stepped up to me and gave me a hug, as if I was his long-lost cousin. "I heard of you, Arthur. Your father told me about you. He's proud of you."

My father was proud of me? I always had the impression he didn't love me. Maybe I was always wrong. My father gave me a look of approval. A second later he turned his attention to Max.

"Max, what do you have?" Just as he said that, I looked over to the back of the store.

"What's that?" I asked myself, as I caught sight of something I thought I recognized. Walking to the back, I saw hundreds and hundreds of boxes stacked against the back wall. I continued walking toward the boxes.

Once I was a few steps from where I left my father, he noticed the direction I was walking and said, "Arthur! Don't go back there! That's where Max keeps his junk."

Max spoke as soon as my father was done, saying, "No, no, don't go over there. Only the scam artists go over there." I didn't stop. I had to see for myself if it was what I thought.

I picked up one of the boxes and couldn't believe it—the $80 sweaters, hundreds of them. The guy with the Brooklyn accent said they came from a high-priced store. "Max, how much are these boxes?" I remembered I paid $35 for two.

"Oh, no Arthur! You don't want those. They're junk. Come back over here."

My father said, "Arthur, come over here, mijo; you don't want that junk."

"I don't want it. I just want to know what it costs."

Max looked up at me with his glasses at the end of his nose. Tilting his head forward a little to take a good look at what I had in my hand, he said, "Those are $1.50; but if you buy a lot of them, I'll give you a better price." $1.50. I paid $35 for two boxes of the sweaters. I even burned my friends at work by selling them these dumb sweaters.

I walked back to the counter, still not believing I had been burned for so much money. In those days $35 was a lot of money. As I was thinking about this, I noticed some merchandise behind the counter, "The Famous Six Perfumes, As Advertised On The Johnny Carson Show." The price inside the package was $60.

I stood there waiting for my father and Max to stop talking, "Hey, Max, how much are these perfumes?"

"Now that's a good deal, $1.50. Those are good; they just came in on a ship. I have a lot of them." I bought 15 to see if I could sell "The Famous Six Perfumes."

"Oh, Pepe, I received these the other day. I don't know if

you're interested." Max took out a small box. The outside looked nice. In red with big letters, "Tiffany" was written on the front of the box. It was black, and it looked as if it was made of leather. He opened the front. It opened with two doors in front, and inside the box was lined with red velvet. It contained in the top corner a small bottle of perfume, in the opposite corner a bottle of women's cologne. On the other corners were two small bars of nicely shaped perfumed soap. My father reached for it.

Holding it, he asked Max, "How much do you want for this, and how many do you have?"

Scratching the back of his head, Max said, "I want $3 each for them, and I have 5,000."

"OK, Max, I'll take them. I'll have a boy come and pick them up in a few days. Let me have about three for samples," my father said.

That was fast. My father must have known what he was doing.

We left the store, and my father directed me to the Alexandra Hotel in downtown Los Angeles. On the way my father was telling me that all he came with on this trip was one $100 bill. That's all he had, and he had to make money fast. "I need money," he said. "So today I'm going to work."

The Alexandra was a first-class hotel. It had a boxing ring, and they held world championship fights there. We went into the lounge and walked to the bar. The lounge was very nice. There was a small stage for a band that played at night. At the other end of the lounge, there was a man and a woman having a drink at one of the tables. Besides them, the only other person in the lounge was the bartender. It was dark. The bartender was doing something when we sat on stools at the bar. He looked up at us. When he saw it was my father, he raised his arms up in the air and became excited.

As he walked toward us, he said with a Mexican accent, "Pepe! It's good to see you! How have you been my friend? My good friend!"

"I'm fine, Beto. I'll only be down for a few days."

"Come and stay at my house, Pepe!"

I sat there on the bar stool. Everybody knew my father, and they all treated him like family.

"Beto, this is my son, Arthur."

Beto looked at me and extended his hand out to shake mine. As he was shaking my hand, he said, "You know, your father is number one around here. He's good to everybody, you know. He helped me out a lot."

My father ordered a drink, and I ordered a Coke. Just then a group of men wearing suits walked into the lounge. I turned and looked at them. One of them glanced our way and said loudly, "Pepe! Hey, Pepe's here!" They all came over excitedly and gave my father hugs. I couldn't believe all these people were my father's friends. He told me on his last visit that his friends were important people, but I thought it was all talk. My father was introducing me to all the men. He stopped by one of them and asked me if I knew who he was.

"Mijo, do you know who he is?"

I looked at the guy, but I had no idea who he was. "No," I said.

Everybody started laughing, and my father asked, "Don't you watch boxing, mijo?"

"Yeah, I always do," I said hesitantly.

"This is Mando Ramos, the world champion!" my father said and laughed with everybody else. He took out his only $100 bill and put it on the bar. "Beto," my father motioned him with his hand, "come here."

"Yeah, Pepe?"

"Here's my $100 bill. Drinks for everybody. Let me know when it's gone, and don't forget to take your tip out of there," he said, pointing to the money.

Beto moved close to my father and put his hand on my father's arm. He said, "Pepe, you don't have to leave me a tip. You have given me enough tips to last a lifetime." In those days $100 was a lot of money.

My father was talking to one of the men sitting next to him about some people they knew and what happened to them. I was just sitting there not talking to anybody, thinking. If my father called this work, this was the kind of work I wanted to find. Then I saw my father reach into his bag. He pulled out a box of Tiffany perfume and handed it to the man.

"This is nice, Pepe. How much do you want for it, and how many do you have?" the man asked as he opened the box to look inside.

"I have 5,000, and I want $5 for each of them."

"Good, I'll take them. I think I can move them."

My father didn't look as if he were excited or anything. "OK, I'll have a boy deliver them to your store in Pasadena tomorrow." And that was it. What a quick deal! I couldn't believe my father made so much money so fast. He didn't even handle the stuff. When we left the bar, my father said he was done working for a couple of months.

I took my "Famous Six Perfumes" to work and sold them in half an hour at lunch. I went back to Max's store repeatedly to buy different things—from sports coats and bath oils to more perfumes and other things. I made a lot of side money and hoped I wouldn't have to work at American Can Company all my life—if I could only do well in sales and be like my father.

I was planning to have an easy job and not work hard. As I watched big trucks go by, I thought to myself, "Someday that's going to be the kind of job I'm going to have."

As time went on, I had to move back to San Jose. My mother was having a hard time with her home on Emory Street. She moved back to Virginia Place and rented the Emory house. The people on Emory were tearing up the place, and she couldn't afford to fix it; therefore, my mother was losing it. The renters who lived there weren't paying the rent, and my mother couldn't make the payments.

Back in Wilmington the American Can Company was preparing for a long strike with the union. The company rented a big warehouse and was stocking up on cans, anticipating a long strike.

My mother called and asked me, "Arthur, if you want the house on Emory Street, you can have it; but you have to come back to San Jose, take it out of foreclosure, and fix it up." It sounded good to me. My life was straightened out enough now that I felt I could handle it.

A NEW LIFE

I made the big move back to San Jose and lived with my mother while I fixed up the Emory Street house. I had no experience in construction repairs, but I had the best help I could get. My mother's sister, Aunt Anabel, was married to Uncle Bob. Uncle Bob went to the house on Emory Street everyday to help me. Because of water damage which occurred, all the ceilings had to be replaced. The San Jose Municipal Airport was just a few blocks away, and the house was under the landing pattern for airplanes. Every time the big airplanes went over the house, the walls vibrated and loosened the ceilings even more.

When I was about five or six years old and living on Spencer Street, Uncle Bob and Aunt Anabel lived in a trailer in our driveway. My uncle was in the Navy and was assigned to the military police. He came home for lunch, and we waited for him to see the criminals in the back of his paddy wagon.

I watched him pull up and would say, "Hi, Uncle Bob."

"Hi, Arthur. How are you today?"

"Do you have any bad guys today?"

"Not today, Arthur, maybe tomorrow." I still didn't believe him, so I made sure he was telling the truth. As soon as he walked down the long driveway to his trailer to have lunch, I snuck up to the paddy wagon. I was very careful, so the bad guys wouldn't see me. It turned out he never had any bad guys.

Later my uncle and aunt moved out of the trailer and bought a house. When I was a little guy, I spent some nights at their home. Almost every time I went, I was hurt while playing; and my uncle and aunt had to rush me to emergency. They always treated us well and were always ready to help anybody with anything they could. They were such good people, they even had my troubled uncle Joe live with them, trying to help him straighten out his life. He gave them a lot of grief.

When I moved to San Jose, we started to fix up the house. As soon as he was off work, he came to Emory Street with his tools and began working. Some days I really didn't want to work on the house, and I drove there hoping my uncle didn't show up. I would be able to take a day off. However, he never missed. I really appreciated all the help he gave me.

Once the work on the house was completed, I moved in and lived there for a few years. My second son Daniel was born during the time I lived on Emory Street.

I started working in different places, but I didn't like the low-paying jobs I was getting. I finally found a job at Owens Corning Fiberglass in Santa Clara. It paid a lot better than my other jobs. I worked rotating shifts, seven days a week, two days off, and then changed shifts. I'd work another seven days, have two days off, and again change shifts. Sometimes I didn't know if I was coming or going.

I was at Fiberglass for five years, trying to take care of my family. One day a job opening came up for a truck driver with the company. This was something I wanted to do. One of my dreams finally came true, having an easy job driving a truck. I drove the Fiberglass truck to the dump. The company had its own truck that took its own rubbish to their landfill.

Everyday I had to drive to the dump at 4 a.m. One morning I went to work and started up the truck as I did every morning. I drove out of the premises to the dump. Lafayette Street was a small country road, one lane going and one lane coming. Most mornings in the winter months, the fog rolled in. I drove the truck through the fog and had to be careful because it was thick. Since my truck was a big rig, the fog reached as high as my windshield. For me there wasn't any visibility problem as I drove. The cars traveled slowly, engulfed in the fog. I came along and saw them, moving at a slow speed. I shot by them, moving a lot faster than the slow-moving cars. They probably thought I was crazy moving so fast. From their view everything was in the fog. I passed car-after-car all the way up Lafayette Street.

On this particular morning as I arrived at the dump in Alviso, everything was quiet and still. The fog was so thick I had to feel for the gate to unlock it. I could only tell where I parked my truck from the sound of the diesel engine. Once the gate was unlocked, I climbed back in my truck and headed up the hill to the dumping area.

The hill was formed from years of trash which had been brought to the landfill. When my truck climbed the hill, I was out of the fog. I backed up the truck and the 40-foot trailer to the area the trash was to be dumped. Stepping off the truck and walking to the back of the trailer, I stood there a minute to look around. I liked to do this in the mornings, to look over all the fog and see the lights all the way from San Jose. It was a beautiful view.

I turned and reached for the handle to open the large back door to the trailer. The handle was horizontal, about nose level. I pulled on the handle, but it wouldn't open. I pulled on it again with all my might. It wouldn't budge because of the pressure from within. All the garbage was pushing against the back door of the trailer. I tried again, and it still wouldn't open. Something more was wrong with it. It must be bent somewhere. I had told one of the mechanics at the plant a couple of days before that the door was harder to open.

I looked around for something, such as a two-by-four or a bar that might be lying around. I saw a board and picked it up. "This will work," I said, talking to myself. I stuck the board behind the steel handle on the trailer and pulled hard, but it didn't open. I tried again. This time I pulled harder; my feet even left the ground. All of a sudden the steel handle popped opened. It happened so fast I didn't know what hit me. It struck me right on the nose!

The next thing I knew, I was 15 feet away from the trailer, rolling around, moaning in pain and lying on the ground full of blood! I stayed on the ground for the longest time.

Before the pain started to subside, I looked around. The engine of the truck was running. The door to the truck was open, and trash was falling out of the back of the trailer. This meant I couldn't just get up, close the door, and drive back to the plant. It was a big job to open the door the rest of the way. I had to hook up an air line from the truck and hook an air gun to a chain to lift the door in order to dump it. Usually it took around twenty minutes to dump the trailer. I didn't know what I was going to do. There were no telephones out here and no two-way radio in the truck. My nose was still bleeding. Every time I tried to get up from the ground, it started to hurt and bleed. What the heck! I figured I would just stay on the ground until the guy who worked there started his shift at 8 a. m.

I lay there for two hours. If I didn't move, my nose didn't hurt. Time passed, I got comfortable, and I waited. The sun came up from over the hill where I was lying. I couldn't believe the view, the marshes looked beautiful—all green grass for miles. While I lay there, I saw the fog clear up. I watched a poor rabbit get chased by three dogs for an hour. While one dog rested, the other dog did the chasing. Finally the rabbit tired. He was torn into pieces by all three dogs.

The blood on my face was drying. As long as I didn't move, my nose didn't bleed. The man who worked at the landfill arrived at 8 a.m. but didn't notice I was on the hill. He thought I had left and didn't close or lock the gate. I could see him from where I was. Since everything was so quiet, he should have been able to hear my truck's diesel engine. The injury was so painful; I couldn't yell out. Finally, he came up and took me to the hospital.

I worked at Fiberglass for five years. I then found another job driving a big diesel Mack truck with a set of doubles behind it. When I was hired for the job, the owner talked to me and asked, "Have you driven these kinds of trucks before?" The one truck at Fiberglass had a 13-speed road ranger transmission and was very easy to drive.

The trucks this guy owned were, well, I didn't know what they were. We were in his office. I answered, "Oh yeah! No problem. I can drive them easy. I've been driving for years. I can drive anything." Then he asked me if I knew how to drive his trucks with a certain type of transmission. I had no idea what he was talking about and didn't say anything. I acted as if I knew all about them. I felt I didn't lie; I just let him do the talking.

FIRST JOB

One summer day when I was eight years old and Eddie was ten, we were awakened early in the morning. "Edmundo, Arturo! Up!" We both got up not knowing what our father had in store for us. It was earlier than usual to get up and to work in the yard. He told us to make a sandwich for our lunch because we were going to work. Work? Where were we working? We had no idea what he planned for us. When we were ready, he told us to go and to wait for him in the car. Obeying his order, we sat in the car, not saying much because we were still half asleep.

My father stepped out of the front door, walked hurriedly to the car, and got in. He didn't say anything at first. Once we left Virginia Place, he started with his customary lecture on what a good worker should be. He told us when he was a young boy, his mother taught him to work. "If there was no work, my mother would get rice and beans, mix them together, and throw them on the ground. Then I had to separate them. If I didn't do it fast enough, my mother would whip me." My father explained his mother was the one who took the lead in raising the family since my grandfather was busy in his professions as a doctor and a lawyer.

My father was driving east on Mckee Road. We turned left on Capital Avenue. All this area was apricot orchards at the time. My father pulled the car over to the northeast corner. This was a country road with no sidewalks.

At first we didn't see a soul in sight. My father told us to get out of the car and follow him. As we got out, I scanned the orchard. The trees were full of apricots. I could see deep into the orchard where people were working. This was the direction my father was walking toward. When we approached the first workers who were walking with tall ladders to their new positions, my father asked, "Who is the foreman here?"

The man gazed down at Ed and me, and he hesitated for a second. I noticed there were no other young boys working in the orchard picking apricots. The man looked over in the other direction and pointed to a man moving some empty boxes. "Over there. The man who is holding the box and wearing the green shirt," the worker said as he started to climb his ladder, not wanting to waste time. He knew the heat of the day would soon start.

"Come on," my father said with his eyes fixed on the man with the green shirt.

We approached the foreman. He stopped what he was doing and looked at us. My father spoke first, "Hola, I need for my muchachos [boys] to work. I would like to leave them with you for the day, so they can learn what it's like to work for a living."

Just as the man was going to respond, my father pulled out a $10 bill. During this time $10 was a lot of money. The man's eyes fell on the bill, and my father continued, "I want a report at the end of the day when I pick them up. I want to know how they did and if they did a good job. And you don't have to pay them; they will work for free. I want them to learn how to trabajar como hombres [work like men]."

As my father was talking, the man's eyes looked down with the saddest expression I had ever seen. His eyes showed he felt sorry for us. He knew we had a strict father who was leaving us with complete strangers to teach us how to work. My father had already taught us how to work at home. Now he wanted us out in the real world. We knew if we didn't cooperate with the foreman, we would receive a whipping in the afternoon; and we didn't want that.

The man agreed and said he would supervise us. My father turned and told us he would return at 3:50 and that he had better get a good report from the foreman.

"Bueno. Muchachos, let's go. Have you ever picked apricots?"

the foreman asked, trying to sound pleasant.

"No," Eddie answered.

"Get that ladder, and you can pick from the low branches. Fill the buckets, and dump them in the box. For every box you fill, I'll pay you."

Ed and I looked at each other. Our father told the foreman not to pay us, but he was going to pay us anyway. "Thanks," we both said as we went for the ladder. The ladder was so tall, it alone was a job for us to handle.

During the day we worked really hard. We wanted the foreman to give our father a good report, plus we were making real money. At lunch we ate the food we brought. By 2:00 p.m. we had earned $2— not bad for two boys who didn't know how to pick apricots.

The lunch truck pulled into the orchard through a dirt road. Some of the workers stopped to eat a snack. Others continued in their work, wanting to make as much money as they could before quitting time. Eddie and I stopped working. We felt so tired, and we had earned $2. The last hour or so we played around, not really working. The foreman looked at us every so often; we hoped he wouldn't report this to our father. The lunch truck took our $2. We sat under a tree and snacked on the goodies we bought. By this time of the day, we were sick of eating apricots.

My father drove up right on time. We were worried the foreman was going to tell him we had been playing around in the afternoon. My father motioned for us to walk with him to where the foreman was standing.

As we approached our father, we said, "Hi, Dad." We knew if we didn't greet him, he would be very unhappy with us.

"Hola. How did my sons do today?" he asked, staring at the man with anticipation.

The foreman responded, looking down at us as if he were talking to us, "Tus muchachos did very well. They are good muchachos and good workers. They worked very hard all day without letting up."

Our father seemed pleased and said, "Then I will bring them back tomorrow."

Our hearts sank to our stomachs. We didn't like this job.

"Oh, I'm sorry, sir. But the owner of the orchard came out

today and asked about these young muchachos. He told me he did not want them to work by themselves. If you want to work with them, then it will be all right."

Our hearts rose back to where they were supposed to be. We knew our father would never accept these conditions. There were many youngsters working in the fields and orchards during this time, but they mostly worked alongside their parents and families. For many, working the fields was the entire family's livelihood.

When we got into the car and drove off, we knew we did all right. My father was in a pleasant mood. From that year on we worked the fields every summer.

* * *

"You have the job. You can start tomorrow," the owner of the trucking company said.

I was there at 6:45 a.m. and ready to go. The yard where the trucks were kept had about 30 large trucks. About 10 of them belonged to the owner, and the rest were individual owners who pulled his trailers.

When the owner saw the new person, me, walk in, he pointed to the big truck I was to drive that day. It was a Mack.

"OK, no problem," I said.

This truck was a lot bigger than the one I drove at Fiberglass. The owner was standing in the middle of the yard talking to a man. He kept looking at me to see what I was doing. Once I checked the water, oil, and the tires, I stepped into the cab of the truck.

"Here I go," I thought.

I turned the key and nothing happened. I heard the truck next to mine make a funny, whining noise; and then the engine started. I started to pull different things on the dashboard to see if I could find the... what did they call it? I remembered someone telling me about it, but I didn't know exactly what it did or how it worked. I was supposed to pull on it, and it was supposed to give the starter more power. The owner kept looking my way, wondering why I hadn't started the truck and probably wondering if I knew how to drive it.

He approached me and asked, "Is everything OK? Are you sure you know how to drive it?"

"Oh yeah. I like to make sure everything is OK with the truck before I take it out," I answered nervously. Just then I put my hand on a handle by my knee and pulled on it. It made the noise I wanted to hear. It sounded as if it made the starter turn really fast. I turned the key, and the engine started right up.

The owner walked back to the middle of the yard. I looked down to see the handle of the transmission, hoping it would be a 13-speed road ranger. No way Jose; it had two shifting handles for the transmission. I tried to figure it out because I had only heard of these. I remembered someone explaining how to operate this kind of transmission with two gear shifts. It's called a transmission with a brownie or an auxiliary transmission which was a lot harder to drive.

I pressed the clutch in, put it in gear, and let the clutch out. Nothing happened. The other trucks started to move out of the yard. As one truck drove in between the owner and me, I let the clutch out again. The truck died, but I restarted it before the owner looked my way. I might get fired before I even started my new job. I was the only guy driving a truck that hadn't left the yard. The owner again walked over to me. He stood next to my cab door.

Because the cab was so high, he looked up at me and asked, "Is everything OK?"

"Sure it is. I like to make sure the truck I'm going to be responsible for is warmed up before I take it out," I said. I had my hand on the other transmission, trying to play with it as he was talking.

With a doubtful look, he said, "Are you sure everything is OK?"

Just then I felt the other transmission go into gear, and the truck jerked a little.

"OK, I'll see you later," I said as I drove out of the yard very slowly. I drove slowly not because I wanted to but because I didn't know which gear the truck was in. If I took it out of gear, I probably wouldn't be able to put it back.

In all my life that was my most difficult day driving the truck. I was stuck on the freeways every little while because I was lost with the gears in the transmission. I had to pull over and start from first gear once more. In a little while I was lost again. All day long it was this way. I remember a few times during the day, my vision was impaired because of the sweat running down my face. Hauling a set of doubles for the first time was a little scary. When I was around a corner, I looked back through my mirror. My trailers were still coming around.

Once, all the trucks picked up their loads of rock at Stevens Creek Quarry. We were returning to our destination. The owner's son, who was one of the drivers, didn't know they had put a two-way radio in my truck. I could hear all the other truck drivers in our company talking.

As we pulled into the job site, he didn't see me behind him. He asked one of the other drivers, "Hey, where's that bimbo Mexican driver my father hired?" He said that because all the others were gavachos [Anglos]. Once we all stopped the trucks, he saw mine behind his.

"There's that bimbo! I don't know why my father hires Mexicans," he said over the radio. I parked my truck next to his, stepped down, and walked over to his side. He saw me walk up to his cab through his mirror and smiled. He motioned with his head, greeting me. I opened his cab door, not saying anything at first. He didn't know what I wanted.

"Hey, what's up?" he asked.

"Look, Junior, my name is Art! Got that?" I waited for his response.

"Yeah," he answered, not knowing why I was telling him this.

"Not bimbo Mexican. My father was born in Mexico, and I am proud of that fact!" His face turned red, and he didn't know what to say.

After about five seconds he said, "I didn't know you had a radio in your truck. I'm sorry."

I looked at him, closed his door, and said, "All right!" As I walked back to my truck, I didn't know if I was going to have a job the next day. However, I did. After that we got along just fine. I continued working for that company for two years.

A GOLD MINE

The first recession hit in the early 70s, and work was very slow. A friend of mine, Leo, kept asking me to go to his company to work with him. Finally I accepted. He talked to his boss and got me on. It was a garbage company, driving a roll-off truck, picking up dumpsters. At the garbage company we drove smaller trucks than I was used to driving.

A roll-off truck has long rails behind the cab. We backed the truck up to a dumpster that was on the ground. With the truck's hydraulic system, we picked up the rails all the way. The back end of the rails touched the ground in front of the dumpster. The truck had a long, big, steel cable that could hold 25 tons of weight. It hooked up to the front of the dumpster. From inside the truck we pulled on a lever that made the hydraulic system work. The truck's steel cable pulled the dumpster up on the back of the truck. Some companies that used roll-off trucks referred to them as piggybacks. We drove the truck to the dump, backed it up to where we were supposed to dump it, opened the back doors of the dumpster, and lifted up the rails. Everything fell out of the dumpster the same way as a dump truck would empty its load.

I had fun working with Leo. The days Leo was training me, he used to stop at the dump to salvage things. On the last day he trained me, he stopped the truck and said, "I'll be right back." He got out of the truck, picked up a cardboard box that was by one of the piles of trash, and walked over to a pile that one of the big trucks dumped on the ground at the landfill. Leo started to pull some telephone wire out of the pile and put it in his box.

He stopped after a minute and yelled out, "Hey, Art, come and get some. There's plenty for both of us!" I was sitting in the cab of the truck.

I looked at Leo and wiggled my finger at him, back and forth, meaning, "No." I thought, "No way, man! I don't need to go in a pile of trash for anything. I'll work for my money." Leo walked back to the truck with a box of insulated wire.

As Leo was tying the box of insulated wire from the telephone company on the side of the truck, he said, "Are you sure you don't want any? There's plenty more over there."

"No, Leo, I don't want any. I don't need that."

"Hey, man, whatever you want," he said. He got in the truck with me, and we drove away.

When we finished work that day, I left with Leo. He had given me a ride to work. "Hey Art, I'm going to stop at the metal company for a minute to turn in my wire."

"Sure, Leo, no problem." Upon arriving at the metal company, we stepped out of his pickup truck. He put his wire on a scale. The guy told him how much it weighed. He said, "$26."

"$26!" I exclaimed, not believing he could receive that much for such a little amount of wire.

The next day I was on my own, driving, and picking up dumpsters. On Leo's third load he drove into the dump. There were some piles of trash all over the place, and the guys who operated the big tractors were on their lunch break. Leo saw my truck parked next to all the piles, but I was nowhere in sight. He stopped his truck next to mine and saw nobody was in it. Leo opened his door and stood on the running board. He looked around and didn't see me anywhere. Thinking maybe I was hurt somewhere, Leo yelled out as loud as he could, "Hey, Art! Art!"

He saw my head pop out from a pile that was dumped from the telephone company. "What are you doing over there? Get out of that garbage," he laughingly yelled, since the day before I didn't want anything to do with salvaging. At first I didn't answer Leo; I was working very fast. In about a minute I yelled back, "Getting money!"

This was the day I started my career in recycling.

I worked for this company for the next ten years. During this time I made my side money, starting with aluminum and wire. My little brother Victor was also hired; therefore, I was able to work with him too. It was a really fun job. One day someone told me the companies from whom we picked up dumpsters threw away a lot of gold. That's right, GOLD! "Why do they throw away gold?" I wanted to know. The guy said the computer companies had so much of it they didn't care. They used the gold on circuit boards and computer chips. Everything that was rejected was thrown into the dumpsters we picked up. He told me one of the guys I worked with, Gab, always sold his to the gold guys. "Gold guys. Who are the gold guys?" I wanted to know. I had been working for this company for a few years and had never heard of this before. I found out who the gold guys were on my route. They were small companies, and all they did was refine gold. I drove by one of these places everyday on my route.

A few days later I picked up a 20-yard dumpster with the truck. While I was putting my tarp over the large box dumpster, I saw some circuit boards that looked the same color as gold. I wondered if they could be. I didn't think they could be gold; there was so much of it. They wouldn't throw so much of it away. I drove the truck to the dump. What I decided to do was to take some of the circuit boards in my dumpster to the gold buyer. If it wasn't gold, all he could do was laugh at me and tell me what to look for. He would also be able to give me some good tips.

Arriving at the dump, I took off the tarp and opened the back doors. It looked as if tons of circuit boards fell out as I opened the back doors of the dumpster. "It just couldn't be," I thought. I looked around, saw some boxes in another pile nearby and picked them up. They were empty Budweiser cases. I grabbed some of the circuit boards with both my hands and shoved them into the box. When it looked as if the box was full, I stuck my foot in it and crushed the contents, so a little more would fit. I did the same thing to the other two boxes. Once this was done, I carried the boxes, one on top of the other, around to the passenger seat of the truck. I went back to finish dumping my load. When it was dumped, there were a lot more circuit boards than I thought there would be. "This couldn't be gold?" I said as I stood there scratching my head.

Driving back down Lafayette Street, I looked at the three boxes of circuit boards sitting next to me. I wondered if I should take them to the gold buyer. The boxes looked like trash. I might make myself look really stupid. "What the heck! What can I lose? I don't even know the guy."

I drove to the back of the building where the shop was located. There was a big bay door, and I saw a man inside the building. He looked over at my truck as I pulled in. I stopped the truck. The guy came out to greet me as I opened the cab door and climbed out. The guy stopped, looked at me, and said, "Hey, I thought you were Gab." Our trucks all looked alike.

"Did you bring me some gold? Gab always brings me gold."

Trying to act as if I knew what I was talking about, I said, "Yeah, I have some. If you give me a good deal, I'll start to bring it to you instead of the other guy." I was trying to make it sound as if I did this all the time.

"Let's see what you have."

"Let me get it out of the truck," I said, hoping I wouldn't make myself look too bad. I walked to the passenger side and opened the cab door. The guy was walking right behind me. I reached into the truck and pulled out the boxes. As I did this, I checked his reaction. So far so good. I bent over and placed the boxes on the ground and watched his eyes as he scanned them. He bent over, and with his hands he grabbed some from the top. He lifted them to look at the circuit boards at the bottom of the box and said, "Yeah, this is good stuff." I was relieved.

But how good? The guy straightened up and looked at me as he pulled out his wallet. I saw it was full of $100 bills.

"Keep bringing me stuff like this; and I'll pay you good money, just like I pay Gab," he said with a smile like a cat who just caught a mouse. He took out a $100 bill and put it in my hand. I held my composure and acted as if this was an everyday occurrence. Then he moved his hand to the other hand that was holding his wallet. He pulled out another hundred and put it in my hand. And another! Then another! At this point I felt like jumping and yelling! He didn't stop. He pulled out two more as he looked at me and said, "Is that fair? Is it OK?" Still holding my composure, I thought of the load I'd left at the dump.

"Yeah, that's good." I said, matter-of-factly.

"Bring me back some more. What's your name anyway?"

"My name's Art, and I will bring back some more," I said hurriedly, thinking of all the gold back at the dump.

"When do you think you'll be back?" he said, eager for more gold.

"In about twenty minutes."

"Good," he replied.

I jumped in my truck and pressed my foot on the pedal, taking it to the floor. I hoped the tractor had not buried the pile that I had just dumped. I never went to the dump without a full load on the truck. That was a no no. If my boss found out, he would have a fit. For as much money as the gold returned, I didn't care if he had a cow.

Arriving back at the landfill, I found my pile was gone. The guys operating the tractors had already pushed it over and buried it. I parked my truck where I dumped the load of gold, looked around the ground, and found only pieces of circuit boards. I picked them up, put them in a box, and left. When I took the dumpster back to the company, I saw the barrels that were ready to go into the dumpster; they were full of gold circuit boards. Everyday I was finding gold or other metals. As I said, this was a fun and exciting place to work!

During this time the City of San Jose was buying all the houses by the airport where I lived. There was a class action suit by a lot of the homeowners in the area. The city made me an offer for the house on Emory Street. I knew if I didn't take what was offered, they would take the house anyway. The day I closed the deal, I went to my mother's home. She wasn't expecting anything from the sale because she had given it to me. I told her when I received the money from the sale, I was giving her half of it. This made her happy, but it made me even happier.

I had to move, and my easy house payments of $65.64 were going to end. "Oh, well, all good things come to an end," I thought.

A year after moving to my new house, my marriage came to an end. It lasted eight years, and we had two children, Artie and Daniel. Things were difficult for a while, since I had custody of my two boys.

However, a very good thing happened in January of 1979. I

met my second wife Flora. She had three children, and I had two. Now I wasn't going to raise only my children but also stepchildren. Tito was ten at the time we were married, Gina was nine, and Elise was three years old. My oldest son Artie was nine, and Daniel was six years old.

Gina and Artie were only weeks apart. At times people who didn't know we had a step family wondered how it was that Artie and Gina were only weeks apart. I told them in a serious tone, "Well, when Flora was in labor, she had Gina. They didn't know Artie was inside of her. A few weeks later I took her back to have the other baby." I must have sounded convincing. They just looked at me, wondering if I were serious.

I continued to work at the same company along with my brother Victor. Victor was a lot of fun to be around. We used to stop every morning at a small cafe in Agnews to have breakfast. The place was full of regulars every morning. Some worked for the same company as we did, and others worked for the City of Santa Clara. We combined our breaks with our lunch and stayed at the cafe for an hour. During that time we had fun telling stories and joking.

After a few years Victor had to leave the company to move his family to Utah. Working there continued to be a pleasure. I was making deals and at the same time doing good work for my employer. Later there was almost a strike between the company and the union. The company was having a war with the union, and the workers were working without a contract. One of the drivers who was working came in late one morning and was fired. We all knew we had to watch our step. It reached the point that management wouldn't greet the workers.

At this company they had three different kinds of jobs. First, a roll-off driver—this was my job. There were about 5 roll-off trucks. Second were the front-loader drivers. These were trucks with big forks in front of them. They picked up small dumpsters, lifted them up and over the top of their trucks, and dumped the small dumpster into the truck's back compartment. Once the truck was full, they drove it to the dump. There were also about 6 or 7 front-loader trucks. Last there were the garbage trucks which picked up garbage at the houses. We had about 20 garbage trucks with about three guys to a truck.

A NEW VENTURE

One evening I received a call from a friend. "Hey, Art, would you like to buy a roll-off truck? I heard there is one for sale in Santa Rosa, and I hear it's really a good deal." He went on to tell me all about the truck. It had a new engine, brakes, tires, transmission—new everything. I liked buying and selling different items. He said the guy wanted to sell the truck with two dumpsters for $12,000. I could turn around and sell it for $20,000.

"Yeah, give me the guy's phone number. If the deal is as you say, I'll probably buy it."

I went to Santa Rosa and looked at the truck. It was just the way my friend described it. I tried to talk the guy down, but he wouldn't budge. He knew he was selling a good truck. After examining it, I was convinced it was worth the money. I knew I could make some money on it. I paid the guy and drove it home to San Jose. Now what was I going to do with this truck? Start my own business? Sell it and make a good profit? I really didn't know.

A few days before I bought the truck, I found out another guy at work had been fired for almost nothing. I didn't think I had anything to worry about because I was a good worker and got along with everyone, even the bosses. A lot of the guys who worked there were alcoholics and were suspended at times for coming to work drunk. I took pride in my work, and I wasn't worried about losing my job.

The day after I bought the truck, I took it to work and parked it around the corner from the company. I wanted to show my friends what I had purchased. When I returned to the yard at the end of the day, I walked to the window where our drivers turned in their invoices. The office was a double-wide mobile home. The lady who worked in the office had been working there as long as I had, ten years. She was sitting behind the window at her desk. I gave her my invoices for the day and told her the problems I had encountered, as I always did. I headed in the direction of the parking lot; the owner of the company stepped out of the office and followed me.

"Hey, Art," he yelled out. As I turned around, I saw him waving his arm, wanting me to return to the office.

I walked back and asked, "Hey, Rick, how you doing?" I had talked to him many times and felt we had a good working relationship.

"Art, I understand you're going into business?" he said in a very nice way.

"Business? Who told you that?" I asked. I was surprised he already knew I had a truck.

"You bought a roll-off truck didn't you?"

Before I answered him, I wondered who told him about my purchase. I had nothing to hide, and I wasn't doing anything illegal; therefore, I said, "Yeah, I bought a truck."

"Are you going into business in this town?"

He sure was asking a lot of questions. I replied, "I don't know what I'm going to do. I might go into business; I might sell the truck. Why? Do you want to buy it?"

"No, I don't want to buy it. But if you do, are you going into business in this town?" He wanted to know because he didn't like competition, and he was the only company that was allowed to do business in the city.

He was sure becoming persistent. I wondered what he wanted. Working for him for the past ten years, I knew his ways. I needed to watch what I said, or I was going to get into some kind of trouble.

"Art, I hope you do well in your new business," he said with a nice, warm expression on his face. When he said this, he extended his hand out to shake mine. This was something he had never done before. I also extended my hand out to shake his.

While we were shaking hands, I said, "I don't know if I'm

going into business, Rick. I might sell the truck. Who knows?" It seemed he didn't hear me.

As he released my hand, he said, "Congratulations, Art!" He turned around and walked away, as if he was in deep thought. I stood there still not knowing what to think.

He sure was nice. I wondered why.

What was I going to do with my new truck? Start a business? It would be nice to be my own boss. All I had to do was have about five dumpsters, and I would be able to support my family. I felt I should try it; it might work out for me. I would also have an easy job. I was thinking about starting a new business all the way home and asked myself some questions, "Can I do it? Will I make enough money since I spent all my money on that truck? I wonder how hard it will be since I don't really know too much about business?"

I parked the big truck in my driveway at home. The manufacturer was White, and the color was white. It was so long that it stuck out into the street. Every little while I checked out of my kitchen window to make sure the truck was all right. I was like a little boy with a new toy. I really hated to sell it; it would be nice to keep. But I thought about my job. I made good money; and besides, I made all the side money from the circuit boards. I took nice vacations, and I always had enough spending money for my family and myself.

The next day I got up and went to work as usual, deciding to drive my car to work and leaving the truck at home. I pulled a lot of loads that day. When I did quality work, I went home feeling good about myself; this day was one of those days.

During the day different guys at the dump and at the yard told me, "All right, Art, you bought a new truck. You're going to put the boss out of business." It seemed as if everybody knew about the truck even though I had only told a few people. Some of the guys congratulated me for buying it, and others congratulated me for starting my business. It seemed they were proud I was undertaking this new venture. Although they assumed I was beginning my own business, at that point I didn't know what I was going to do.

Mike, one of the other roll-off drivers, was a good friend. When we stopped for breakfast that day, we discussed different names I could give my business. We sat there at Agnews Cafe, and he said, "How about 'The Dumpster Company,' 'A-1 Disposal!' or 'Number

One Disposal'?" He went on and on.

"Stop! Stop, Mike! The name you said I liked the best was 'Number One Disposal!' If I start a business, that's the name I want."

At the end of the day, I drove my company truck into the yard. I parked it by the mechanic's garage because I had a flat on one of my tires. Flats happened practically every day because of all the junk the trucks ran over at the dump.

"Hey, Pudgie, I have a flat in the back," I said, climbing out of the cab.

"Art, you bought a truck, huh? Are you going into business?"

"I don't know what I'm going to do, Pudgie."

I had my invoices in my hand and headed to the window to turn them in. As I approached the window, it looked as if Jane, the lady I worked with for ten years, was crying. She had a tissue and was wiping her eyes.

I opened the small window and said, "Here's my work for the day, Jane. What's wrong? Are you OK?"

She looked up at me, put the tissue down, and said forcefully, "You should have lied to him, Art. You should have lied to him!"

Not knowing what in the heck she was talking about, I said, "Lied to whom? What are you talking about, Jane?"

She stopped crying at this point and picked up a letter from the top of her desk. She said, "You should have lied to Rick!" I looked at her, wondering why she was so upset. I had never seen her like this.

"Jane, I've worked with you for ten years; and you know I don't lie to anyone!"

Jane looked at me and said sadly, "You should have lied to him and told him you didn't have a truck. Now I have to give you this!" She stretched out her hand and gave me a white envelope.

"What is this, Jane?" I asked, having no idea what it was. My thoughts went back to when I first drove my company truck into the yard. I saw Rick come out of his office, jump in his pickup truck, and drive away.

I reached for the envelope. Jane started to cry again. I closed the window and turned around, opening the envelope and wondering what it contained. In a few steps I had it opened and took out a paper that had the company letterhead, "To Whom It May Concern: Art Rodriguez is terminated, due to being in direct competition with this company." I read it again, thinking I must have misunderstood. Wait a minute. This couldn't be right. I had been working there for ten years and had never had a write-up. I was there at work every day and had maintained a good relationship with everyone.

I walked back to the window and opened it. I asked Jane, "What does this mean?" I still couldn't believe what I had just read.

"I told you. You should have lied to him, Art." I felt my face turn red, wanting to beat up the owner. I remembered he had left. I walked away, still not believing I was fired.

"Fired?" I asked myself in a low voice. That didn't sound right. I had grown to like working for this place. Fired? What was I going to tell my wife when I arrived home? Fired? For what? What did I do? My work was not good enough? No, my work was good. It was because I made a deal for a truck that had nothing to do with my job. I shouldn't feel bad. I wasn't fired because of my work; it was for wishing to better myself.

Now what was I going to do? Was I going to look for another job driving a truck for a while? No, I had a truck and two dumpsters. I might as well start my own business right away. I was going to go into business, and Rick wasn't going to stop me.

I didn't know the first thing about owning my own company. With whom was I going to place the dumpsters? Where was I going to buy more dumpsters for my business? I didn't have any more money. I spent the money on the truck and planned to live from paycheck-to-paycheck for a while. Now I didn't have a paycheck. What was I going to do about my house payment, the gas and light bill, the food? I was in a fix!

I told my wife Flora I was planning to start my own business.

"Whatever you want to do, I'll help you and do whatever I can," she said. She was willing to back me up and help me manage the business.

The next evening after I was fired, I received a call from an owner of one of the other companies. "Art, I really felt bad when I heard what happened to you. I found out this morning when I came to work. I'm really sorry, Art. If there is anything I can do for you, just let me know." This man was a very good person. Whenever someone needed some kind of help, he was always there. At times he didn't even know the person; he just heard of situations and was always willing to help.

I thought, "If he's offering, I might as well ask." Therefore, I asked, "Look, I've seen all those junk dumpsters you have lying around. Would you like to sell me some?" Used dumpsters were hard to find. Everybody in the business was looking for them. To buy a used 20-yard dumpster, it cost between $1,000-$1,500. At that time a new 20-yard dumpster cost about $2,300. A new 30-yard dumpster cost about $2,500.

"Sure, Art, I'll sell you eight of them. How does that sound?"

"That's good."

"What I want you to do right away, Art, is paint them your color. I don't want them to look like my dumpsters. I'll sell them to you for $100 each, and you can pay me later when you have the money."

What a generous man! The junk dumpsters were in pretty bad shape, but they just needed a little work. I went the next day with my truck to pick them up. He said I had to paint them my colors. What were my colors going to be? Other companies had all different colors. I wanted one that no other company used.

I had seen blue, white, different shades of brown, and different shades of green. Black! I had never seen black out there. This was going to be the color of my dumpsters. That was it; they turned out to be black. The corners and the top railings were painted yellow.

I placed our first dumpster through a friend who knew someone who needed one. Our friend told them I had dumpsters. I took my first delivery by Alum Rock Park. Here I was driving my own truck to deliver my own dumpster. This was something I thought could never happen.

I arrived home with the first money and my first receipt. Flora and I sat on the sofa and looked at each other; we knew our business had started. Through the years we have kept that first receipt; and every so often, we stop to look at it. We remember the first days of starting Number One Disposal.

Within the first week after being fired, I called the union. "Yeah, they fired me for that!" I said in a vengeful tone.

"Don't worry, Art; they can't do that. We'll get them for this. That's not a good reason to fire you. I'm going to make an appointment with the company, and we'll see what we can do," the business agent said.

The next morning I received a call from the union representative. "Art, can you be at the company in an hour? I have a meeting with them to talk about your job?"

"Sure, I'll be there." What if he gets my job back? Would I give up my plans to start my business? I had a truck, two dumpsters, plus eight more. In this short time I really didn't know if I wanted my job back.

We walked into the company's office. Jane and the other girl who were in the office acted cold with me.

"Hi, Jane. How are you?"

"I'm, OK, thank you. How are you?" she asked.

Jane was probably in a bad position under the circumstances. She probably wanted to talk to me, but she needed to keep her loyalty to the company. If she appeared to be really nice with me, it would make her seem as if she was on my side.

The supervisor showed us into one of the back offices. I had never been in that office. This was where the owner kept himself most of the time. The room was really luxurious, with a very large oak desk. The other furniture in the room was expensive; and the room had plush, green carpet. The supervisor who walked into the room with us closed the door and sat behind the desk. The union man and I sat on chairs in front of the desk. I didn't notice the owner around the premises. His pickup truck wasn't around either.

The company supervisor started off. "What can I do for you?" he asked coldly. The company and the union hated each other at that time. We had heard the union called the Internal Revenue Service on the company. We also had heard the union had called the Highway Patrol on the company and told them the company had unsafe trucks. The last two days before I was fired, there were two Highway Patrol officers in the company yard checking the trucks; therefore, the company owner was furious.

"Well," the union man said, "why did you fire Art?"

The company supervisor replied with a hard look on his face, "It's on his paper. Can't you read?"

The union man became angry. "Hey, now, you don't have to get smart! This isn't about you and me. It's about Art. He has a family to take care of. Why don't you give him back his job?"

"He started his business, and we can't have him working against us." This supervisor was playing the hard guy. I didn't think he really wanted to talk to us, and he sure sounded as if he wasn't about to give me my job back. The union rep reached behind me, put his hand on my back, and said, "Give the poor guy his job back, please."

I didn't like this, the rep begging for my job. I thought he wanted to talk to the company supervisor to make them rehire me because they fired me for an unfair reason. The supervisor didn't know what to say. He wouldn't look at me. I had always gotten along with him in the past and never had any problems. I knew right then what the problem was. He couldn't give me my job back even if he wanted to. I knew he had orders from the owner not to rehire me because of his battle with the union.

For the third time the rep said, "Please, give the poor guy his job back!"

I had to stand up. I couldn't take the begging! I stood up knowing this man had his orders from Rick, and he was not going to hire me back. This was not because of my work or my buying a truck. It was because of the war he was having with the union.

"Let's go. They don't want to give me back my job," I said with pride.

The union rep and the company supervisor started arguing about the reason we were there and almost ended up in a fist fight. We walked out of the office. Everyone was quiet, no good-byes and no I'll-see-you-laters. We walked out to the parking lot and stood by our cars.

"Art, this is the first step. Now we're going to take care of business. They weren't supposed to fire you like this. There was no reason. We're going to make an appointment with the union lawyers."

"The union lawyers? Do you think they can make the company hire me back?"

"Well, let's talk to them first." As he got into his car, I thanked him. He said he would contact the lawyers.

As the weeks went by, I rented a small yard not far from where I lived. I kept my truck and the dumpsters there while I ran an ad in the local newspaper. The plan was working, placing my dumpsters with companies and people in the neighborhoods to clean up their yards. Things started improving; and I really didn't know if I wanted my job back, even if they offered it.

One day I received a call from the union to inform me of my appointment the next day with the lawyer in San Francisco. I was surprised to find that the attorneys for both the company and the union were in different high-rise buildings in downtown San Francisco. The lawyer told me we were going to sue the company for unjustifiably firing me, and we would have our first court hearing in a couple of weeks. They said winning was a sure thing. I was going to get my job back with full back pay and money for damages.

In the meantime my new business was starting to take off. I had some customers who wanted the services of dumpsters on a regular basis. We were also getting new contractors and roofers who were using us on a daily basis. I was doing all the driving, and my wife was taking care of our home office. We had a lot to learn about owning our own business.

One day I received a call from John who built dumpsters for different companies all over the area. When I worked for the company I was fired from, I found old dumpsters or old compactors that were not being used anymore. Since I went to the back of all the buildings to get the dumpsters, I spotted old dumpsters and called John on the telephone. He went to these businesses and made an offer for the old dumpster or compactor. He then reconditioned them to sell to someone else. He paid me about $200 as a finder's fee.

"Hello," I said, answering the telephone.

"Art, I'm really sorry about what happened to you."

"Yes, John. All I did was buy a truck, and the guy got paranoid. So he gave me no choice but to start my own business."

"Well, that's really good, Art. Maybe that's a blessing in disguise."

"Who knows? Maybe your right, John. Things are getting better all the time. I'm getting more work."

"Art, do you need anything? Do you need dumpsters?"

"Yes, I do need more; but the problem is I don't have any money."

"Money? Art, your word is like money in the bank. You tell me how many dumpsters you need, and I'll build them for you. I'll have them to you in six weeks. Do you need five, ten? Tell me how many?"

"Oh, let me think. I can use ten. Maybe five, 20-yard dumpsters and five, 30-yarders."

"You got it. And you can make payments. Send mc $1,000 a month. How does that sound?"

This wasn't bad. If I placed ten dumpsters in one week, after dump fees I would make a $1,000 a week, since I only left the dumpsters at one place for one week at a time. Sometimes when I was busy, the dumpsters moved every day.

"Sure, John, that sounds good," I responded as I thanked him.

What a great guy. I really didn't know him that well, and he gave me $20,000 credit.

I received my new dumpsters within six weeks as he promised. I was on my way to beginning my business.

During this time I went to court with the union lawyer twice. They told me it was going to take about a year-and-a-half to win this case. They were almost certain I was going to win because it wasn't legal that they fired me for no reason.

The union was still fighting with the company, and the men were still working without a contract.

THE CRASH

One rainy morning I had three loads to deliver. The yard I rented to store my truck and dumpsters was on Towers Lane. It was one block from Aborn and King Road. When I arrived, I parked my pickup truck and went to unlock the gate.

Cab-over trucks have an automatic locking device that locks the cab-over when it's brought down. My truck was a little older. Instead of an automatic locking device, it had a chain that was supposed to be hooked manually when the cab was lowered onto the truck, to check the oil or to check the water. At times when I left the yard, I hit a bump on the road and realized I had forgotten to hook the cab down with the chain. I had to stop and secure the cab with the chain. It was a scary feeling. If I were to get on the road and it was not locked down, the cab could swing up and over. The windshield would hit the ground, with me behind it.

Once, I opened the gate. I pulled the cab over to check the oil and water. Everything looked perfect that morning. When I was done checking the engine compartment, I pulled the cab down and over. Then I walked around the truck to check the tires. This was my regular morning routine. When I was done, I climbed into the cab of the truck and was ready to go to work on that rainy morning.

I drove out of the small yard, put my wipers on, and stopped the truck outside the gate. I climbed out of the cab to lock the gate before leaving. I drove on the dirt road very slowly. Usually by the time I reached Towers Lane, I would notice I hadn't locked the cab. When I arrived behind the Target store, I saw there weren't any cars waiting at the stop sign to get on Capitol Expressway. I approached the expressway very slowly, and I didn't make a complete stop at the stop sign. If I had made a complete stop, I would have felt the cab bouncing as if it were going to go over. At times when it did do this, I wondered how it would feel if the cab were to go over at a high speed on the street. I knew if this were to happen, I would have big problems.

I stayed on the lane to get on the freeway and put my foot on the pedal to pick up speed. I was traveling at about 30 miles an hour on the ramp to approach the freeway. At that point the rain was really coming down. In San Jose we have signal lights at the entrance of the freeways, as do many metropolitan cities. The signal lights are to control the traffic which enters.

The diesel engine was picking up speed for the merge onto the freeway. All of a sudden I saw the lights on the signal in operation. Three cars were in line waiting to get onto the freeway. I took my foot off the accelerator and applied the brake a little. When my foot touched the brake, the cab moved. It wasn't locked down! How could I have forgotten to do that? When my brake took hold, the cab lifted up. It felt comparable to floating on air. Now I knew I was going to have big problems in the next few seconds.

Cars were stopped at the signal light about 300 feet in front of my truck. Instantly I saw what looked like children in the back seat of a car which was last in line. I had to think fast! What was I going to do? I could turn off the road and crash over the curb. What if I didn't make it over the curb and continued toward the car with the kids in it? The car was now only 50 feet in front of my truck, and I was moving 30 miles an hour. If I tried to apply my brakes a little at a time, I wouldn't have time to stop my truck. The cab would start to move over, and I would lose control. The only thing I could do was put my foot on the brake and hold it down as hard as I could until I blacked out. At that point I didn't have any time to decide if this was a good or bad idea. I was going to experience impact in a matter of seconds.

I hung onto the steering wheel as hard as I could. With all my might I put my foot on the brake and held it down. Instantly the truck brakes locked up, and the cab lifted me up and over! I remember seeing the windshield in front of me as the steering wheel was bending. I was holding onto it very tightly. Then I saw the pavement passing in front of the windshield. I was almost upside down at this point. My body was being squashed! The last thing I remember was pushing my toes on the brake, trying to stop the truck before I was out of it. I didn't want to kill the kids in front of me. CRASH! Everything went black.

"A BOX! I'm in a box! Where am I? There's glass all over the place. Is this a cave or a box? Where am I? I can't remember," I mumbled to myself.

"Hey, are you OK? Are you hurt?" a voice called.

"Who is that? What do you want?" I asked.

My cab was almost upside down, and I was knocked unconscious for only a second. I had blood all over my hands and didn't know where the blood was from.

"Are you OK in there?" someone was calling out to me.

The cab windows were wet and fogged. Someone was wiping off the window on the passenger side. Whoever it was had his hands next to his face up against the window, trying to look inside the cab. "Are you OK?" he screamed.

"Where am I? What is this? What happened? Where is all this blood coming from?"

The cab was rocking, and someone else was trying to pull the door open on the driver's side.

The other person was still calling out to me on the passenger side, "Are you OK in there? Can you hear me?" Within seconds I started to get my memory back. I remembered I was in the cab of my truck—wrecked and with the windshield in pieces.

"But what happened? I can't remember."

Someone opened the door and looked at me. "Are you all right? Come out of there!" He grabbed my arm and pulled me out. When I was pulled out of the cab, I remembered where I was and what happened. I looked around. In front of me was the car with the kids. It was about 10 feet in front of the truck. I was relieved I didn't kill the kids. My truck had good brakes.

"But, my poor truck! My only truck! What was going to happen to my business now?" I thought.

Within a few minutes the fire department arrived. Before arriving, one of the men who helped me out of the truck asked if I was OK and gave me something to put on my head to stop the bleeding. I asked the man if he could do something for me.

"Sure, I'll try to do whatever I can," he said, wanting to be helpful.

"Can you go to Towers Lane?" I asked, pointing toward the location of the street.

"You'll see a big house with a mechanic's yard. The mechanic's name is Manuel. He's the guy that works on my truck. I need him to help me get it back to my yard. Do you think you can go and get him for me?"

"No problem. I'll leave right now."

I never was able to thank that man.

The Highway Patrol wanted to tow my truck away, and they wanted me to be taken to the hospital. I wouldn't go to the hospital until my truck was taken care of. The mechanic arrived. With his pulling tools and cables, he pulled the cab right-side-up and towed the truck to his yard. I was then taken to the hospital and had fifteen stitches on my forehead.

At the scene of the accident, the damage seemed worse than it actually was. The truck's windshield had to be replaced. All the air lines and hoses were reconnected, and the steering wheel had to be bent back to its proper position. My truck was ready to go back on the road. The top of the cab had a visor that was part of the truck. When the top hit the pavement, the visor protected the face of the truck from sustaining more damages than it would have if it didn't have the visor. My business was saved! I knew I had to buy another truck as a backup in case something like this happened again.

One day I received a call from the union. They wanted me to go to San Francisco to talk to the union lawyers. "Sure I'll go see them," I said. Once there, I was taken to one of the attorneys' offices.

"Art, we wanted to meet with you and let you know what happened. The union settled with the company, and now the union is working with a contract. The company is making you an offer. They said they'll give you back your job, and they'll also give you your back pay. As you know, it's been a few months, almost a year. The only thing they're asking is that you give up your business. We think it's a good offer. What do you say?"

I sat there in deep thought, thinking, "Why should I have to give up my business anyway? They're the ones who fired me. I actually started my business when they fired me. I can't do this. My business is doing well now."

I looked at the lawyer and asked, "Can I think about it? I wasn't expecting this offer."

"Sure. Take your time. If you want your job, it's there waiting for you."

I stood up and made my way to the door. The lawyer shook my hand and said, "Try to call me in the next couple of days."

The next day I decided to talk to the attorney to ask some questions about the company's offer. When I called, the receptionist said the attorney was out of the office.

"Can you have him call me when he gets in?" I asked, hoping to talk to him later.

"Sure. What is your name and telephone number?"

I waited all day for his call, but I didn't receive it. I called again the next day, and the receptionist took my name down again. The third day I called again, and the receptionist said the attorney was with a client.

"Is it OK if he calls you when he's free?"

"Sure," I said, thinking at least he's in the office now. He had never returned my previous phone calls.

The next day I called the union, and the receptionist said she would give the business agent my message. "He'll probably call you this afternoon."

"No problem. I'll be waiting for his call," I said. No one wanted to talk to me. I wondered why. I had heard that lately the union was at the company offices attempting to work things out. It went on like this for weeks. I would call the union and the attorney, but I couldn't get them to talk to me.

One of the guys whom I worked with at the company told me the union sold me out. They made a deal. I was the card the union used to make a deal on other issues the union wanted. Three weeks later I was trying to call the union and the attorneys. I still couldn't get through; they wouldn't return my calls.

I saw the guy I worked with, Mike, a few weeks later. He told me they had a union meeting, and someone asked about me.

"Is Art going to get his job back?" one of the guys asked during a question-and-answer session at the union hall.

"Art said he didn't want us to get his job back, and he hired his own lawyer," the union rep said from the platform.

"Hey, Mike, that's a lie. I don't have another attorney."

That's where it stayed for a while. I was working hard to get my business going and not worrying too much about my job. My wife's uncle was a negotiator for companies and was getting ready to retire during this time. One day he came from Fresno to visit. I was getting ready to hire an attorney here in San Jose to sue the company and the union; I learned the union could be sued for not representing me properly.

I asked Flora's uncle, "Hey, Tommy, what do you think about my situation? I was fired for buying my truck. I had not started a business yet, and the guy fired me. I'm thinking of suing the company and the union. What should I do?"

He wanted me to tell him the whole story. I sat there and gave him the details about the conversations I had with the union and the attorneys.

When I finished, he asked, "And how is your business doing right now?"

"Tommy, my business is doing well. I'm having regular customers call me, and I think I'm going to make it."

"Well, do you have $50,000?" he asked, already knowing the answer. "Because that's the minimum it's going to cost you. It might go as high as a $100,000 or more, and that's no promise you're going to win. You might spend all that money on attorneys and lose the case. Not only that, but you have to remember all the worrying and the anxiety you're going to have over the next few years. That's how long it's going to take. No, Art. I think if you're doing well, you should just forget about the company and the union and put all your effort in your business," he said, raising his arms. He continued, "You can do without all of that. Having a business is enough anxiety."

He was right about that. This older man sure had a lot of wisdom. I'm glad I took his advice.

THE HEART ATTACK

My father's work involved selling medical supplies to doctors in small towns in Mexico. He was self-employed. One day I received a call from a doctor in a small town in Penjamo, Mexico.

Speaking in Spanish, he said, "Is this Arthur Rodriguez?"

"Yes."

"Well, I'm calling to tell you your father is here right now. He just had a heart attack. He's not doing very well; he's doing badly. I don't think he's going to make it," he said in a consoling way.

I couldn't imagine my father dying. He was just in San Jose visiting us two months earlier, and he was just fine. The last time he was here, he was so proud of me and my business. He was full of questions.

"Mijo, how much do you charge for one of these dumpsters? What about the truck, did you pay cash for it? When are you going to buy more of them?" My father looked over the truck proudly.

"I don't know when I'm going to buy more trucks, Dad. Would you like to come with me to pick up a dumpster at a job site then go with me to take it to the landfill?"

"Yes," he answered proudly.

As we were driving down the freeway in the big truck, I turned and looked at my father who was sitting on the passenger seat. He was bouncing, and his hair was blowing in the wind. He looked around the interior of the cab. There he was, going with me to the dump where he once had forbidden me ever to go.

THE FORBIDDEN PLACE

I was ten years old. My friend Philip from down the street came to my back door and knocked. "Hey Phil, what do you want to do today?" I asked as I greeted him.

Philip and I spent the summers having fun in the neighborhood.

"I found some really neat things when I went with my uncle to the dump. They have everything there. I was going to go back and get some more stuff. Do you want to go with me?" Phil asked excitedly.

"What kind of stuff?" I asked, wondering what could be found at a dump. I had never been to one.

My mother had to take care of some errands, and my father would not be home until later. It was 10 a.m. "Yeah, I'll go," I said as I stepped out of the door.

My parents didn't mind if we went out with our friends as long as we were around when my father arrived home from work; and, of course, as long as we put in our time working in the yard pulling weeds.

Getting to the dump was an easy walk. It was on Story Road just east from Senter. At this time the area was all country roads.

Arriving at the dump, my nostrils picked up a bad odor. We went in the back way, so no one would tell us anything. We walked through the field; there were no fences to keep kids out. I saw piles and piles of trash.

"Hey, Arthur," Phil yelled. "Over here. Look what I found!"

Philip held something up. I couldn't make out what it was that he was so excited about. Walking towards Phil, I saw somebody's old coat in his hand. It seemed to be in good condition.

"Wow! That looks new!" I said as I reached to examine it.

"There's a lot of things here. Look!" Phil said, pointing around the ground where we were standing.

I looked down and could not believe what I saw: blankets, kitchenware, clothes, and books. I reached down and picked up a large clock that looked as if it worked. "Look at this!"

"I know; that's what I have been telling you about this place. It's full of things like that," Philip said as if he had struck gold. "Come on. Let's get some boxes and get some of these things. My mother will never know they came from the dump," he said, convinced he was doing a good thing.

I looked at Phil and thought the same. Then I wondered if my father would know where I found all the junk. My father would never approve of my being at the dump. Once my mother wanted to try to save money and went with a friend to the secondhand store. When my father found out, he had a fit. He made her throw out all the things she bought. As I stood there thinking what my father would say about what I was doing, a chill ran up my back.

"Hey. Get some boxes and start putting stuff in them," Phil said.

Worried about my father, I answered, "Whatever I take home, I'm going to tell my mother you gave them to me. I'll say your aunt gave them to you, and you gave them to me. All right?"

"Sure. If she asks me, that's what I'll tell her. Hurry! Get those pots and pans. Look!" he said, pointing to another pile. I saw a box with an electric blanket, and it was in its original box. It was almost new. Electric blankets were something special in those days.

Once we had our boxes packed with junk, then came the hard part. I wondered how in the heck we were going to get all this stuff home. "Can we carry all this home, Phil? I don't think it will be that easy."

"Hey, it'll be easy. Hitchhike!" Phil said confidently.

That sounded easy enough. We were used to hitchhiking. We did it all the time when we returned from Alum Rock Park.

Getting to Story Road was difficult. We had to make two trips to move all of the junk to the road. I thought my mother was going to be really happy with all the things I was getting for free.

We put our boxes next to the road where the big eucalyptus trees were, not too far from Coyote Creek. We stood next to the boxes and put out our thumbs. We were both very grimy-looking since we had been digging through the piles and getting dirty. The first car was traveling fast down the road toward us. I looked at the man in the driver's seat as he passed. He didn't look at us. He didn't want to pick up two dirty kids who had just left the dump. The next car was coming; I put my thumb out, hoping he would stop. I didn't want anyone who knew my family to see me out there. It might get back to my father, and this thought sent another chill up my back.

"Hey, what time do you think it is?" I asked, thinking about my father.

"I don't know. Around 3, I think."

My father would soon finish his shift at the American Can Company on Fifth and Martha. I didn't think he would go straight home on Story Road. The only time he did this was when he stopped at Ralph's Bar on Keyes Street, a continuation of Story Road. Ralph's Bar was one block away from his work.

"I hope my father doesn't come home this way today," I said.

Phil looked over at me. He hadn't thought of this. He felt sorry for me, knowing how strict my father was. "Na, I don't think so. Doesn't he go home on San Antonio Street?"

"I think," I said as the next car approached. We both extended our thumbs out as the car neared. The man in the driver seat slowed down as if he were going to pick us up. When he caught sight of the trash boxes next to our legs, he didn't stop. He put his finger up and wagged it at us as if he were saying, "No, no, no!" He also nodded his head in disgust at the same time.

Just as he passed, another car approached us. The first thing I saw was a head from a distance. As it came closer, I saw whoever was driving sit up as if he caught sight of us. Maybe he was going to give us a ride, since in those days people stopped easily to give a couple of boys a lift. The next thing that caught my attention was the color of the car. It looked very familiar. I heard Phil say in an undertone, "Oh no!"

Then I saw it. My father's frown! He was driving his green

Pontiac, moving fast when he saw us. He came to a sudden stop, expressing a look of shame and disgust. I looked over at Phil; he had an expression of regret for taking me to the dump.

My father stepped out of the car and looked to see if anybody was around. He stood there looking down at my box. "Arturo, what is this?"

I didn't know if I should greet him before I answered, since that's what we were taught to do. "Hi, Dad! This stuff is Phil's. I was just helping him take it home."

My father looked at me not knowing if he should believe me. I just knew I was going to be beaten when I arrived home. "Are these things yours?" he asked Phil.

If my father believed him, I thought maybe I wouldn't be hit. I knew I might get whipped just for being at the dump. Then again, I reasoned. I was never told I could not go to the dump.

"Yes, my mother said it was all right if I took things home," he lied.

My father opened the trunk and did not say anything. He didn't like taking all this trash and putting it in his trunk. However, he wasn't going to leave my friend Phil in the street.

On the way home my father was quiet. I wanted to say something to ease things and maybe put my father in a better mood. Phil didn't say anything either. He knew how my father was and that I probably was going to be whipped when I arrived home. We stopped at Phil's house on Virginia Place to drop him off. I stepped out of the car and helped him with the boxes.

"I'll give you your stuff later," he said in a whisper, not looking up at me. He didn't want my father to see him talking to me.

"No, I don't want any of it. Keep it. If he finds out it's mine, he'll kill me!" I whispered.

I really wanted to walk the rest of the way home, since it was only a few houses away. I told Phil good-bye, stepped back in the car, closed the door, and my father drove down the street to our house. As we drove into our driveway, my father turned and looked at me. His expression was scary, and his frown was intense. He said in a stern voice, "I never, never want you to go there again! Do you understand, Arturo? Never!

"I won't, Dad. I promise I won't," I said, feeling afraid of what he might do.

He gave his sarcastic laugh, "Ha, ha, ha. If I find out you went there again, Arturo, do you know what will happen to you?"

I knew and didn't want him to tell me.

"I buy you your clothes and everything you need. If you ever go over there again, you are going to see what will happen to you, Arturo!"

And now, my dear father was so proud to have his son in the same kind of business he had once forbidden me to enter.

* * *

Not believing the doctor, I asked, "Who is this?" I thought someone was playing around. My father was one to make us feel bad for him by saying he was very sick. He would put someone on the phone to confirm it. He did this because he wanted his children's attention.

"This is the doctor speaking."

"Is my father right there with you?" I asked, wanting the playing around to stop.

"Yes, he's right here."

"Can you put him on the phone? I want to talk to him," I said. I didn't know why my father liked to play around like this.

"I'm sorry, mister," he said in Spanish. I'll never forgot the words he said next. "Pero tu papi esta muy grave. No puede hablar." ["I'm sorry, mister, but your daddy is very serious. He can't talk."] The doctor said this in a sad tone that didn't make my father's condition seem good at all. When I heard this, I knew my father wasn't just trying to get my attention.

"Mr. Rodriguez, I have to go. I just wanted to call you and let you know of the situation." Before he hung up, I got his phone number. Once I hung up the phone, I tried to call my sister Tita and my brothers Victor and Eddie. Eddie was at a friend's funeral in LA. Tita was out and so was Victor. I was trying to locate Eddie by calling different numbers where he was supposed to be. By this time I thought I'd better call the doctor back and get an update from Mexico. It had not been more than half an hour that the doctor had called me.

"Hello, this is Art Rodriguez calling from California. I'm calling to see how my father is doing," I said in Spanish.

"Oh, Señor Rodriguez, I'm sorry to tell you; but your father is dead."

I was shocked! I couldn't believe it at that instant. It took a few seconds for it to sink in. Then I cried and cried and cried. So did my brothers and sister. We grew to love my father a lot. Even though he was abusive when we were young, he was a good man. He had a good heart. He just had his ways and was brought up in a hard way—in the traditional Mexican style. He thought it was the only decent way to bring up his children.

When I married Flora and before she met my father, I told her, "I want you to know that when you meet my father, you'll find he's different."

"What do you mean, he's different?" she asked, not knowing what I meant.

"You'll see later. I just wanted to let you know."

Well, later when she met him, she told me, "Now I know what you mean."

View my Picture Album at www.EastSideDreams.com

Order the Monkey Box...

The Monkey Box is about a family's history as well as a love story. Travel with the writer as he takes you to the 1800's in Chiapas, Mexico. Experience the hardships of young lovers. Art Rodriguez's great grandfather, Francisco, and great grandmother, Lydia, struggle to be together in spite of the efforts of Lydia's guardians to prevent their relationship.

Follow the family history with their son, Romulo. See how the previous family documents that were stored in the monkey box were destroyed and lost forever. Go with Romulo and Luzita's son, José, as he makes a new life in San José, California, and falls in love.

A story that appeals to both young and old, this author relates experiences about real people in a real time. Live their lives and feel their feelings.

"They both sat and smiled, dreaming the happy, contented visions of young lovers. Mildred visualized her four future children: Eddie, Arthur, Mildred, and Victor. They were married one month later with the blessing of Ben and Frances."

You may order The Monkey Box through Your local bookstore. Publisher: Dream House Press (408) 274-4574 fax (408) 274-0786.

You may order The Monkey Box through Your local bookstore or from the last page of this book.

For bookstores and Libraries: Distributor/Wholesaler: Ingram, Baker & Taylor, Partners West, Jay O' Day Inc, Follett, Blackwell's Book Service, Brodart, Midwest Library Service or your own book jobber.

Order
www.eastsidedreams.com

Order Forgotten Memories. . .

"Turbulent Teenage Years! But Life Goes On!"

Are you having difficult teenage years? Does life go on? Travel with Art Rodriguez as he takes you through his teen years. You will see that life does get better, even though it appears confusing and harsh at times. You will enjoy his stories of growing up in San Jose, California. He will take you for a stroll; as he does, you will experience with him fun times and hard times. You will enjoy this sequel to East Side Dreams.

You may order Forgotten Memories through Your local bookstore or from the last page of this book.

For bookstores and Libraries: Distributor/Wholesaler: Ingram, Baker & Taylor, Partners West, Jay O' Day Inc, Follett, Blackwell's Book Service, Brodart, Midwest Library Service or your own book jobber.

Order
www.eastsidedreams.com

Sueños Del Lado Este

*V*iaje usted con Art Rodríguez, conforme sueña su pasado. Art experimenta una desagradable niñez, llena de obstáculos difíciles que pudieron haber disminuido sus oportunidades para desarrollar una vida normal. La vida aparece para él como una vida sin esperanza durante esos años de la juventud cuando se esfuerza para descubrir quien es realmente, al mismo tiempo que vive una continua batalla con un padre dictatorial. Viaje con él y acompáñelo a través del sistema carcelario de California, la cárcel para jóvenes delincuentes.

No obstante que creció bajo semejante estado general de tensión, él encuentra todavía disfrute y alegría al crecer en San José California, acompañando a sus amigos adolescentes en Virginia Place, en el lado Este de San José. Experimente con él su niñez, conforme recuerda los tiempos pasados de infelicidad y los momentos agradables. En esta historia capaz de hacerlo llorar y de reir; tanto los jóvenes como los adultos pueden encontrar ánimo sabiendo que cuando la vida parece desolada y aparenta no haber esperanza, las circunstancias pueden cambiar. Existe escape de una situación desesperada. Vea como una mala relación entre un padre y un hijo puede cambiar, desde el resentimiento a una relación afectiva.

Esta historia es un estímulo para los jóvenes y para los adultos porque en ella pueden descubrir como Art deja su vida de delincuente y se impulsa hacia un futuro con promesas.

En 1985, Art Rodríguez comenzó un exitoso negocio en San José, la ciudad en la que nació. ¿Cómo pudo este hombre, un ex delincuente, comenzar un negocio con semejante pasado? Descubra junto a él y acompáñelo en el relato de su vida y experimente el sufrimiento, la privación y luego el éxito de su nueva empresa.

Those Oldies but Goodies

One of Art Rodriguez's passions is sharing his inner thoughts with his readers. As he writes, he shares more of life's adventures. Come and read as he transforms life's negativities into positive and pleasurable memories. He will take you through some of life's pleasures, balancing them against life's obstacles that can be overcome with endurance, self-sacrifice, and time. You will enjoy this book as you read Art's simple style of writing. This story is an exciting page turner. You will want to read Those Oldies but Goodies to its end!

Follow this young adult when he is released from the California Youth Authority. Read and find that he marries and only finds sadness and hurt. Go with him as he becomes a businessman and at the same time toys with organized crime. Does he find the woman of his dreams? Did this young man survive his ordeal with the difficulties of life? If you go through related events in your life, can you endure? Read this book and find the answers to these questions.

➤This story will keep you entertained throughout!

➤This tale should encourage someone in your family to write their story.

Art Rodriguez has been honored by The New York Library System to be on the *"2001 Books for the Teenage List."* He was also presented with *"The Mariposa Award — Best First Book"* at the **Latino Literary Hall of Fame in 2001.**

New York Public Library: *"Please keep your terrific books coming!"*

The Monkey Box was entered into the **Latino Literary Hall of Fame for 2002 Book Awards** and won *"Best Biography and Best Cover Illustration."*

Other books authored by Art Rodriguez include **East Side Dreams**, translated into Spanish, *Sueños del Lado Este*. **Forgotten Memories** is the sequel to **East Side Dreams**.

Order
www.eastsidedreams.com

ORDER FORM

Give a person a Gift.

No. of Copies:

_____**East Side Dreams by Art Rodriguez.** (Inspirational Story About Growing Up.)
. . . . $13.95

_____**The Monkey Box by Art Rodriguez.** (Romantic Family Story.) $12.95

_____**Forgotten Memories by Art Rodriguez.** (Sequel to East Side Dreams.) . $12.95

_____**Sueños del Lado Este by Art Rodriguez.** (East Side Dreams in Spanish.) . $12.95

_____**Those Oldies but Goodies by Art Rodriguez.** (Sequel to ESD.) $13.95

Shipping & handling, first copy $4.00 plus $1.00 for each additional copy.
Five books or more, Shipping & handling, NO CHARGE. *We are prompt about sending books out.*

If you are paying with a credit card, you may fax or send to address below.

❏ Visa ❏ MasterCard ❏ American Express ❏ Discover Card

Card Number _____

Expiration Date _____

Signature _____

Check No. _____

Make checks payable to **Dream House Press**.

Your Name _____

Street _____

City _____

State _____Zip _____

Phone (_____) _____

Send to:
Dream House Press
2714 Ophelia Ct., San Jose, CA 95122
Phone: (408) 274-4574
Fax: (408) 274-0786 www.EastSideDreams.com